T0330467

Preparing for High Impact Organizational Change

ELGAR GUIDES TO TEACHING

The Elgar Guides to Teaching series provides a variety of resources for instructors looking for new ways to engage students. Each volume provides a unique set of materials and insights that will help both new and seasoned teachers expand their toolbox in order to teach more effectively. Titles include selections of methods, exercises, games and teaching philosophies suitable for the particular subject featured. Each volume is authored or edited by a seasoned professor. Edited volumes comprise contributions from both established instructors and newer faculty who offer fresh takes on their fields of study.

Preparing for High Impact Organizational Change

Experiential Learning and Practice

Edited by

Gavin M. Schwarz

Professor of Management, University of New South Wales, Australia

Anthony F. Buono

Professor of Management and Sociology, Bentley University, USA

Susan M. Adams

Professor of Management, Bentley University, USA

ELGAR GUIDES TO TEACHING

Cheltenham, UK • Northampton, MA, USA

Published by
Edward Elgar Publishing Limited
The Lypiatts
15 Lansdown Road
Cheltenham
Glos GL50 2JA
UK

Edward Elgar Publishing, Inc.
William Pratt House
9 Dewey Court
Northampton
Massachusetts 01060
USA

A catalogue record for this book
is available from the British Library

Library of Congress Control Number: 2019930813

This book is available electronically in the **Elgar**online
Business subject collection
DOI 10.4337/9781788116954

MIX
Paper from
responsible sources
FSC   FSC® C013604

ISBN 978 1 78811 694 7 (cased)
ISBN 978 1 78811 695 4 (eBook)

Typeset by Servis Filmsetting Ltd, Stockport, Cheshire

Printed and bound by CPI Group (UK) Ltd, Croydon, CR0 4YY

Contents

Figures

Tables

Contributors

Susan M. Adams is Professor and former chair of the Management Department at Bentley University, USA. Her research, published regularly in practitioner and academic outlets, and her consulting efforts to more than 100 clients, focus on changes needed for business success with rewarding careers for employees. Adams has edited two books, most recently *Time for Solutions: Overcoming Gender Related Career Barriers.* Since 2003, she has co-authored The Boston Club's annual *Census of Women Directors and Executive Officers.* Adams has served on and chaired boards of companies and non-profit organizations, was on Governor Deval Patrick's Women in the Workforce initiative task force, and developed and supported implementation of Governor Patrick's Women in the Workforce Fellowship Program. She is also a member of the United Nations Principles for Responsible Management Education (PRME) Gender Equality Working Group. Adams is a former Chair of the Management Consulting and Careers Divisions of the Academy of Management, and a member of the American Psychological Association and former Senior Director of Bentley's Center for Women and Business. Her PhD in Management is from Georgia Institute of Technology.

Anthony F. Buono is Professor of Management and Sociology at Bentley University, USA. He is also a former Chair of Bentley's Management Department and the founding Director of the University's Alliance for Ethics and Social Responsibility, which he oversaw from its inception in 2003 through 2013. Tony's primary research, teaching, and consulting interests include organizational change, inter-organizational strategies, management consulting, and ethics and corporate social responsibility. He has written or edited 21 books including *The Human Side of Mergers and Acquisitions* (1989, 2003), *A Primer on Organizational Behavior* (7th ed, 2008), and most recently, *Intervention Research* (2018) as part of his Research in Management Consulting series (Information Age Publishing). His articles and book review essays have appeared in numerous journals, including *Academy of Management Learning and Education, Administrative Science Quarterly, Human Relations, Journal of Business Ethics,* and *Journal of Organizational Change Management.* A two-time Chair of the Academy of Management's Management Consulting Division, Tony has received Bentley's highest honors for both teaching and research. He is actively involved in the United Nations Global Compact-sponsored Principles for Responsible Management Education (PRME) and was honored as a PRME Pioneer at the 2017 Global Forum on Responsible Management Education.

Nicole M. Zwieg Daly is the Director at the Center for Ethics in Practice at the Opus College of Business, University of St Thomas, USA. She has nearly 20 years of business management, relationship management, and organization development experience. She has held a variety of leadership and management roles including being the start-up Chief Executive Officer and sole proprietor of a sales and consulting firm where she worked with international manufacturers and retailers of all sizes, from small firms to Fortune 500. Before starting her own company, Nicole worked as Director of Operations for an international manufacturing company in Minnesota where she was responsible for the operations, financial management, and human resources departments of both domestic and international branches. Her work has been presented at the Organization Development Network and Western Academy of Management. She frequently speaks to national associations, government agencies and businesses on the topics of principled leadership and ethical decision-making. Nicole holds a doctorate in Organization Development and Change from the University of St Thomas, a BA from the University of St Thomas with a double-major in Business Management and Journalism–Public Relations, and was among the first class to graduate from the St Thomas School of Law.

Richard Dunford is Professor and Associate Dean, International and External Relations, in the UNSW Business School, University of New South Wales, Australia. As a scholar, Richard has widely published in top tier journals including *Academy of Management Review*, *Administrative Science Quarterly*, *Journal of Organizational Behavior*, *Journal of Management Studies*, *Long Range Planning*, *Human Relations*, and *Organization Studies*. He has also been the recipient of multiple federal (Australian Research Council) research grants and has many years' experience teaching strategic management and organizational change, primarily in MBA and Executive MBA programs. As well as working within the university sector, Richard has worked in business (the oil industry) and government (technology policy), and has provided consulting services on strategy, managing change, and executive education to a wide range of companies in Australasia and South-East Asia.

Ann E. Feyerherm is a Professor of Organization Theory and Management at Pepperdine Graziadio Business School, USA. She teaches in the Master of Science in Organization Development (MSOD) program, as well as courses on human behavior, organization change, and leadership. Her research focuses on the role of leadership in inter-organizational collaborations, emotional intelligence, and organization development. Her work has been published in the *Leadership Quarterly, Journal of Applied Behavioral Science, Graziadio Business Report, Organization Dynamics*, and the *OD Practitioner*. Ann was a past chair of the Organization Development and Change Division of the Academy of Management and has served in various leadership capacities at the Graziadio Business School. She is a two-time recipient of the John Nicks Memorial Service award, and has also received Pepperdine University's Howard A. White teaching excellence award.

George W. Hay is the Associate Chair and an Associate Professor in the Business Psychology Department of the Chicago School of Professional Psychology, USA, teaching in its PhD programs in Organizational Leadership and Business Psychology. George received his PhD in Organization Development from Benedictine University, USA. His academic publications focus on how scholar-practitioners close the theory–practice gap by securing breakthrough organizational results and generating new scholarly knowledge. Prior to joining the Chicago School, George was a Director of Global Consumer and Business Insights at McDonald's Corporation. Over his 15 years at McDonald's, he led domestic and international research initiatives that delivered the consumer insight and foresight which supported McDonald's brand improvement and business growth. George is interested in furthering his career as a scholar-practitioner of management through the practices of collaborative management and business research, the publication of scholarly and practitioner articles on organizational change, and the teaching of the next generation of organizational leaders. He is active in the Organization Development Network, serving on the editorial review board of the *OD Practitioner*.

E. John Heiser is Chief Executive Officer of LabVantage Solutions, Inc. LabVantage is a leading global developer of laboratory information management systems. Prior to joining LabVantage, John served as President and Chief Operating Officer of Magnetrol International, Inc., a global leader in level and flow process control instrumentation. Magnetrol pioneered liquid level instrumentation for industrial applications in 1932 and continues to provide advanced measurement and control solutions across a wide product and technology portfolio. John began his career as an attorney in private practice before transitioning into business, where he has held numerous leadership positions in legal, government affairs, sales, and marketing with DuPont Merck Pharmaceutical Company, DuPont

Pharmaceuticals, Merck & Co., Inc., and Bausch & Lomb. John earned his BA degree in Political Science/Sociology from the University of Iowa, a JD from Tulane University, an MBA from the Kellogg School of Management at Northwestern University, and a PhD from the Center for Values Driven Leadership at Benedictine University, all in the USA.

Keith Hunter is an Associate Professor in the Department of Organization, Leadership and Communication at the University of San Francisco School of Management, USA. He is a military veteran and former software engineer, holding a PhD in Organizational Behavior and Management from Carnegie Mellon University, USA, as well as master's degrees in Public Policy and Computer Science. He is committed to active and experiential learning techniques in his instruction of courses that fall under the areas of organizational behavior and organization development. Dr Hunter has authored both teaching cases and teaching exercises for multiple peer-reviewed journals including the *CASE Journal, Case Research Journal, Organization Management Journal, Journal of Critical Incidents*, and *Management Teaching Review*. Consistently linked to his content and approach are his primary research topics of organizational networks and organizational culture and leadership.

David W. Jamieson is Professor and Chair of Organization Development Programs at the University of St Thomas, USA. He is also President of the Jamieson Consulting Group, Inc. and a Distinguished Visiting Scholar in other organization development programs. He has nearly 50 years of experience consulting to organizations on leadership, change, strategy, design, and human resource issues. He is a past National President of the American Society for Training and Development, and past Chair of the Management Consultation Division and Practice Theme Committee of the Academy of Management. He was the recent recipient of the Lifetime Achievement Award from the Organization Development Network, and the Distinguished Scholar-Practitioner Career Achievement Award from the Academy of Management. Dave is co-author of numerous works, including *Managing Workforce 2000: Gaining the Diversity Advantage* (Jossey-Bass, 1991), *The Facilitator's Fieldbook* (AMACOM, 2012, 3rd edn), and *Consultation for Organizational Change Revisited* (IAP, 2016). He holds a PhD in Management from the University of California, Los Angeles (UCLA), USA, majoring in Organization Design and Development; and a BS in Business Administration from Drexel University, USA, with a Behavioral Science minor.

Michael R. Manning is Director of Research and Professor of Leadership, Strategy and Change at the Center for Values-Driven Leadership, Daniel

L. Goodwin College of Business, Benedictine University, USA. He is also a doctoral faculty member in the School of Leadership Studies at Fielding Graduate University, USA. He has held previous faculty appointments at New Mexico State University, Case Western Reserve University, and the State University of New York at Binghamton, all in the USA. Michael has dedicated his professional career to educating and developing executives and managers, consulting with and designing effective organizations, and creating applied action research processes and intervention techniques. He consults extensively with business owners and top corporate officials in both public and private sectors throughout the United States and internationally in Mexico, Europe and the Baltic States, the Middle East, and the Far East. His research focuses on issues of occupational stress, the role of emotions in processes of change, and whole systems change, and has been published in numerous academic journals. Michael is also a past Division Chair of the Organization Development and Change Division of the Academy of Management. He currently serves as associate editor of *The Journal of Applied Behavioral Science*, an editorial board member of the *Journal of Change Management* and the *Business Forum*. He holds a BA in Mathematics and an MA in Applied Behavioral Science from Whitworth College, USA; and a PhD in Administrative Science from Purdue University, USA.

Robert J. Marshak, PhD is Distinguished Scholar in Residence Emeritus, School of Public Affairs, American University, USA, where he taught courses in organization theory for 40 years. He has published three books and more than 100 articles and book chapters on organizational consulting and change. Bob's contributions to the field of organization development have been recognized by numerous awards including the Organization Development Network's Lifetime Achievement Award, and the Distinguished Educator Award from the Organization Development and Change Division of the Academy of Management.

Cynthia A. Martinez is an administrator, educator, and consultant. She has more than a decade of experience in higher education as a student affairs administrator. In her current role as Dean of Students at the Keck Graduate Institute, USA, she is responsible for developing and implementing the strategic plan for the division of student affairs, and has demonstrated experience in managing and communicating change, problem-solving, decision-making, conflict resolution, negotiation, and counseling. As an educator, she currently teaches in the Master of Communication Management Program at the USC Annenberg School for Communication and Journalism, University of Southern California, USA. In addition, Dr. Martinez has previously taught graduate and undergraduate courses at the USC Rossier School of Education, and the University of San Diego School of Leadership and Education Sciences, USA. She is also certified to train, coach, consult, and administer the EQ-I Emotional Quotient Assessment, the Change Style Indicator, and the Global Mindset Inventory.

Jackie M. Milbrandt is a doctoral candidate in organization development and change at the University of St Thomas, USA. Jackie has more than 15 years of experience as a business manager, consultant, educator, and researcher in the United States and abroad, working in for-profit, government, and nonprofit organizations. She has published several book chapters and journal articles, and is an active member of a number of professional groups including the Organization Development Network, Academy of Management, and Family Firm Institute. Jackie also serves on the editorial board of the *Organization Development Review* (formally the *OD Practitioner*) and is a peer reviewer for the *Journal of Management Inquiry*. Her long-term projects and interests include whole-scale strategic change, family business resilience, organizational culture and values, practice-values in the field of organization development, and collaborative advantage in family firms.

Matt Minahan has worked for more than 35 years at helping organizations build capacity. He works with senior executive teams on enterprise-wide change programs to meet new business challenges in their external and internal environments, develop new business strategies, and redesign their organizations from the bottom to the top. Matt's work includes collaborative design and facilitation of strategic planning, organization design, organization structure, leadership development, communications, business process simplification, and culture change. These change programs often include Action Research-based interviews and focus groups, a frank self-assessment by the organization of its strengths and weaknesses, stakeholder analysis, external benchmarking, and work on alignment among the organization's business strategy, values, mission, and leadership philosophy. He served on the board of trustees of the Organization Development Network for seven years from 2009 to 2015, including as Vice-Chair, Co-Chair, and Chair. He is currently an active volunteer and former board member both of NTL Institute and the Chesapeake Bay OD Network. Matt has written dozens of articles and book chapters, and is an author and co-editor of the *Handbook for Strategic HR: Best Practices in Organization Development from the OD Network* (Amacom, 2013).

Philip H. Mirvis is an organizational psychologist whose studies and private practice concern large-scale organizational change, the workforce and workplace, and business leadership in society. An advisor to companies and non-governmental organizations on five continents, he has authored 12 books including *The Cynical Americans* (social trends), *Building the Competitive Workforce* (human capital investments), *Joining Forces* (human dynamics of mergers), *To the Desert and Back* (business transformation), and *Beyond Good Company*. Mirvis serves as board member of PYXERA Global and formerly Foundation for Community Encouragement and Society for Organization Learning. He received a career achievement award as Distinguished Scholar-Practitioner from the Academy of Management. He teaches executive education (Exec-Ed) in business schools and firms globally, and leads a study of corporate social innovation.

Mary M. Nash is Vice President, Organization Development and Learning, for NYU Langone Health, a nationally ranked academic health system. Mary has more than 30 years of experience as a leader and consultant in healthcare and other industries, including technology, manufacturing, construction, financial services, retail, education, and government. She is an executive coach holding the Professional Certified Coach (PCC) credential of the International Coach Federation, and has taught courses in change, power and influence, coaching, and other leadership topics at universities in the United States (George Mason University, Virginia Commonwealth University/Medical College of Virginia, Fielding Graduate University) and abroad (Helsinki School of Economics and Helsinki University of Technology (now Aalto University), and ITESO). Mary has published several chapters and peer-reviewed articles, including in *The Journal Of Applied Behavioral Science*. Mary earned a bachelor's degree in Fine Art from James Madison University, master's degrees in Education (James Madison) and Psychology (Longwood University), and a PhD in Human and Organizational Systems from Fielding Graduate University, all in the USA.

Melissa Norcross is a veteran strategy and leadership consultant currently holding a strategy role at USAA, an organization proudly serving the military community. With a career that has spanned three continents and multiple industries, she has helped organizations achieve profitability and performance at both strategic and operational levels, particularly in the areas of innovation, manufacturing, and product development strategy. Her work at McKinsey, Integral, and now with Eighty Twenty, spans industries that include retail, technology, consumer products, financial services, manufacturing, and pharmaceuticals. In addition, she has served as the Chief Strategy Officer for Ontario Systems, a technology company in the finance and revenue cycle space. During tenure at Ontario

Systems, she undertook a number of strategic initiatives including a financial turnaround, acquisition of its largest competitor, and the sale and recapitalization of the company under new private equity ownership. Since 2007, Melissa has served as a moderator for executive councils at Creative Good. Melissa holds a BS in Engineering from MIT, an MBA from Harvard Business School, and a PhD in Values-Driven Leadership from Benedictine University's Center for Values-Driven Leadership, all in the USA.

Eric J. Sanders is a scholar-practitioner in organization development. He has a PhD in that field from Benedictine University, USA, along with an MBA with concentrations in Economics and International Business, an MA in Economics, and a BS in Psychology. His research and publications are on the characteristics and practices of scholar-practitioners, organizational culture, diversity and inclusion, and change management. He serves on the review board of the *Journal of Applied Management and Economics* and is associate peer review editor for the *Organization Development Journal*. Sanders has practiced as a consultant since 2004 with clients in financial services, manufacturing, healthcare, and non-profits, and worked in retail sales and management for 20 years prior to that. He has taught for most of the past 20 years in several different business schools including Benedictine, the University of Illinois at Chicago, USA, and Marquette University, USA. Courses have included organization development, leadership, general management, human resource management, international business, and economics. He is an active member of the Organization Development Network, and the Academy of Management where he is currently beginning the second year of the four-year leadership track of the Management Consulting Division.

Gavin M. Schwarz is Professor in the School of Management at the UNSW Business School, University of New South Wales, Australia. His research and work interests include organizational change and organizational inertia, with a particular interest in better understanding how organizations fail when changing, and developing applied strategies for dealing with failure to change. He is also interested in exploring how knowledge develops in organizational and change theory, and has published in numerous journals including *Academy of Management Learning and Education, Journal of Management, Group and Organization Management, British Journal of Management*, and *Administrative Science Quarterly*. He is an associate editor for the *Journal of Applied Behavioral Science* and the *Journal of Change Management*, and sits on several editorial boards.

Ramkrishnan (Ram) V. Tenkasi is Senior Professor of Organization Change with the PhD program in Organization Development and Change at the Goodwin School of Business, Benedictine University in Chicago, USA. He is a Fulbright Senior Research Scholar and has authored more than 120 articles and chapters across many leading journals. His article with Professor Richard J. Boland, "Perspective Making and Perspective Taking in Communities of Knowing," is one of the most influential articles to impact the fields of information systems, knowledge management, and organizational change based on citation index counts. Ram also serves as a continuing Funding Panel Review member of the United States National Science Foundation, the Department of Defense, the National Institutes of Health, the American Association for Advancement of Science, and the Netherlands Organisation for Scientific Research. In addition to research, where he has been funded more than US$3 million from federal and private agencies, he has consulted on issues of learning, knowledge, innovation, and large-scale change with many global, large-cap organizations.

Gary Wagenheim is Adjunct Professor of Management at the Beedie School of Business at Simon Fraser University, Canada and Aalto University Executive Education, and former professor of organizational leadership in the School of Technology at Purdue University, USA. His research, teaching, and consulting interests are reflective practice, individual and organizational change, leadership, and organizational behavior. He has published one book and 25 academic journal articles in the *Management Teaching Review, Journal of Management Education, International Journal of Teaching and Learning in Higher Education*, and *Reflective Practice: International and Multidisciplinary Perspectives*. He owns Wagenheim Advisory Group, which provides training and development programs. He presently serves as Vice-Chair of the board of trustees of Fielding Graduate University, USA, and is a member of the advisory board of the Department of Technology Leadership and Innovation in the Polytechnic Institute at Purdue University. Gary received a PhD in Human and Organizational Systems from Fielding Graduate University, USA.

Therese F. Yaeger, Professor, PhD in Organization Development, and MS in Management and Organizational Behavior program at Benedictine University, USA. She has authored several papers and articles, and 11 books. Her publications include *Global Organization Development: Managing Unprecedented Change* with Sorensen and Head (2006), and "Assessment of the State of Appreciative Inquiry: Past, Present and Future," in Woodman and Pasmore's *Research in Organizational Change and Development* (2005). She is an editorial board member of *Journal of Management Inquiry,*

Journal of Leadership and Organizational Studies, OD Practitioner, and *Revue Sciences de Gestion/Management Sciences*. Yaeger has served on the executive boards of the Southwest Academy of Management, the Midwest Academy of Management, and the Management Consulting Division of the National Academy of Management. She is a past President of the Midwest Academy of Management, and a past Division Chair of the Academy of Management's Management Consulting Division.

1. Preparing for high impact change: the critical role of experiential learning and practice

Anthony F. Buono, Susan M. Adams, and Gavin M. Schwarz

This book is intended to help prepare change leaders – at all organizational levels – to effectively deal with the myriad challenges inherent in the process of organizational change. While it has literally become a well-worn cliché that organizations and their management face unrelenting demands for change (Kerber and Buono, 2018), the simple reality – which is not so simple in terms of its impact on organizational life – is that the majority of change efforts fall well short of their intended goals. Despite a literal avalanche of research and managerial attention devoted to conceptualizing and empirically testing an array of change management practices (see Abrahamson, 2000; de Caluwé and Vermaak, 2002; Jamieson et al., 2016; King and Wright, 2007; Kotter and Cohen, 2002), successful organizational change often remains an elusive quest. Unfortunately, many of our educational efforts to develop the capabilities of students and early career executives to successfully deal with the subtleties, nuances, and complexities of organizational change similarly tend to fall well short of the need. Thus, in a "back to the future" spirit, this volume seeks to confront this challenge by resurrecting a powerful hands-on, immersive pedagogy: high impact change-related simulations and experiential exercises.

Effective organizational change involves a combination of understanding, learning and unlearning, and practiced behavior as part of the underlying conceptualization, formulation, and implementation processes. The book presents a series of exercises – each with background context, explicit directions, facilitator suggestions, and debriefing guidelines – that promote learning and developing readiness for change, from preparing people for change, understanding and managing resistance, grappling with cultural confines and confusion, dealing with communication challenges, and coping with change-related obstacles, to seeking buy-in for the change. Emphasis throughout the book is placed on developing change-related competencies.

Some background for the volume is in order. It has long been recognized that change is an intrinsic factor in the long-term success and survival of organizations, leading to extensive frameworks and ways to deal with and manage organizational change, from such allegorical tales as Johnson's (1988) *Who Moved My Cheese?* and Kotter and Rathgeber's (2016) *Our Iceberg is Melting*, to conceptually oriented frameworks (e.g., Jamieson and Armstrong, 2010; Kerber and Buono, 2005, 2018; Kotter, 1996), to more empirically based approaches (see Beer, 2006; de Caluwé and Vermaak, 2002). The accepted view is that for the business world as well as society as a whole, the magnitude, speed, impact, unpredictability, and consequences of change are greater than ever before. Consequently, organizations face a whirlwind of changes in trying to keep their balance between the need to perform in the present amid the pressures of change moving forward. Yet, as noted above, evidence suggests that most organizational change efforts fall well short of intended targets, more often than not failing in some form.

On an individual level, despite this lack of success, we all experience continuous and repeated change in the workplace, which has led to the development of the field of change management: a systematic approach aimed at shaping the thinking of students, practitioners, and educators on the process of organizational change. This training and focus, however, has created a conundrum: when it comes to training people for organizational change, most attention is given to examining how to manage and lead change, often focusing on the impact of change. Based on the evidence of its failure, however, it seems that we still do a poor job at preparing people for the realities of change and the process of change itself. An underlying problem is that the themes and approaches in discussing "how to" change have remained constant for the past several decades. *Plus ca change, plus c'est la meme chose* – the more things change, the more things remain the same? Yet, at the same time, a rich tradition in preparing people for change – embedding them in exercises and experiences that simulate various aspects of the change experience – has seemingly faded from view, despite it being an increasingly necessary part of how we transfer knowledge.

With its focus on facilitating change, this book takes a step back in deconstructing and presenting a series of hands-on approaches to engaging change. On a personal level, if you have ever wondered how you can engage better with organizational change, whether you would like to instill a healthier response to the next change you face, or if you want to better understand how change can be a positive vehicle for organizations, then this book is perfect for you. Educators will find it useful in helping to create an active learning environment, directly engaging participants in the nuances and subtleties inherent in change processes. Grounded in experiential learning, it presents a forum for a broad array of stakeholders – educators, researchers, consultants, and practitioners – showcasing high impact methods for engaging with organizational change in its many contexts.

This book is the culmination of a series of successful Professional Development Workshops (PDWs) during the Academy of Management annual meeting for more than a decade. Beginning in 2005 in Honolulu, we honestly did not know what to expect when we ran the first PDW – "That Was Great! High Impact Activities, Exercises and Approaches for Teaching or Consulting on Organizational Change" – co-sponsored by the Organization Development and Change Division and the Management Consulting Division. At an 8:00–10:00 am session on a Friday morning, with the lure of Diamond Head and Waikiki Beach dangling in front of Academy members, well over 100 people showed up to an overfilled room. Participants experienced five abbreviated exercises or simulations accompanied by interaction, facilitator suggestions, questions, and discussion. The session was energetic, with a noted buzz throughout the room and more than a few "Aha!" moments punctuated with laughter, openness, and sharing among colleagues. We clearly hit a need. We have run the PDW every year since then with similar sized audiences and reactions, at this point culminating in Chicago in 2018 – and our decision to co-write and edit this volume.

The objective of the book is to provide educators, consultants, and practitioners as well as students with a set of coherent and rigorous perspectives to better understand organizational change and change-related processes through high impact exercises. At its foundation, while we acknowledge that there is a history of practitioners, educators, and scholars (especially those working in organizational development) engaging in techniques and exercises to help raise self-awareness of learning (see, e.g., Pfeiffer and Jones, 1972), this type of publication – a collection of techniques for experiential learning – is far less relevant today. Yet, paradoxically, our research suggests that people experiencing change both seek it out and avoid it, a dynamic that is often lost in academic and practitioner approaches. Most academic attention focuses on understanding the nature, content, and processes of change, often through applied cases; in essence, better understanding what change and its make-up look like, and how it was handled in a particular instance. In contrast, most practitioner interest has resulted in an emphasis on "toolkits" for managing change and change-making tactics from client experience. This book seeks to engage these two foci, personalizing the change experience through role play, simulation, and experiential exercises.

The overarching theme is learning from the change experience, focusing on the challenges involved in implementing and facilitating the change process: learning (about change) by doing. After establishing the basis of learning from change, the set of exercises presented and deconstructed encompass the fundamental features of organizational development and change in facilitating the improvement of an organization's problem-solving and renewal processes, through more effective and collaborative management of change. The range of exercises provides facilitators options for reaching those with learning styles which are often ignored. This collection raises the odds for giving everyone a chance to learn their own way (Boyatzis and Kolb, 1995) and to have a more lasting recall of the lessons.

A quote that has been attributed to Confucius – "I hear and I forget, I see and I remember, I do and I understand" – is still very relevant today, as individuals typically prefer different modalities for learning. As an example, Barbe et al. (1979) suggest that there are preferences to learn visually, auditorily, or kinesthetically – in other words, from seeing, listening, or doing. The choice, of course, need not present an either/or challenge. Kolb's (2014) model of the learning process, for example, envisions a cycle of learning that begins with concrete experience, followed by reflective observation, abstract conceptualization, and more active experimentation. This book offers exercises that capture the "doing" dimension of the learning cycle, supporting a hands-on approach to experiencing various aspects of the change experience in "safe" environments. The volume's emphasis on the importance of debriefing these exercises captures Kolb's notions of reflective observation and abstract conceptualization; examining and processing one's own experience and the experience of other participants. Within this context, it is important to remember that learning to understand and lead change from doing it in the classroom (or in training simulations) is much safer than in the organizational world where the impact of failure is much higher.

THE VOLUME

The book is divided into four parts that explore various ways to enhance our understanding of change through experiential learning, from initial thoughts about getting started in the process, to self-learning and personal development, and the challenges related to communicating change, to exploration of the human side of the change experience on multiple levels. The final part provides explicit direction for experiential learning's "end game" – a critical debriefing of the experience and exploration of lessons learned.

Experiential Learning as a Pedagogical Tool: Getting Started

The first group of exercises, in Part I, has three chapters that set the stage for experiential learning. Following this introduction, Chapter 2 offers a historical perspective on the field of organization development (OD) that orients the rationale for this volume, focusing on the competencies of successful scholar-practitioner change agents. Ram Tenkasi, George Hay, and Eric Sanders describe how the pursuit of high impact change is a familiar quest within the field of organization development and change (ODC). Expectations that the results of any change initiative must be impactful are quintessential in today's organizations faced with pressure to demonstrate their financial value in hyper-competitive, global markets. Tenkasi and his colleagues assert that high levels of change impact can be realized through theoretically informed practice, implicitly drawing upon a key founding principle of ODC, "there is nothing as practical as a good theory" (Lewin, 1945, p. 126).

In contemporary times this basic Lewinian idea is expressed in the notion of actionable scientific knowledge. This concept refers to processes of knowledge creation that fulfill the criteria of the scientific community and also impact the business needs of the organization. Actionable scientific knowledge outcomes are both theoretical and practical, serving theoretical advancement while simultaneously impacting business needs of organizations. While there are multiple agents of actionable scientific knowledge, the chapter's focus is on ODC scholar-practitioners who are concerned with organizational change, applying theory to organizational change practice to create successful impact for both theory and practice. These professionals approach ODC from an integrated role as theoreticians, researchers, and change agents who use theory to influence practice. The chapter draws on two studies that reveal the competencies of these successful scholar-practitioners.

In Chapter 3, volume co-editor Anthony Buono looks at the use of icebreaker exercises as a way of initially engaging participants, opening them up and setting the stage for learning, reflection, and sharing. As he suggests, an underlying problem is that many, if not most, exercises of this nature typically make people feel ill at ease: instead of engaging them, they make participants feel awkward and uncomfortable. It is not that such exercises do not work or should not be used – as he suggests, "they can and they should" – but they need to be clearly related to and focused on the topic under study. As an example, the chapter presents a word association exercise – the Reaction-to-Change (RTC) inventory – that sets the stage for examining people's reactions to change, on both a general level as well as in relation to a specific change, and serves as a foundation for the type of learning upon which the volume is focused.

Concluding this part of the book, Robert Marshak examines the power of experiential learning in enhancing theory-oriented courses. As he suggests, instructors in such courses are often challenged to communicate abstract concepts in ways that generate interest and enhance internalization, getting participants to focus on application rather than concept memorization. Yet, despite advances in learning methodologies, he argues that the read–lecture–discuss method still tends to be the preferred vehicle for conceptual learning. Unfortunately, the result is often people who can recite theories chapter and verse, but have difficulty finding any use for this knowledge beyond demonstrating that they are "educated." His chapter begins with a discussion of the importance of theory as a practical tool for engaging the world around us. Noting that when experiential methods are used, they are typically placed in sequential combinations with cognitive readings and discussions, Marshak proposes an alternative approach, one that seeks to simultaneously combine experiential and cognitive learning about theory, illustrating this approach with various design examples and offering suggestions for debriefing a simultaneous cognitive and experiential learning design.

Self-Learning and Beyond through Change Exercises

Part II includes four chapters that focus on specific experiential exercises with an emphasis on self-learning about the change process. Each of the chapters introduces and explains a seminal change theme, highlighting the change, its different mechanisms, and the value of different approaches to dealing with such change. The chapters detail the theme and potential for high impact change, explaining its basis and theoretical framework. The contributors deconstruct their high impact exercises, providing the reader with the basis for the exercise and its history (for example, classic exercise, a derivation from core theory), with a hands-on explanation of the exercise and method for debriefing. The chapters conclude with reflection on the underlying insights into our learning about the change.

Beginning with Chapter 5, Philip Mirvis focuses on enhancing self-awareness through storytelling and mask-making. The exercise involves participants creating personal autobiographies, telling stories about themselves, and creating masks that reflect how they see themselves, cultivating introspection and reflection. Drawing on specific instances where he used this approach, Mirvis illustrates how these exercises can engage emotions as well as cognitive understanding for the participants as well as others in their surroundings. As he suggests, enhancing self-awareness can also serve as a bridge to change; both self and organizational. Drawing on his experience, he notes that it is common for people to follow up such self-reflection with specific action plans, from self-improvement initiatives to ways to adapt to new organizational requirements.

Chapter 6 by volume co-editor Susan Adams shares a card game that involves multiple rounds of simulated organizational changes, with participants physically moving to different groups based on "winner" and "loser" status. The game gives participants opportunities to observe their own behaviors and emotions during change and to experience how others react; both to each other, and perceived norm violations. The debriefing discussion links these observations to change-related triggers as well as potential management techniques to counteract such tendencies. As she notes, by focusing on our reactions to change, the exercise increases awareness on multiple levels, from forming a better understanding of our own personal reaction to change and the different ways in which individuals react to change, to group influences on reactions to change and our own reactions to others' change-related reactions.

In Chapter 7, Matt Minahan outlines two related activities – the Argument of Obviousness and Dealing in Decades – that are designed to assist organizations in differentiating and integrating various parts of the system involved in an organizational change. As he argues, a significant need in any change effort, especially in terms of large-scale change, is to align the beliefs and perceptions of the myriad stakeholders involved to better enable the organization to take concerted action going forward. The underlying challenge, he points out, is facilitating conversations that help build a common understanding among people who may not know each other and may even feel threatened by those others, as well as building the necessary trust to allow such conversations to take place. The exercises in the chapter are intended to assist organizational members in establishing that trust, realizing and capitalizing on system complexity and the two underlying, seemingly contradictory, dimensions of organizational life: differentiation and integration.

The concluding chapter in Part II, Chapter 8 by Michael Manning and Melissa Norcross – the Mads, Glads, and Sads exercise – was originally designed as part of a large-scale change initiative, focusing on getting the "whole system in the room" to engage in system-wide action planning. The exercise creates the context for groups of any size to reflect on their personal organizing experiences – both emotionally as well as cognitively – with the intention of enhancing participant engagement and commitment in the change process. The exercise has an explicit focus on the central role of emotions in terms of dealing with, managing, and activating change.

Communicating Change

The two chapters in Part III share exercises that focus on challenges related to communicating about and within change. In Chapter 9, Richard Dunford's Symbols exercise illustrates several of these challenges, from recognizing the importance of clearly communicating the objective of the change, to understanding the individual and organizational effects of mis-communication, including misunderstanding (management's objectives), frustration (even anger), demotivation, and underperformance against objectives, to understanding how inadequate communication can lead to the (mis)attribution of meaning to specific activities by organizational members. In the exercise, groups will only be able to complete the task by deciphering codes in their "rules," emphasizing the need to pay attention to how others communicate, understand how information ebbs and flows in an organization, and to take the time to understand the associated meanings of comments and the behavior of others.

Cynthia Martinez's Ball Game exercise in Chapter 10 presents an exercise using tennis balls to help participants experience the chaos of change, consider the different variables and/or circumstances affecting the change process, and the challenge of creating strategies and actions for change-related planning, implementation, and evaluation. The Ball Game introduces critical dimensions of change, getting participants to experience what it feels like to encounter change and work through the important change-related communication functions, methods, and processes.

The Human Side of Change: Strategy, Culture, and Change Recipients

The five chapters in Part IV focus on the interpersonal side of change, offering exercises related to resource dependency, negotiating, conflict management, collaboration and the influence of individuals, culture and social networks.

In Chapter 11, Mary Nash, Michael Manning, and John Heiser apply Kurt Lewin's Force Field Theory to facilitate SWOT (strengths, weaknesses, opportunities, threats) analysis. Their methodology promises to be beneficial for a range of users, from leaders and managers, to organizational members and other stakeholders involved in the strategic planning process, as well as facilitators (internal or external) of such initiatives. Their approach also provides a useful road map – with possible routes and barriers – in planning for change, which can readily inform preparations for change and provide a starting point that can be revisited during change implementation.

Chapter 12 by Ann Feyerherm presents an exercise that faces participants with the opportunity and challenge of physically dealing with diminishing resources, in the form of paper squares on the floor that are taken away during the exercise. The task is to find creative solutions to problems precipitated by the removal of the squares. While simple (and somewhat reminiscent of the children's game of Musical Chairs), the exercise simulates reactions to typical resource decline, serving as a potential springboard to innovatively dealing with change. As Feyerherm emphasizes, the experience brings the phrase "necessity is the mother of invention" to life in a very real way.

In Chapter 13, David Jamieson, Jackie Milbrandt, and Nicole Zwieg Daly describe an exercise called the Culture and Change Challenge. The experiential activity is intended to help participants develop the awareness and skills needed to anticipate, observe, and leverage culture in organizational change. As participants explore the dynamics of culture and change through the exercise – described as an accelerated learning experience with differences, disorientation, and disconfirmation – they build greater cultural awareness, thinking, and strategies necessary for planning for, responding to, and successfully managing change in a complex world.

Chapter 14 by Keith Hunter presents an exercise that explores the factors that drive the emergence of social networks as well as the extraction of value from those networks. The underlying objective of the simulation is to enhance participant understanding of social capital, exchange, and power in social networks. The exercise is built around a simple game using standard playing cards in which participants examine rather complex and influential processes that are associated with the accumulation, adoption, and sustaining of organizational change. As Hunter underscores, much like in a real organization, a group of participants is composed of individuals who operate under a need to maximize their local interests; with their capacity to do so highly dependent on exchange relationships with at least some others who have their own local priorities. By engaging in multiple dyadic interactions with the aim of maximizing the value of the resources (cards) they hold, participants experience the need to negotiate with their counterparts to obtain resources (cards) that will improve their respective situations.

Therese Yaeger concludes Part IV with Chapter 15, focused on generational conflict as participants experience how workers from different age cohorts present themselves as the "best person" for a new leadership role. The basic objective is to gain appreciation of perspectives and challenges of four different generations in today's workforce. Through an experiential role play, participants uncover greater insight into the values and needs of different age groups and how those differences can impact decisions. As Yaeger concludes, through the role play exchanges an underlying hope is that participants will also realize their own shortcomings and biases when working with other age groups.

The Experiential Exercise End Game: End-Point Engagement

The final part of the volume, Part V, provides guidance for debriefing experiential exercises. We believe that the debrief is the most crucial part of the learning process associated with using experiential exercises, which unfortunately is often cut short due to time constraints. Deconstructing an exercise in real time, directly following the participants' experience while it is fresh in their minds, is obviously the preferred approach. A challenge with experiential exercises, however, is that they can be very seductive, engaging participants (and facilitators) at such a level that time seems to slip by, leaving little time for true exploration and reflection of the experience. An all too common refrain – "That was fun" – often seems to surpass what was (or was not) learned. Thus, while what might be thought of as immediate teachable moments might be preferable, planned teachable moments still provide powerful learning experiences: in essence, starting the next class or training session with a look back at what transpired in the previous exercise, ensuring sufficient time and attention to the underlying takeaways and lessons from the experience.

In Chapter 16, Gary Wagenheim provides a general framework for thinking about "the debrief," the process by which students are encouraged to critically analyze their individual experience, with the goal of gaining further insights into their learning. Although each of the exercise presentations in the earlier chapters include debriefing guidelines for that particular activity, Wagenheim extends these recommendations though an explicit set of guidelines based on objective, reflective, interpretive, and decisional questions that guide participants in their own personal self-exploration. As he suggests, these four sets of questions are not intended to be as linear as they might initially suggest. In practice, students tend to drift between questions, get stuck on issues, get distracted or run out of energy, and think in ways that may run counter to the sequence. As he argues, given that this type of dialogue is circular – often "messy and sticky, and occasionally dull" – as the facilitator it is important to prompt students to dig deeper with those questions that resonate with them, probing for more information and insight and even simply moving on to other questions if there are no responses. The goal is to prompt student ownership of their learning, helping to promote the ever-important and desired life-long reflective learner.

Chapter 17 by Anthony Buono explores the idea of a Three-Part Journal as a way of enhancing concept application and reflective learning. The chapter presents a structured journaling technique originally created by our Bentley University colleague Edward Zlotkowski as a way of enhancing student experience and development in service-learning engagements.

Certainly relevant to organizational change, this activity captures: (1) participant thoughts about the experience (written in regular font); (2) how that experience relates to course (or training session) concepts and frameworks (bold face font); and (3) focused reflection (italics), pushing participants to delve into their own feelings and personal aspects of the learning process, from testing assumptions and beliefs, to contemplating new attitudes and behaviors as part of their own growth and development.

The volume concludes in Chapter 18 with some brief reflections by the editors, delving into the value of learning about change through personal experience. Focusing on the integrative development and place of using games, exercises, and simulations in order to better engage with organizational change, the concluding discussion counterbalances the toolkit approach. In this way, the book is a resource for understanding change through experience.

ACKNOWLEDGMENTS

As noted in the first section of this introductory chapter, this book was inspired by more than a decade of successful Professional Development Workshops (PDWs) at the annual meeting of the Academy of Management (AoM). Two key AoM divisions – the Organization Development and Change Division and the Management Consulting Division – were continually and highly supportive of our efforts, sponsoring the PDWs year after year. We would also like to thank the presenters as well as the participants in these sessions. Our presenters (many of whom are contributors to the volume) were fully open in their willingness to share their materials, engage with the audience, and in general, inform and have fun along the way. Similarly, this book would never have happened without the good-natured participation and involvement by those who attended the workshops, in many instances multiple times over the years. Their reaction to the exercises and subsequent discussions and feedback prompted us to capture the experience in this volume.

The PDW was initially created by Gavin Schwarz with Ian Palmer and Richard Dunford, who played central roles in developing the underlying idea and plan for the workshops. As Ian and Richard gravitated toward academic administration roles, Anthony Buono and Susan Adams became co-developers, working with Gavin to continue the insightful work of our Australian colleagues. Co-writing and editing this volume has been one of the more enjoyable writing projects that we have experienced. It is our hope that the book – and the PDWs that inspired it – will help to stimulate a revival of experiential learning as an important pedagogical approach, helping readers and users to more fully understand and appreciate the complexities, nuances, and possibilities inherent in the change process. And still have some fun along the way.

REFERENCES

Abrahamson, E. (2000). Change without pain. *Harvard Business Review*, 78(4), 75–79.

Barbe, W.B., Swassing, R.H., and Milone, M.N. (1979). *Teaching through Modality Strengths: Concepts Practices*. Columbus, OH: Zaner-Bloser.

Beer, M. (2006). *High Commitment High Performance: How to Build a Resilient Organization for Sustained Advantage*. San Francisco, CA: Jossey-Bass.

Boyatzis, R.E. and Kolb, D.A. (1995). From learning styles to learning skills: the executive skills profile. *Journal of Managerial Psychology*, 10(5), 3–17.

de Caluwé, L. and Vermaak, H. (2002). *Learning to Change: A Guide for Organization Change Agents*. London: SAGE Publications.

Jamieson, D. and Armstrong, T. (2010). Consulting for change: creating value through client–consultant engagement. In A.F. Buono and D.W. Jamieson (eds), *Consultation for Organization Change* (pp. 3–13). Charlotte, NC: Information Age Publishing.

Jamieson, D.W., Barnett, R.C., and Buono, A.F. (eds) (2016). *Consultation for Organizational Change Revisited*. Charlotte, NC: Information Age Publishing.

Johnson, S. (1988). *Who Moved My Cheese? An Amazing Way to Deal with Change in your Work and in your Life*. New York, NY: G.P. Putnam's Sons.

Kerber, K.W. and Buono, A.F. (2005). Rethinking organizational change: reframing the challenge of change management. *Organization Development Journal*, 23(3), 23–38.

Kerber, K.W. and Buono, A.F. (2018). The rhythm of change leadership. *Organization Development Journal*, (Fall), 1–18.

King, S.B. and Wright, M. (2007). Building internal change management capability at Constellation Energy. *Organization Development Journal*, 25(2), 57–62.

Kolb, D.A. (2014). *Experiential Learning: Experience as the Source of Learning and Development*. Hoboken, NJ: Pearson FT Press.

Kotter, J. (1996). *Leading Change*. Cambridge, MA: Harvard Business School Press.

Kotter, J.P. and Cohen, D.S. (2002). *The Heart of Change: Real-Life Stories of how People Change their Organizations*. Boston, MA: Harvard Business School Press.

Kotter, J.P. and Rathgeber, H. (2016). *Our Iceberg is Melting: Changing and Succeeding under any Conditions*. New York: Penguin Random House.

Lewin, K. (1945). The research centre for group dynamics at Massachusetts Institute of Technology. *Sociometry*, 8, 126–35.

Pfeiffer, J.W. and Jones, J.E. (1972). *The 1972 Annual Handbook for Group Facilitators*. Iowa City, IA: University Associates Press.

PART I

Experiential learning as a pedagogical tool: getting started

2. The competencies of successful scholar-practitioners

Ramkrishnan (Ram) V. Tenkasi, George W. Hay, and Eric J. Sanders

There is agreement that one sign of a successful spanning of science and practice is the production of actionable scientific knowledge. According to Adler, Shani, and Styhre (2003, p. 84), *actionable scientific knowledge* refers to the knowledge creation processes that meet the criteria of the scientific community and the business needs of the organization. The recent decades have seen the rise of new intermediate professionals between the world of theory, research knowledge, and its application. These intermediaries, including scholar-practitioners, consulting firms, and professional groups, now serve as bundlers and co-producers of knowledge, creating alternative pathways for translating and integrating scholarly knowledge to practice across a variety of disciplines (Bartunek and McKenzie, 2018; Bartunek and Schein, 2011; Martini et al., 2012; Mohrman and Lawler, 2011; Reed and Hocking, 2013). They have changed society's perception of the research-scholar, who has gone from the primary or sole agent responsible for translating and applying scholarly knowledge to practice, to one of several agents involved in the process.

Scholar-practitioners are uniquely positioned to cultivate high impact change since they hold unique competencies that enable the production of actionable scientific knowledge. An exploration of their bridging strategies to inter-relate theory and research to practice, and an understanding of their personal characteristics, can be useful for other scholars and professionals in producing such actionable insight.

This chapter focuses on scholar-practitioners and how they apply theory and research knowledge to practice to produce outcomes for an organization while advancing scientific knowledge in the process. Scholar-practitioners are actors who have received traditional academic training, and who apply their knowledge of theory and research to an organization's particular challenges to resolve business problems. Astley and Zammuto (1993) label scholar-practitioners an intermediate cadre of professionals who, by virtue of belonging to both the practice and academic communities, can effectively bridge the incommensurate worlds of scholars and practitioners. Huff and Huff (2001) view scholar-practitioners as intermediate boundary-spanners who have one foot in the world of practice and the other in the world of theory and research. Scholar-practitioners can also be classified as a subtype of the "engaged scholar," as defined by Andrew Van de Ven (2007).

Being a scholar-practitioner transcends the boundaries of a specific work context. It does not matter whether a scholar-practitioner is employed as a professor by a college or university, as an executive by an organization, or as a consultant by a consulting firm. Three roles define a scholar-practitioner, regardless of their employment, as: agents of change through their work within organizations; researchers of change through their documentation and study of this work; and theoreticians of change through the use of extant theory to design initiatives, as well as the use of their results to advance new theory.

Within this context, the thrust of this chapter is on answering three questions concerning scholar-practitioners as intermediate agents:

1.   How do scholar-practitioners successfully translate and apply theoretical and research knowledge to resolve organizational problems, and what is the underlying process they employ to enable this integration?
2.   What are the key competencies that scholar-practitioners require to effectively integrate theory with research and practice?
3.   What are the personal characteristics that enable these boundary-spanners to apply themselves fully in both academic and practitioner communities?

THE BRIDGING STRATEGIES OF SUCCESSFUL SCHOLAR-PRACTITIONERS FOR INTER-RELATING THEORY TO PRACTICE

The scholar-practitioner's intermediate role has both historical and contemporary precedent in Aristotle's concept of *phronesis* (Aristotle, 1961) and Van de Ven's (2007) notion of engaged scholarship. To understand this integration, we turn to an inductive qualitative study of 11 cases reported in some detail in earlier publications (Hay et al., 2008; Tenkasi, 2011; Tenkasi and Hay, 2004, 2008, 2013), and a second study of 41 scholar-practitioners from organization development and change (ODC) and medical and health translational research (Sanders, 2015). Both studies sought to understand not only the theory and practice the scholar-practitioner brings to the table, but also how they go about linking theory to practice in organizational projects. Table 2.1 includes a description of different scholar-practitioner projects and outcomes with dual relevance.

All cases from both studies were analyzed using an iterative approach of going back and forth between the data and the emerging theory to develop a model (Eisenhardt, 1989; Elsbach and Sutton, 1992; Silverman, 2001; Yin, 1994). The cornerstones of our analyses were to: (1) develop a narrative sequence of events for each case; (2) employ a within- and across-case analysis of all cases to identify similarities and differences across events; and (3) systematically develop and employ an emergent coding system to methodically discern and elaborate on the common dynamics of theory–practice integration observed across the cases based on the logic of replication.

Project Definition and Planning Stage

Framing the problem
The scholar-practitioners frequently used theory and research findings to frame and give direction to a broadly expressed change mandate from the organization's leadership, looking for the resolution to a perceived organizational crisis or the realization of a desired future state. This stage is frequently where scholar-practitioners step in, using their theory and research knowledge to analyze the situation and to frame and define the problem in more precise terms (Van de Ven, 2007).

One scholar-practitioner took the chief executive officer's (CEO) vision to make his manufacturing plant a center of excellence by defining the program as one of bolstering the aging workforce's effectiveness and productivity through principles of motivation and employee involvement (Lawler, 1986). In a second case, the scholar-practitioner framed the CEO's mandate to make the R&D organization more effective as better systems and processes for knowledge management, enabled by a non-routine socio-technical systems (STS) framework.

Conjecturing an appropriate pathway to resolve the problem
After top management accepted the scholar-practitioner's framing as an appropriate problem definition (Van de Ven, 2007), the scholar-practitioners used their theory and research findings to conjecture a pathway (Bunge, 2004), perceived as most suitable for resolving the problem in light of the local contingencies.

In the first case, the CEO's mandate for the manufacturing plant to become a center of excellence, the scholar-practitioner could have addressed the issue using various mechanisms, including better manufacturing processes or materials management, both scientifically validated pathways

Table 2.1   A description of scholar-practitioner projects and outcomes of dual relevance

Purpose of project	Practical outcomes	Theoretical outcomes
1. Increasing the innovation effectiveness of the research and development (R&D) center of a high technology firm	A practical model of the critical deliberations that new product development projects should undertake based on project life stage and the essential knowledge domains required to be involved at each stage. A key impact among others was reduction in product development cycle time.	Several presentations at forums such as the Academy of Management and journal publications
2. Leadership alignment across a multi-divisional global consumer products firm	A training program and a model that could be used to assess and develop transformational leadership behaviors among the many managers and supervisors of each division or unit. Key impact were observed uniformity in transformational leadership behaviors across the different business units.	Presentations at academic and practitioner conferences, journal publications, and working papers that assessed the relationship between transformational leadership and emotional intelligence
3. Establishing a Center for Manufacturing Excellence in a heavy engineering firm	An internal organizational model of the stages involved in realizing self-managing team effectiveness and training interventions that will accelerate movement to each stage. Key impacts were improvements in cost and quality indices.	Paper presentations at practitioner and academic conferences on self-managing teams, book chapter, and a dissertation
4. Creating effective practices and processes for mergers and acquisitions (M&As) in an electrical products firm	An internal workbook highlighting procedures, processes, and training interventions for post M&A integration drawing on social constructionist principles. A major aspect of the model was achieving strategy or vision consensus about the merged organization between the two parties. Key impacts were quicker and effective cultural integration as indicated in post-survey measures.	Presentations at Academy of Management, journal article, and a dissertation

Table 2.1 (continued)

Purpose of project	Practical outcomes	Theoretical outcomes
5. Transitioning four brownfield manufacturing units into high performance work systems of a global equipment manufacturing firm	An internal process model based on appreciative inquiry and incorporating best practices and training interventions drawn from a study of four pilot sites, to help evolve other brownfield manufacturing sites into high performance work systems. Key impacts were improvements in cost, quality, and productivity indices.	Presentations, conference proceedings, and a dissertation
6. Piloting a whole-systems design model for radical organizational change in one region of a multi-regional wireless company	A process model for whole-systems design developed from learnings of the pilot region for use in other regions. A key impact was increased market share based on restructuring of business operations, particularly the customer service function.	Presentations, journal articles, and a book on large group interventions
7. Assessing differential implementation success rates among four business units or regions of a corporate-driven global organizational change program in a worldwide food services firm	An internal model of change communication that takes into account interpretive differences among the multiple constituents who are parties to the change. A key impact was a revised change communication protocol from the corporate office for tailoring change messages by taking into account the cultural and interpretive background of regions or units.	Presentations, conference proceedings, and a dissertation
8. Designing optimal organizational structures for new product development effectiveness and efficiency in a global communications firm	An internal organization design model for structuring new product development units largely derived from a meta-analysis of existing new product development research literature.	Presentations, journal publications, working papers, and a dissertation

9. Improving restaurant effectiveness and efficiency in the US Midwestern region of a worldwide food services firm	An internal process model based on appreciative inquiry and a template that can be implemented in other regions for improving restaurant effectiveness and efficiency. A key impact was improvement in restaurant service effectiveness.	Presentations, conference proceedings, and a dissertation
10. Transitioning a centralized global information technology (IT) company into decentralized customer-focused business teams	Successful reorganization of company, with buy-in of key stakeholders.	Working papers, presentations at practitioner conferences, and a dissertation
11. An assessment of peer mentoring on effective sharing of organizational knowledge in a global communications firm	Evaluation of peer mentoring program and identification of best practices in knowledge sharing.	Conference presentations, journal article, and a dissertation

to achieve manufacturing excellence (BMP Center of Excellence, 1998). But the scholar-practitioner saw that the real issue was motivating an aging workforce and enhancing their effectiveness through principles of employee involvement. She made this choice based on several local considerations. First, the older workforce had high levels of camaraderie and a collective identity as a group distinct from their supervisors. The scholar-practitioner saw that the best way to heighten awareness of quality, cost, and schedule was to let the employees take ownership of these issues through self-governing teams instead of relying on supervisory mandates, which had been ineffective in the past. Second, the scholar-practitioner chose the team-based design to allow for multi-skilling and job rotation, which would give team members variety and challenge in an otherwise routine environment. This approach would also be more cost-efficient, given the high capital costs involved with installing computer-aided manufacturing software or a new material management software. The question really was how to motivate a skilled workforce who were ultimately demotivated at being a "cog in the wheel" (Hackman and Oldham, 1980), and potentially would have refused to faithfully appropriate the requirements and demands of the new software (DeSanctis and Poole, 1994).

Influencing and legitimizing the chosen pathway

Conjecturing the pathway and considering why one mechanism works better than others helps to legitimize the pathway, since it is based on both theoretical and practical considerations. Influencing and legitimizing frequently involved distributing articles and books from practitioner sources that carry legitimacy in the business world, such as the *Harvard Business Review* or *Sloan Management Review*, and readable article summaries from academic sources such as the *Academy of Management Journal* and *Organization Science*, condensed by the scholar-practitioner. Occasionally, the scholar-practitioner also brought in experts, including practitioners with hands-on experience of implementing the conjectured pathway in similar environments, and scholars who had written practical books or articles on the topic. Sometimes the experts were hired as consultants to guide the project, but in most cases we observed they came in as additional sources to influence and legitimize the chosen pathway and acceptance of it among concerned stakeholders.

The Project Implementation Stage

Activating the conjectured pathway

Once the causal pathway or preferred strategy for change was established and accepted by relevant stakeholders, based on the cost-efficiency of involving the workforce and the danger that they may unfaithfully appropriate the new software guided requirements, the fourth function of theory and research in informing practice was in activating the conjectured pathway. To activate the project, the scholar-practitioner often used the theoretical, research, and practice literature, including expert opinion on the chosen platform (whether self-managing teams or non-routine STS), as guiding frameworks. This frequently meant creating training programs for the community to enact the details of the chosen pathway for change that preceded implementing the intervention. Often scholar-practitioners also used training programs as pre-assessment forums, using survey instrumentation, qualitative interviews, or in several cases, both, to create baseline information before enacting the change.

Making sense of the activated pathway

Scholar-practitioners used surveys, interviews, systematic observations, and, in one case, personal diary recordings to monitor and assess the pathway's ongoing progress. For the STS knowledge management project, the scholar-practitioner used systematic research methods such as surveys and interviews to assess whether the quality of internal deliberations – an intervention created within the teams – helped them to meet monthly goals in cost, quality, and schedule over one year. Whether hypothesis-driven or based on evolutionary insights, the scholar-practitioners' hallmark was using systematic research methods to gauge the efficacy of the conjectured pathway.

Project Realization/Closure Stage

Demonstrating impact of the chosen pathway in achieving the change

Finally, the scholar-practitioners applied research knowledge to demonstrate impact. Applying systematic research methods to activate and make ongoing sense of the conjectured pathway also helped to demonstrate that the organizational project successfully achieved practical results, whether that meant changing mindsets, behavior, or other hard metrics. A selection bias is clearly at work in the successful projects we chose to study. Nonetheless, demonstrating business impact required collecting data and analyzing it using systematic research designs in the project execution phase. Scholar-practitioners used quantitative evidence to show shifts in hard performance measures before and after change. Likewise, the scholar-practitioners used qualitative data, particularly context-sensitive quotes or verbatim comments, to show changes in perspective or behavior. For example, the scholar-practitioner who set up self-managing teams used many quotes from team members to demonstrate that they were engaged in the kinds of behaviors involved in team self-management.

Meta-Strategies for Relating Theory and Practice

In a majority of cases, what was most salient and needed attention in the minds of management was the business problem. Our interviews with scholar-practitioners suggest that consulting is seen as adding value to the organization's business problem, while research is seen as an abstract act that is not practically relevant. For many scholar-practitioners, "research" was a term they preferred not to use but rather to integrate into the process. As one aptly summarized:

> My CEO wants us to become a center of manufacturing excellence. I have convinced him that the best way to achieve it is to create self-managing teams. He wants them to happen, and if I tell him I want to conduct a research project on testing a theory of self-managing team effectiveness, I will probably be out of the door tomorrow. We don't have the luxury of presenting a research proposal but have to build research principles into the way we consult. But if I do write a few articles from this project, he is okay with it as long as I show practical results.

"Turns" are reframing moves and tools that help to make an element more familiar, legitimate, and palatable to the concerned audience. Turns achieve this by locating the element in a community's "systems of meaning" (Fleck, 1981). For example, "research" (the academic phrase) gets translated into "demonstrating results" (the executive phrase). In our observation, successful scholar-practitioners used theory-to-practice turns to make the unfamiliar familiar to the practitioner community during all stages of the project.

In a few cases scholar-practitioners used another, less common meta-strategy known as "scaffolding" across a project's life cycle. Commonly associated with construction, the word "scaffolding" typically means a "platform made for workers to stand on when they want to reach higher parts of a building to add on to or modify the structure of the building" (*Cambridge Dictionary*, 2003). For scholar-practitioners, scaffolding means carefully selecting a theory-based platform that helps to frame the problem at hand, guides practice, and, has the potential to realize subsequent theoretical and empirical outcomes by seeking to answer new research questions. For example, the scholar-practitioner who framed the CEO's vision to make the manufacturing plant a center of excellence used the theory-based platform of self-managing teams to direct action and conduct systematic research on the gap she identified in the teams' research literature (that is: What is the evolutionary pathway in becoming a self-managing team? Why can some teams but not others successfully transition into self-management? And why are some faster at it?) (see Figure 2.1 for a synthesis of the process).

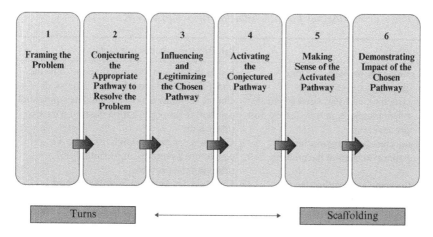

Figure 2.1   A process model of strategies for inter-relating theory with practice

THE COMPETENCIES OF SUCCESSFUL SCHOLAR-PRACTITIONERS

Our observations indicate that while scholar-practitioners use theory and research knowledge to inform practice and produce outcomes of dual relevance, we also see that theory and research knowledge, a critical component of the scholar-practitioner's repertoire, is just one of a set of "know that" (knowing about something) and "know how" (knowing how to do something) (Ryle, 1949) in successfully impacting organizational change practice (see Table 2.2).

In connecting with organizations, scholar-practitioners bring certain kinds of "know that" (current literature, social science theory, principles of research design), and certain kinds of "know how" (designing research and data analysis). They also understand the importance of merging this knowledge with the "know that" (contextual conventions, norms, rules, power relationships, routines, and established procedures) and "know how" (influencing, legitimizing, project management) specific to the organization. Scholar-practitioners demonstrate distinct competencies to effectively bridge theory and research knowledge with practice that invoke different sets of "know how" and "know that."

Table 2.3 provides a summary of the key competencies of scholar-practitioners. First, they are familiar with the *universals* (the larger scientific discourse pertaining to theory and research) and can articulate what is known and what needs to be known to advance knowledge from a

Table 2.2   Strategies for inter-relating theory to practice

Strategy	Inter-relating theory to practice
Framing the problem: A strategy employed to bound and structure, an otherwise equivocal phenomenon in more concrete and precise terms	Using theory and research findings to frame and give direction to a broadly expressed change mandate from leadership as a potential solution to an organization crisis or a desired future state
Conjecturing the appropriate pathway to resolve the problem	Using theory and research findings to conjecture a pathway most suitable for resolving the problem
Influencing and legitimizing the chosen pathway: A strategy used to justify and convince relevant stakeholders that a concept, idea, model, or course of action was most appropriate for a situation	Using theory as a tool to influence and legitimize the need for a certain kind of practical action often garnered from a review of current literature around the topic of interest
Activating the conjectured pathway	Using theoretical, research and practice literature including expert opinion on the chosen platform as guiding frameworks
Making sense of the activated pathway: A reciprocal dynamic where theory is used as a tool to make sense of practice, and practice to make sense of theory	Using theory as a tool to make sense of practice such as applying systematic principles in the assessment, diagnosis and sense making preceding implementation of interventions, and making sense of implementation experiences by drawing on a background of theoretical and research knowledge
Demonstrating impact of the chosen pathway in achieving change: A strategy that co-mingles theory and practice elements to demonstrate impact and results	Using research-based quantitative and qualitative evidence to demonstrate proof that the organization project was successful in terms of achieving practical results: that there was a change in mindsets, behavior, or metrics of effectiveness such as return on investment (ROI) or profitability
Turns: A strategy of reframing that helps to make a theoretical element more familiar, legitimate, and palatable to a practitioner audience by locating it within the community's systems of meaning	Turning the knowledge of current literature to information from best practices in the industry and other organizations, or turning representative sampling as a broader strategy for involvement of employees
Scaffolding: A strategy that can be likened to a platform that helps in subsequent building activities	Including a theory-based platform at an earlier stage of a project that, while helping in guiding practice, also ensures subsequent theoretical outcomes in seeking to answer new research questions

Table 2.3   Key competencies of scholar-practitioners that enable them to produce actionable scientific knowledge by inter-relating theory to practice

Key competencies	Knowledge and skills
Familiarity with the *particulars* of the organization	Knowledge of local theories of action including awareness of organizational history, insights into social dynamics, interpretive conventions, norms, and power relationships within the organization.
Familiarity with the *universals* or the larger scientific discourse pertaining to both theory and research	Knowledge of generalizable theories of action derived from mastery of theory and research in domains such as organizational behavior, organization theory, strategy, organizational development and change, and research methods including qualitative, quantitative, and mixed.
Influence in the organizational system to move projects within the organization	Understanding of how to build credibility and legitimacy with top management and relevant stakeholders, and the skills to influence them. Practical knowledge and skills to move projects toward completion within organizations.
Ability to play the role of *semiotic brokers* and act as effective bridges between the research and practice contingents of the organization	Skills in translating between communities and locating concepts and ideas from one community within the meaning systems of another. Includes ability to take elements of theory and express it in terms that would be more familiar and legitimate to a practice-based community, while also taking practical contingencies and framing them for their theoretical and research possibilities to a research community.
Ability for *mutual sense making* between theory and practice	Skills in using theory to activate and make sense of practice; and when executing practical organizational projects, using evolving practice insights to make sense of the theory at hand. This important reciprocal dynamic often leads to relevant outcomes for practice and theory.

theory and research vantage. Second, they are familiar with the *particulars* of the organization – local theories of action, organizational history, social dynamics, norms, and power relationships – a unique competency that successful scholar-practitioners are adept at. When these two sets of competencies unite, scholar-practitioners are able to find appropriate causal mechanisms that can move the system to its desired state, achieving practical outcomes while enhancing scientific theory. Third, to put causal pathways into motion, scholar-practitioners need credibility, legitimacy, and influence in the organizational system, particularly among top management and other stakeholders. These actors have deep practical knowledge of how to move projects in the organization. Fourth, a critical skill of scholar-practitioners is the ability to adeptly translate theory regarding its practice implications, and to frame practice contingencies in terms of their theoretical potentials. Fifth is the competency to inter-relate theory and research to practice that can help in mutual sense-making. Scholar-practitioners frequently use theory to activate and make sense of practice. When executing practical organizational projects, scholar-practitioners' evolving practice insights re-enable them to make sense of the theory at hand. This important reciprocal dynamic often leads to relevant outcomes for practice and theory.

When considering how the scholar-practitioners developed the "know-that," "know-how," and "know-why" referred to in prior paragraphs, it is noted that these competencies developed within a crucible of applied experience and engaged scholarship. These scholar-practitioners were seasoned practitioners with considerable expertise as change leaders. They were also committed to executing applied research that would lead to new knowledge about organizational change. Some were in the midst of a PhD program in Organization Development. As tautological as this sounds – learning to be a scholar-practitioner stems from acting as a scholar-practitioner – it also emphasizes the teleological nature of mastery. Competent scholar-practitioners emerge because they choose to be scholar-practitioners. They embark on a quest to create and produce actionable scientific knowledge.

There are a variety of practices that support and enhance a successful quest for actionable scientific knowledge. Scholar-practitioners set aside time to generate new ideas and insights. Although many of these ideas and insights arise from a critical reflection on prior work experiences, they also reflect an immersion in the published theoretical and applied literature. There is a constant comparison between what is happening and what might happen. Scholar-practitioners learn by doing: they put their ideas into action to see how they work. Sometimes the learning-by-doing requires political skill and personal courage in order to launch an unfamiliar or unpopular course of action. There is collaboration with other professionals as projects are executed and evaluated. Ad hoc discussion with others augments the sense-making. Perspective-taking is frequent, as the scholar-practitioner actively seeks to look at the experience from different vantage points. This is enhanced further as scholar-practitioners commit to documenting and writing up their experiences for other scholar-practitioners. The combination of reflection and writing, plus presenting cases and theories generated in professional conferences and other gatherings, builds the knowledge base of the scholar-practitioner, as well as those involved in the discussions and presentations.

Personal Characteristics of Scholar-Practitioners: Use of Self and the Ability to Thrive in both Academic and Practitioner Communities

Our second study was qualitative research with 41 scholar-practitioners: 27 in organization development and 14 in medical translational research (Sanders, 2015). It confirmed the strategies used by scholar-practitioners in two different fields. Further, our research suggests that scholar-practitioners' sense of self is critical, regardless of their competencies as theoreticians, change agents, and/or researchers. In essence, who successful scholar-practitioners are is as important as what they do. There are two key aspects to their use of self in this context: one is how scholar-practitioners approach their multiple roles, and the other deals with their personal characteristics.

Approaching multiple roles

Executing multiple roles means living simultaneously in multiple communities. Often for scholar-practitioners this challenge is portrayed as a linear continuum between being a scholar (doing research) and being a practitioner (executing work). Wasserman and Kram (2009, p. 18) show how this is too narrow a definition, and develop a more fluid model with cyclical movement between and across the roles of "scholar" and "practitioner" with permeable boundaries in the integrated role where they perform both roles simultaneously. In our second study of 41 scholar-practitioners, we confirmed that these roles varied and flowed based both on time and on research and client needs. In addition, the ability to seamlessly flow between the roles and blend them as needed was based on the personal characteristics of the scholar-practitioners and their use of self, which is discussed below.

If we add the third role of being a *change agent* and put it in the context of the use of self, the model of how the scholar-practitioner works expands to a much more dynamic model (Figure 2.2). A key point here is that the scholar-practitioners rarely performed all three roles at once; but did so occasionally. They expand and contract certain roles over time in order to maintain personal harmony. They have a place somewhere in the flow between the roles where they are most comfortable, which Wasserman and Kram (2009, p. 19) describe as "a place called home." However, even that place varies over time; for instance, Edgar Schein said that earlier he would have put himself right in the middle of the model, but now he is more of a

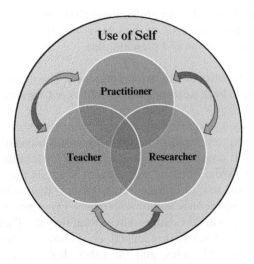

Figure 2.2   Expanded scholar-practitioner model

scholar, focused on writing rather than practice or teaching. As the saying goes, "home is where your heart is." Different stages of life and careers can change not only our physical homes, but our professional ones as well.

Personal characteristics
To enable themselves to excel in their multiple roles as scholar-practitioners, we found that five key characteristics describe successful scholar-practitioners as people: they are adaptable, collaborative, passionate, holistic, and wise (see Table 2.4). Consent was obtained to use both names and actual quotes from these scholar-practitioners to demonstrate the value they placed on these characteristics. These personal characteristics will be discussed in alphabetical order, as we did not have enough data to prioritize them.

The "adaptable" category includes agility, creativity, and use of intuition, all of which show the ability to be flexible to the client or patient needs, and to adapt to the situation at hand. Judith Katz, a noted consultant on diversity and inclusion (along with her long-time colleague Fred Miller, both winners of the Organization Development Network's Lifetime Achievement Award), described a five-year engagement with a global pharmaceutical company in which she and her partner helped to change their culture around diversity and inclusion. They did that through leadership development and adapting their materials to fit the existing language and culture of the firm. In her own language:

Table 2.4   Scholar-practitioner characteristics that enable use of self

Characteristic	Definition	Example
Adaptable	The ability to be flexible to the client or patient needs, and to adapt to the situation at hand	Adjusting the interventions used with a client in real time as client needs change
Collaborative	Being comfortable acknowledging when you need help, and working with others to achieve a goal	Engaging outside specialists when your personal skills and abilities do not fulfill client needs
Holistic	Someone who looks at the world as a system of systems, and considers all levels of a situation	Bringing together a cross-functional and/or a multi-level team to engage all parts of the system
Passionate	Fiercely committed to helping clients and making a difference in the world	Courageously working on issues or interventions that you feel are important
Wise	Having extensive learning and the ability to use it in practice	Life-long learning, and carefully applying knowledge gained through practice over time

The foundation of the work, was really helping them think about inclusion as a "How?" versus inclusion as a "What?" What was important about that too, was linking it to whatever they had already going on. They did a lot of work with Lean Six Sigma. The critical element was taking Lean Six Sigma – if you think about that as a tool – and really adopting and saying Lean Six Sigma looks at the processes and systems, and eliminating waste in those systems and processes, and inclusion eliminates waste in the interactions.

What we did was really tried to link it to something that they knew, to something that they were going to bring in to the culture. I think because the Lean Six Sigma work was so embedded in their language, in their approach, and in their culture, it was easier for them to then take the inclusion work as a "How?" because they already had standard work around the manufacturing processes . . . So we were taking a known framework and bringing our work into a framework that could also be known in a similar way around standard work. (J. Katz, personal communication, January 7, 2015)

This work also relates to the strategy of turns or bridging, which was described in greater detail in a prior section.

All of the scholar-practitioners noted the importance of being collaborative with others in their work. Part of the reason for collaboration is the complex work environment, whether it is in getting the data and expertise to run a business or to treat an illness. Scholar-practitioners need to be comfortable acknowledging what they do not know and getting help from others in order to be successful for the client. For example, many of the medical and health translational researchers talked about how they would engage people from different medical specialties, as well as molecular biologists, geneticists, epidemiologists, and frequently biological statisticians, in their studies. Each of these people adds a different perspective and greater depth to the research and helps to find solutions that are otherwise unavailable. Benjamin Kipp, Associate Professor of Laboratory Medicine and Pathology at the Mayo Clinic, put it this way:

> We have started to set up weekly meetings . . . It used to be, the surgeons did their surgeries, and pathologists signed out their cases, and molecular geneticists did their things, but it's becoming more difficult to sign-out or to interpret genomics without more collaborative information about the patient and their tumor(s). Since geneticists and the pathologists identify the genetic abnormalities and determine histologic tumor type, genotyping of tumors is now forcing them to come to the table and understand more about each other's fields. The same thing can be said about the collaborations between clinicians (e.g., surgeons, oncologists) and pathologists/laboratory professionals. New discoveries and the abundance of new data are really forcing medical professionals with different areas of expertise to sit down at the same table to better help the patient. (B. Kipp, personal communication, March 13, 2015)

A final point regarding collaboration is that in addition to helping deal with complexity and adding outside perspective to their work, many of the scholar-practitioners said they collaborated with others because it made the work more enjoyable. Following are examples from Terry Armstrong and Peter Sorensen, two long-time scholar-practitioners who epitomize the ideal of fulfilling collaboration:

> Any of us could have probably done the work without the others, but it's just more fun to do it as a team or as a group. Also, you learn from each other. It's a great way to continue your learning. Even when I was working with people who didn't know anything about OD [organization development], like with the engineers, I learned a lot about engineering and operations management, and they learned a lot more from me in terms of how to interview, and how to just get along. So it was very mutual. I found it very rewarding. I prefer to work with somebody. Even if I can't do that, I'll try to find someone in the organization, maybe a younger person, and contract them to work with me. (T. Armstrong, personal communication, February 9, 2015)

> I've written hundreds of articles and papers. I think maybe I've done 5 alone, because it's no fun doing it alone. (P. Sorensen, personal communication, January 30, 2015)

Being holistic, or having a holistic perspective, is another interesting characteristic that was common across all of the scholar-practitioners.

As scholar-practitioners in today's complex world, they usually deal with units that are part of larger systems, and, without a systemic perspective, whatever interventions or treatments proposed are likely to be ineffective. This was equally true in organization development and medical and health translational research, as the two following quotes show, from Brenda B. Jones (a global OD scholar-practitioner who is current President of the Lewin Center for Social Change, Action and Research, and past President of the NTL Institute), and Benjamin Kipp:

> When we go from practice to theory and when we talk about use of self, when we talk a lot about the role of the consultant, I'm very clear about what my work is at all levels of the system. But learning more about unintended consequences in this particular group of about 15 people – and it was in fact their whole unit – helped me learn more about working with larger systems, and what that meant in terms of issues that come up and how they need to be addressed. (B. Jones, personal communication, February 10, 2015)

> There is a very wide spectrum of people that need to work on these types of large assays like this. So, I work very closely with a group of oncologists and that group was kind of set up just to determine what genes we should be testing. We work very closely with our pathology colleagues, because again, they are the ones making the first diagnosis; and the third group at the table was the clinical molecular geneticists, and the reason for that is that this assay is actually performed in a molecular genetics laboratory and they do the clinical interpretation of the report. So again, as the assays become more complex, it's really forcing all the clinical groups to work together nicely. (B. Kipp, personal communication, March 13, 2015)

The epidemiologists in our research noted the same, as they deal with environmental factors as well as smaller scale biological causes of disease. Without a holistic view, causes of disease and potential treatments can easily be overlooked.

While it was not a surprise, the passion behind the work that these scholar-practitioners do was striking. They are fiercely committed to their fields, their clients or patients, and to making a difference in the world. These are brilliant people who have put a lot of time and energy into developing "a better mousetrap" in their areas of choice. That was captured especially well by Patti Gravitt, who is conducting research on the incidence of human papillomavirus (HPV) over a woman's lifespan, especially latency through middle age and then reoccurrence of the disease in older women, and how that affects their risk of developing cervical cancer.

She has conducted some tremendous studies on the topic literally around the world, and is now working to use animal models to test her hypotheses before further work with humans. Since her work spans both cancer and infectious disease, she has supporters and detractors for her work, as it is challenging traditional assumptions about the way HPV and cervical cancer are related. Her passion for the work helps her to overcome those challenges and was captured not just in the volume of her research work, but in her tone of voice and in the amount of information she shared in an hour-long conversation (P. Gravitt, personal communication, March 12, 2015).

Similar conversations around diversity and inclusion were had with Judith Katz; about organizational culture and its relationship with leaders' career anchors with Edgar Schein (Professor Emeritus from MIT and well-known organizational scholar-practitioner); about organizational design and organizational culture with David Jamieson (Professor and Director, Doctorate in OD and Change at University of St Thomas); about coaching and peer-to-peer networks with Mila Baker (a long-time leader in the organization development community who was Director of Leadership and Human Capital Management programs, and Academic Chair of the MS in Human Resource Management and Organization Development program at New York University's School for Continuing and Professional Studies when she passed away in 2017). These scholar-practitioners think broadly and care deeply, and it shows in their personalities and in their work.

An important part of executing one's passion is being courageous. These scholar-practitioners are not fearless, but they are willing to push past their fears and live with the discomfort of working in the unknown. Franchee Harmon, a consultant and doctoral candidate at Benedictine University, understood this well, and was researching this very topic when her life was cut short by cancer. It seems only appropriate to quote her here:

> Jeff Bezos is right. We don't choose our passions; our passions choose us. Still, we have to have the courage to use them. Let go of your fears, use your instincts, go "act out" your environment with others who share your dreams, and let your passion find you. Then, and only then, can purpose begin its work. (Harmon, 2006, p. 245)

These scholar-practitioners have the courage to take the leap into the unknown, and let their passions guide them to the greater good.

Last, but certainly not least, these successful scholar-practitioners are *wise*. The *Oxford English Dictionary* (2015) definition of the term includes three key concepts related to our context: "having or exercising sound judgment or discernment . . . having the ability to perceive and adopt the best means for accomplishing an end; characterized by good sense and prudence."

All of the scholar-practitioners are life-long learners. Many went back to school after working for a number of years to pursue their graduate studies. All continue to read the journals in their areas of expertise, attend and present at conferences, and teach regularly. They affirm the adage that the teacher always learns more than the students, as described by Connie Fuller, an organization development consultant who followed Marvin Weisbord at Bethlehem Steel, and worked in several other firms before becoming a Professor in Business Psychology at the Chicago School of Professional Psychology, now retired:

> The way I integrated was pretty much the same thing that I do now in terms of taking my work experiences into the classroom, and taking new learning experiences from the classroom into my work situations. I never have a class where I don't learn something new, even if it's a topic I have talked about a hundred times. There are nuances there, new situations to apply it to. I learn something every time I'm in class. I often think back to my work practice in the corporate world, and think "Well, I wish I had been smart enough to figure that out when I was there." (C. Fuller, personal communication, December 15, 2014)

This emphasis on ongoing learning may also explain their longevity in the field. Ten of the people interviewed had been working for more than 40 years, and all continue to work to this day. Their minds are active, and they continue to want to use them to help others.

A final and key point on how these wise scholar-practitioners became so is that they learned from their mistakes. One of the most important lessons that many of them learned was best expressed by Warner Burke, one of the leading practical theorists in the OD field, when asked to describe a failure and the lessons learned from it. In that project, he was trying to help the head of Human Resources (HR) for a Fortune 50 company to be more successful and to change the HR function of the company to be more effective. What he found over the course of a year was that the HR leader was more concerned with his interactions with the other senior executives than with the people in his department. By continuing to look upward instead of downward, the leader could not make any effective changes in his organization, and Burke could not find a way to change the leader's perspective. That led to Burke's key lesson learned:

> As a consequence of that failure, I realized that I was really quite good at team building and group stuff, and I was not as effective one-on-one as I wanted to be. And that was before there were coaching programs. What I did was to go to the Gestalt Institute in Cleveland, and got myself trained as a Gestalt therapist although I've never practiced therapy, but that was extremely helpful to me with respect to my future ability to be an effective coach. I've used that training the rest of my life.
>
> But you understand the point I'm trying to make. The failure led to my making a change about myself because I couldn't change the Head of HR. But I could change me. (W. Burke, personal communication, February 20, 2015)

That type of introspection and the subsequent personal development, to ensure that he avoided a similar failure in the future, was common across all of these wise scholar-practitioners.

CONCLUSION

The growing number of executive PhD programs, as well as the number of working professionals from diverse positions who are enrolling in these programs, show that scholar-practitioners play a key role in organizations today (Mathiassen and Sandberg, 2012; Wasserman and Kram, 2009). Executive PhD graduates are building careers within these profit and non-profit organizations as the landscape for traditional academic employment shifts. In addition to being effective intermediaries in the knowledge-to-practice value chain, they can help these organizations to secure high impact change. From an Aristotelian legacy, practitioner-scholars are the modern representation of the *technites*, who carefully blend the traditions of theory and practice to solve problems of scientific and social concern (Tenkasi and Hay, 2008).

Keeping in mind the unique competencies of the scholar-practitioner as a professional who understands the inter-relation of theory to practice strategies, and as a person who is committed to this charge, will well serve those who seek alternative pathways to enable high impact change. The production of actionable scientific knowledge is not the sole purview of doctoral-level scholar-practitioners. Other change agents, consultants, scholars, executives, and students are invited to learn about theory–practice bridging strategies by doing them. They are invited to reflect upon the "learning by doing" through the lens of their use of self in order to cultivate the personal characteristics that are essential for the management of change initiatives. Share freely of what is learned from these experiences; this will fulfill the promise of actionable scientific knowledge to deliver effective results and generate new insights into change theory and practice.

While many of the participants in our studies learned these skills on the job initially, they further developed them through readings, courses, and planned experiential learning. As education and training for scholar-practitioners becomes more robust, more experiential learning through exercises, simulations, and supervised action learning projects can all help to build a strong foundation upon which to develop the craft of assisting clients to succeed in transformational change. This chapter, and the others in this volume, will help those who pursue this path to improve themselves and the clients they serve.

REFERENCES

Adler, N., Shani, A.B., and Styhre, A. (2003). *Collaborative Research in Organizations*. Thousand Oaks, CA: SAGE Publications.

Aristotle (1961). *Metaphysics*. H. Tredennick (trans.), Loeb Classical Library. Cambridge, MA: Harvard University Press.

Astley, W. and Zammuto, R. (1993). Organization science, managers, and language games. *Organization Science*, 3, 443–460.

Bartunek, J.M. and McKenzie, J. (2018). *Academic–Practitioner Relationships: Developments, Complexities and Opportunities*. New York: Routledge.

Bartunek, J.M. and Schein, E. (2011). Organization development scholar-practitioners: between scholarship and practice. In S.A. Mohrman and E.E. Lawler (eds), *Useful Research: Advancing Theory and Practice* (pp. 233–250). San Francisco, CA: Berrett-Koehler.

BMP Center of Excellence (1998). Best manufacturing practices report. College Park, MD: BMP Center of Excellence. Available at: http://www.bmpcoe.org/ (accessed October 1, 2006).

Bunge, M. (2004). How does it work? The search for explanatory mechanisms. *Philosophy of Social Sciences*, 34 (2), 182–210.

Cambridge Dictionary (2003). Cambridge: Cambridge University Press.

DeSanctis, G. and Poole, M.S. (1994). Capturing the complexity in advanced technology use: Adaptive Structuration Theory. *Organization Science*, 5 (2), 121–147.

Eisenhardt, K. (1989). Building theories from case study research. *Academy of Management Review*, 14 (4), 532–550.

Elsbach, K. and Sutton, R. (1992). Acquiring organizational legitimacy through illegitimate actions: a marriage of institutional and impression management theories. *Academy of Management Journal*, 35, 699–738.

Fleck, L. (1981). *Genesis and Development of a Scientific Fact*. Transl. by F. Bradley and J. Thaddeus. Chicago, IL: University of Chicago Press.

Hackman, J.R., and Oldham, G.R. (1980). *Work Redesign*. Reading, MA: Addison-Wesley.

Harmon, F. (2006). *Making Purpose Work: The Challenge of Growing Ourselves and Our Companies*. Chicago, IL: HPH Publishing.

Hay, G.W., Woodman, R., and Tenkasi, R. (2008). Closing the ODC application gap by bringing ODC knowledge closer to ODC practice. *OD Practitioner*, 40 (2), 22–26.

Huff, A. and Huff, J. (2001). Refocusing the business school agenda. *British Journal of Management*, 12 (Special Issue), S49–S54.

Lawler, E.E. (1986). *High-Involvement Management: Participative Strategies for Improving Organizational Performance*. San Francisco, CA: Jossey-Bass.

Martini, A., Gastaldi, L., Corso, M., Magnusson, M., and Laugen, B.T. (2012). Continuously innovating the study of continuous innovation: from actionable knowledge to universal theory in continuous innovation research. *International Journal of Technology Management*, 60 (3), 157–178.

Mathiassen, L. and Sandberg, A. (2012). How a professionally qualified doctoral student bridged the practice–research gap: a confessional account of Collaborative Practice Research. *European Journal of Information Systems*. Available at: http://www.palgrave-journals.com/ejis/journal/vaop/ncurrent/full/ejis201235a.html (accessed April 6, 2013).

Mohrman, S.A. and Lawler, E.E. (2011). *Useful Research: Advancing Theory and Practice*. San Francisco, CA: Berrett-Koehler.

Oxford English Dictionary (2015). Retrieved from http://www.oed.com.libweb.ben.edu/.

Reed, K. and Hocking, C. (2013). Revisioning practice through action research. *Australian Occupational Therapy Journal*. Available at: http://onlinelibrary.wiley.com/doi/10.1111/1440-1630.12033/abstract (accessed April 6, 2013).

Ryle, G. (1949). *The Concept of Mind*. London: Hutchinson & Company.

Sanders, E.J. (2015). A comparative analysis of the roles, strategies and tactics used by scholar-practitioners in organization development and medical translational research to simultaneously create research knowledge and help clients achieve results. Doctoral dissertation. Lisle, IL: Benedictine University.

Silverman, D. (2001). *Interpreting Qualitative Research* (2nd edn). Thousand Oaks, CA: SAGE Publications.

Tenkasi, R.V. (2011). Integrating theory to inform practice: insights from the practitioner-scholar. In S.A. Mohrman and E.E. Lawler (eds), *Useful Research: Advancing Theory and Practice* (pp. 211–231). San Francisco, CA: Berrett-Koehler.

Tenkasi, R.V. and Hay, G.W. (2004). Actionable knowledge and scholar-practitioners: a process model of theory-practice linkages. *Systemic Practice and Action Research*, 17 (3), 177–206.

Tenkasi, R.V. and Hay, G.W. (2008). Following the second legacy of Aristotle: the scholar-practitioner as an epistemic technician. In A.B. Shani, N. Adler, S.A. Mohrman, W.A. Pasmore, and B. Stymne (eds), *Handbook of Collaborative Management Research* (pp. 49–72). Thousand Oaks, CA: SAGE Publications.

Tenkasi, R.V. and Hay, G.W. (2013). Understanding the essential principles for integrating theory and research knowledge to the realm of practice: lessons from the scholar practitioner. In G.D. Sardana and T. Thatchenkery (eds), *Reframing Human Capital for Organizational Excellence* (pp. 224–241). New Delhi: Bloomsbury Publishing.

Van de Ven, A. (2007). *Engaged Scholarship: A Guide for Organizational and Social Research*. New York: Oxford University Press.

Wasserman, I. and Kram, K. (2009). Enacting the scholar-practitioner role: an exploration of narratives. *Journal of Applied Behavior Science*, 45 (1), 12–38.

Yin, R. (1994). *Case Study Research: Design and Methods*. Thousand Oaks, CA: SAGE Publications.

3. Using icebreaker exercises: futility and possibility – assessing reactions to organizational change

Anthony F. Buono

Classroom instructors and trainers often rely on icebreaker exercises to engage people, encouraging them to "open up," to set the stage for sharing and reflection – in the classroom to make students feel more at ease, or in company training programs to engage employees with the goal of creating stronger, more effective teams. The Internet is full of readily downloadable "Best Icebreaker Activities" that promise to get sessions off to a good start, creating a foundation for the learning and development that is to follow. An underlying problem, however, is that most people are ill at ease being involved in such exercises. From such seemingly intrusive prompts as "Say your name and your spirit animal" to asking people to share their "favorites," these kinds of icebreakers can stress people out, making them feel awkward and more than a little uncomfortable (e.g., Qian, 2018). Moreover, many of these starters are simply not appropriate for effective development and teamwork training, and there is little academic research regarding the efficacy of such openers (see Casper, 2017).

It is not that icebreaker exercises do not work or should not be used – they can and they should. The key is to ensure that they are clearly related to and focused on the topic under study, in essence, that they have demonstrable pedagogical value in the classroom (Freeman, 2017). "Introduction to . . ." type exercises tend to be very effective in drawing people into the topic at hand, prompting early reflection prior to the presentation of any course content (Arnold, 2015; Snider and Southin, 2016). They are also helpful in creating a norm of dialogue and discussion, signaling to participants that their own perspectives are valid points of data. A well-thought-through icebreaker exercise can provide students with a perspective on what the course or training session is about, what topics will subsequently be covered, and how it relates to the reality of organizational life.

ASSESSING REACTIONS TO CHANGE

One particularly useful icebreaker for gaining insight into people's thoughts about change is the Reaction-to-Change (RTC) inventory, based on the work of DeMeuse and McDaris (1994). The exercise is designed to examine people's reactions to change, on both a general level as well as in relation to a specific change. I have successfully used it as an introductory icebreaker exercise in graduate courses on organizational change and in consulting engagements (for example, with an executive team gauging comparative reactions to a potential acquisition), and with mixed results at the undergraduate level (largely due to their experience base). It can be used on two levels:

1. As a non-threatening way to prompt people to explore their initial thoughts and reactions about change, creating a basis for understanding and potentially modifying their own responses to change. It also encourages people to reflect on what it takes to bring about change in a positive manner.
2. The RTC exercise can also serve as a diagnostic instrument, exploring how people are reacting to a specific change in the workplace, providing insight into their views and perceptions as a starting point for better preparing them for the change, keeping them informed, and getting them involved in the process. It can also provide a basis for examining the potential reactions of their managers, subordinates, and peers.

The exercise quickly engages participants and prompts them to share their thoughts and experiences about how change is perceived and experienced in organizational life, probing their expectations about change and the change process. Students are asked to complete a simple word association exercise about their feelings about organizational change. Participants then "score" their reactions based on whether their associations are positive, neutral, or negative. This assessment is then used as a basis for discussion about reactions to change and their ramifications for organizations and their management.

The Exercise

Box 3.1 provides the basic RTC exercise. Students are asked to complete a simple word association inventory, circling the words that on a personal level they most frequently associate with the idea of organizational change. Students are encouraged to circle as many (or as few) words as they feel appropriate. Each of the words connotes a certain view of change:

BOX 3.1   THE BASIC REACTION-TO-CHANGE EXERCISE

Circle the words that in general on a *personal level* you most frequently associate with the idea of *organizational* change.

Adjust	Different	Opportunity
Alter	Disruption	Rebirth
Ambiguity	Exciting	Replace
Anxiety	Fear	Revise
Better	Fun	Stress
Challenging	Grow	Transfer
Chance	Improve	Transition
Concern	Learn	Uncertainty
Death	Modify	Upheaval
Deteriorate	New	Vary

- Words that conjure positive images of organizational change are given a value of +1.
- Words that cast change in a neutral light are given a 0.
- Words that depict change in negative terms are given a value of –1.

Box 3.2 provides the exercise scoring sheet, with results in the –10 to +10 range.

Once students have completed and scored the inventory, the next step is to take a poll of the class as to how many of them fell into each of the scoring categories, from strong (+5 to +10) and moderate (+2 to +4) support, to willingness to comply (–1 to +1), to moderate (–2 to –4) and strong (–5 to –10) resistance (see Figure 3.1). The results are tabulated and shared with the class (blackboards and whiteboards still have a place in the classroom). The discussion then explores why they reacted to the idea of organizational change as they did. After students in each of the groupings share their thoughts, follow-up questions focus on what might make organizational change easier for them, or more difficult. What does it take to inspire commitment to change? How might organizations harness the enthusiasm of supporters to help promote change? What will it take to deal with resisters?

As part of the discussion, it is also useful to explore the reactions of participants in the extreme groupings: strong support and strong resistance. For example, those with strong support ratings might be prompted to consider potential dangers in being overly enthusiastic (high expectations) about change. Similarly, those with highly resistant ratings can be asked to explore the underlying reasons and what it might take to

BOX 3.2   RTC INVENTORY SCORING SHEET

Reaction-To-Change Inventory: Scoring Sheet

The following values are associated with each term in the inventory. Words that conjure positive images of organizational change are given a 1; words that cast change in a neutral light are given a 0; and words that depict change negatively are given a –1.
Total the values of all the words you circled.

Adjust (0)	Different (0)	Opportunity (+1)
Alter (0)	Disruption (–1)	Rebirth (+1)
Ambiguity (–1)	Exciting (+1)	Replace (0)
Anxiety (–1)	Fear (–1)	Revise (0)
Better (+1)	Fun (+1)	Stress (–1)
Challenging (+1)	Grow (+1)	Transfer (0)
Chance (0)	Improve (+1)	Transition (0)
Concern (–1)	Learn (+1)	Uncertainty (–1)
Death (–1)	Modify (0)	Upheaval (–1)
Deteriorate (–1)	New (+1)	Vary (0)

Scores in the +5 to +10 range suggest strong support for organizational change.
Scores in the +2 to +4 range suggest moderate support for organizational change.
Scores in the –1 to +1 range suggest a willingness to comply with organizational
     change.
Scores in the –2 to –4 range suggest moderate resistance to organizational change.
Scores in the –5 to –10 range suggest strong resistance to organizational change.

Why do you think you react to organizational change the way you do?
What might make organizational change easier? More difficult?

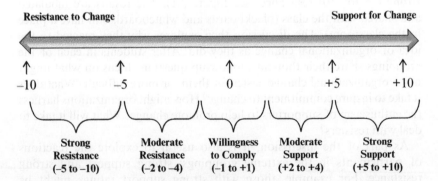

Note: Reaction-to-Change Inventory: Scoring and Debriefing.

Figure 3.1   RTC participant summary

moderate such opposition. Participants can then brainstorm about what it would take to manage people in these different categories. Instructors can also guide the discussion toward comparative analysis, exploring why people react differently to different changes as well as differently from each other relative to the same change. As DeMeuse and McDaris (1994) suggest, it is important to underscore that there are no right or wrong answers or ways to respond to the word inventory. Rather, it is designed to capture the range of reactions to the idea of change in general or in response to a specific change – not to label people as "supporters" or "resisters" per se.

During the debrief (see Gary Wagenheim's thoughtful guidance in Chapter 16 in this volume), I have found that Dilbert cartoons provide a humorous way to place the discussion in a broader context, underscoring that many of the points and concerns that people raised are reflected in how others see organizational change. The exchange between Dilbert and his Pointy-Haired Boss in one of my favorite strips nicely captures the essence of the change challenge:

Pointy-Haired Boss: We're hiring a Director of Change Management to help employees embrace strategic changes.
Dilbert: Or we could come up with strategies that make sense. Then employees would embrace change.
Pointy-Haired Boss: That sounds harder.

Exercise Variations

Several variations of the exercise are possible, going from a general assessment of organizational change to perceptions of specific change initiatives, personal assessment versus perceived reactions of subordinates, and so forth. As examples:

- Change-specific RTC: Circle the words that you most frequently associate with the [organizational change in question].
- Comparative RTC:
  - Step 1: Think about a current or impeding change in your organization. Circle the words that on a personal level you most frequently associate with this change.
  - Step 2: With the same change in mind, draw a box around the words that you feel represent the ways in which the majority of people in (your organization, department, and so on) will associate with the change.

General Observations

Based on my experience, I have had more success with the exercise with graduate students and managers than with undergraduates. Many undergraduates do not have comparable experience in dealing with organization change as their more senior counterparts; and they are often strong supporters of the idea of change in general, questioning why anyone would resist change. Recent successes with undergraduates, though, suggest the potential of framing the exercise around changes they are experiencing – for example, campus changes that have an impact on their lives, or drawing on their internship experiences – rather than their perception of organizational change in general.

Over the years, another observable trend in results suggests that although people are supportive of the idea of organizational change on a general, non-specified level, reaction to specific changes reflect more resistant attitudes. It appears that the way in which particular changes are managed leaves quite a bit to be desired: from how managers respond to employee concerns and a lack of stakeholder engagement around the change, to the extent to which success metrics are clarified and resistance to the change is allowed to surface and be discussed (see Kerber and Buono, 2005; Schantz, 2018).

Finally, there also appears to be a hierarchy gap with respect to perceptions of change: higher-level executives tend to have more positive views of a current or impending change than those below them in the hierarchy. To some extent this might be viewed in terms of a corporate "credibility gap" as employees feel that they were promised one thing and experience something quite different, perceiving a violation of their psychological contract with the organization (Rafferty and Jimmieson, 2017). It can also reflect timing-related factors. Especially with respect to strategic change, senior-level people have typically been wrestling with the proposed change for some time, working through their own issues with respect to the change. At this point, they are ready to move on. Organizational members below them, however, are just being exposed to the change and are just beginning to process the change and its ramifications.

CONCLUSION

As research suggests, how people experience change is dependent on a broad array of factors, from the employee–management relationship and one's personality traits, to the level of participation in the decision-making process and perceptions of job security, among other factors (Amarantou et al., 2018). Change, in and of itself, can spark powerful emotions; as such, it is important to work with participants to help them make sense of and gain control over these emotions. As noted by DeMeuse and McDaris (1994), individuals differ in their overall comfort level and ability to respond during times of change – an observation that can be facilitated through the use of the exercise. Individuals who perceive themselves as having the ability to adapt easily to change, for example, may be more receptive to organizational change efforts and be more likely to view the organization's readiness for change as favorable. This simple exercise is very effective in getting people to reflect on their own perceptions of general and/or specific changes – and as an icebreaker to set the tone for sharing and dialogue for the sessions that follow.

REFERENCES

Amarantou, V., Kazakopoulou, S., Chatzoudes, D., and Chatzoglou, P. (2018). Resistance to Change: An Empirical Investigation of its Antecedents. *Journal of Organizational Change Management*, 31 (2), 426–450.

Arnold, R. (2015). Where's the Diplomacy in Diplomacy? Using a Classic Board Game in Introduction to International Relations. *Political Science and Politics*, 48 (1), 162–166.

Casper, W.C. (2017). Teaching beyond the Topic: Teaching Teamwork Skills in Higher Education. *Journal of Higher Education Theory and Practice*, 17 (6), 53–63.

DeMeuse, K.P. and McDaris, K.K. (1994). An exercise in managing change. *Training and Development Journal*, Feb., 55–57.

Freeman, M.E. (2017). Pushing the Envelope of Pedagogical Gaming: Dark Networks. *Political Science and Politics*, 50 (4), 1083–1088.

Kerber, K.W. and Buono, A.F. (2005). Rethinking Organizational Change: Reframing the Challenge of Change Management. *Organization Development Journal*, 23 (3), 23–38.

Qian, S. (2018). On Spirit Animals and Community. *University Wire*, April 11. Accessed via *ProQuest*. Document ID No. 2023606768.Web.

Rafferty, A.E. and Jimmieson, N.L. (2017). Subjective Perceptions of Organizational Change and Employee Resistance to Change: Direct and Mediated Relationships with Employee Well-being. *British Journal of Management*, 28 (2), 248–264.

Schantz, J. (2018). How Can Leaders Manage Change Successfully?. *Leadership Excellence Essentials*, 35 (1), 8–9.

Snider, B. and Southin, N. (2016). Operations Course Icebreaker: Campus Club Cupcakes Exercise. *Decision Sciences Journal of Innovative Education*, 14 (30), 262–272.

4. Teaching theory experientially*

Robert J. Marshak

One of the more difficult challenges facing instructors in theory-oriented courses is how to communicate abstract concepts in ways that generate interest and enhance internalization, focusing on the ability to meaningfully apply this material to organizational life rather than relying on rote memorization to pass a test or exercise. The former leads to "theory in action," while the latter often produces little more than recitation and test-taking ability that lacks insights into how the theory can be useful in "the real world."

Despite considerable advances in learning methodologies, the read–lecture–discuss method still tends to be the preferred vehicle for conceptual learning. This is particularly true when the concepts address organizational versus individual or interpersonal behavior. Unfortunately, the result is too often people who can cite theories and concepts chapter and verse, but have difficulty finding any use for this knowledge beyond demonstrating that they are "educated."

In response to this challenge, the discussion addresses ways to communicate theory experientially as an aid to internalization and practical application. The chapter begins with a brief discussion of the importance of formal and informal theories as practical tools for engaging the world around us. It then discusses using experiential methods in sequential combinations with cognitive readings and presentations. An additional approach that seeks to simultaneously combine experiential and cognitive learning about theories is then introduced and illustrated with three example designs. Some suggestions for how to debrief a simultaneous cognitive and experiential learning design are also briefly presented.

THEORIES AS PRACTICAL CONCEPTUAL TOOLS

It is important to keep in mind that as cognitive creatures people think about the world around them. They do not just experience it. In conducting their thought processes people order their world with beliefs about cause and effect relationships, assumptions about what is important and less important, and they create myriad categories to collect and store data. This ordering process is guided and influenced heavily by such factors as early value formation, socialization, and education. The end result is people with fairly clear, but usually implicit, beliefs about the world in which they live. These beliefs guide or determine what people will look at, what they will see, how they interpret what they see, and, therefore, how they will act. While perhaps not fitting the formal definition of a theory, these beliefs are nonetheless a person's "theory of how the world operates." Consequently, everyone, at all times, at some level, acts from theory. The underlying questions are: "What theories guide our thinking?" and "How explicit are they?"

Viewed in this manner, formal theories and concepts can become important tools for dealing successfully with the world around us. As with other tools, their effectiveness is enhanced if different types are available to meet a variety of needs and situations. The fewer the tools that are available, the greater the likelihood for overuse, abuse, or difficulty in getting the job done effectively and efficiently. As with many jobs, sometimes several tools need to be tested before the one that is most helpful in a particular situation is found.

Formal theories – for example, about organization, management, human behavior, and change processes – may be more explicit than everyday belief systems, but they are no different in complexity or use. Each is nothing more nor less than a conceptual system to understand various phenomena and guide behavior. The advantage of formal theories and concepts lies in their explicitness, which makes them easier to learn and understand than implicit beliefs. Their variety provides a diversity of possibilities for literally every occasion. Their liability, of course, is that like other belief systems, they may be inaccurate, incomplete, or misapplied. The skilled user of such tools, however, soon learns each instrument's particular strengths and weaknesses, while discarding outmoded or ineffective ones.

The value of learning formal theories and concepts is straightforward and utilitarian: they can be useful tools for effectively addressing management challenges, problems, and emerging situations. For illustration, consider the manager of a department confronted with poor performance from one section. The manager can: (1) view and analyze this situation based on their implicit beliefs about human behavior, motivation, performance, productivity, change processes, and so forth; (2) reach a conclusion; and (3) then act on that inference. The resulting action may prove effective or ineffective, but it will always be limited by the single conceptual tool used by the manager.

On the other hand, the manager could view and analyze the same situation using a variety of conceptual tools, in addition to the implicit belief system. Use of several theories and concepts will provide a greater variety of perceptions to guide action than one theory or belief system alone. The resulting action may again prove effective or ineffective, but it will benefit from the greater opportunity to discover new insights and understandings. In fact, used in this way, some of the liabilities of formal theories – their proliferation and contradiction of each other – can be turned into assets. Each provides a different perspective and understanding of the same situation, creating a rounder and more complete view of the problem and the opportunities for action.

If theories and concepts are useful for their practicality, then it is essential that they be learned in ways that demonstrate utility and application. Reliance on the read–lecture–discuss method alone is unlikely to do this. Discovering the usefulness of theories and concepts requires putting them into practice, and that means experiential learning is needed in addition to cognitive learning.

EXPERIENTIAL LEARNING OF THEORIES AND CONCEPTS

Experiential learning as an educational methodology is not new, although it has suffered from a stereotype that it is non-rigorous and skill-oriented, rather than demanding and concept-oriented. In reality, the methodology is neutral. In its application to various learning objectives, it can take on rigorous or non-rigorous, skill- or concept-oriented characteristics. Limitations and opportunities, therefore, are related to how it is applied, not its inherent properties. In turn, how experiential learning is applied becomes more a question of the skill and creativity of the instructor than subject-based limitations.

Furthermore, the range of approaches an instructor can draw upon for experience-based learning is broad, including: field projects, case studies, application exercises, simulations, role plays, and structured experiences. All of these are valuable methods or serve as adjuncts to cognitive readings and lectures. They also add a plethora of learning possibilities and combinations to the realization of theory-based learning objectives.

In theory-based learning, then, how experience-based means are used – rather than whether they should be used – is the critical issue. In typical practice there are two dominant ways in which cognitive and experiential processes can be combined for theory learning. One can begin by providing cognitive input followed by an experience; or alternatively creating an experience followed by cognitive reflection. For example, participants might first hear a lecture about someone's theory of change, followed by a case study application of the ideas and principles. Second, they might participate in a classroom simulation and then reflect on how different theories or concepts of change might apply, based on previous or subsequent readings and/or lectures. A variation of this sequence would be to have the participants in the exercise in post-event discussions generate their own theories and principles about organizational change based on their simulated experience.

It is important to note that in both combinations the different modes of learning are separate from each other: for example, now cognitively, then experientially. The separation compels the learner to establish the linkages between the two. This assessment, however, is made difficult by the linear sequence of the combinations, which creates a boundary, a separation of the two learning modes. The learner, then, has trouble establishing the necessary connections required for successful internalization and ability to apply the concepts in real-life situations. This problem is not a serious defect as long as learners are able to bridge this gap. Unfortunately, learners are left to their own devices and, more importantly, must do so intellectually; in essence, they must think about how the two are related. This can be a particular problem in learning theories and their practical use, since the contrast between conceptual abstraction – for example Lewin's (1947) three-stage change process of unfreezing, movement, freezing – and the richer texture of real-life situations tends to be strong. When the contrast is too great, the ability to make the necessary connections will be impeded. The learner will be able to intellectualize about how the two are related, but without experiencing and internalizing the linkage.

Simultaneous Cognitive and Experiential Learning

One approach to this difficulty is a third combination: simultaneous cognitive-experiential learning. In short, both learning modes occur at the same time. The advantages to this third combination are significant. First, it reduces the boundary between abstraction and specifics. Second, the two modes of learning are mutually reinforcing. Third, the process itself models the linkage between theory and action. Fourth, the learning is synergistic rather than linear. Fifth, different learning styles or preferences of learners are simultaneously addressed. Finally, learners not only think about the linkages, but directly experience them intellectually, psychologically, and emotionally. Therefore, the probability of successful internalization and the ability to apply the theory or concepts are increased.

For example, consider a course covering various leadership theories where several small 8–10 person groups are assigned the task of creating a 1 to 5 rank-ordered list of the most important actions for leaders to do to involve workers in problem-solving a work challenge. A leader for each group's task is then assigned, volunteers, or is selected in some manner. Each group is given a time limit to complete the rank ordering (for example, 30 minutes). Afterwards each member of the group debriefs their experience of leading and being led. Focus should be placed on what worked well and less well, and the extent to which their experience validated any of the theories they studied and/or the rank order list they created. In this example, the participants not only think about important leadership principles, but also simultaneously have a specific focused experience of leading and being led. This design potentially realizes many, if not all, of the potential advantages of the simultaneous cognitive-experiential exercise.

This approach combines at the same time thinking about and actively experiencing leadership in a problem-solving group. Because participants are thinking about and justifying the leadership actions that are most important, while at the same time experiencing the impacts of leadership actions and non-actions, the two modes are potentially mutually reinforcing and synergistic (theory reinforces experiences, which reinforce theory in a form of recursive learning). Actively experiencing one or more leadership theories may also help to suggest the sometimes subtle linkages between principles in the abstract and in practical experience. Furthermore, the combination of the two modes allows people who learn better through abstract reflection or by hands-on experience to simultaneously have their preferences met to some degree. Finally, because the exercise involves real behaviors, emotions, reactions, and outcomes, learners engage theory and action intellectually, psychologically, and emotionally. Naturally, of course, how well these advantages are realized depends on the quality of the debriefing part of the exercise and the instructor's facilitation skills.

DESIGNING SIMULTANEOUS COGNITIVE-EXPERIENTIAL LEARNING EVENTS

Designing a simultaneous cognitive-experiential learning event is not easy, but the difficulty may be associated more with the creativity and skills of the instructor than anything else. The principal design consideration is how to create a situation in which participants think about a theory or set of concepts cognitively while simultaneously experiencing them. This can be done in three main steps:

1. Identify the essence of the theory or concepts to be learned, leaving out the frills, flourishes, and elaborations.

2. Identify situations that will generate and highlight the phenomena described by the essence of the theory or concepts identified.
3. Merge the first two steps into a structured situation in which the task focuses on the conceptual content, while the process and dynamics replicate the phenomena described by the theory or concepts.

Emphasis should be placed on essence and simplicity to keep all data and dynamics highly focused on the main point(s) to be learned. The more complex the situation and theoretic point(s), the greater the likelihood that extraneous data and dynamics will be generated, which will confuse the learning point and impede the desired connections. This may mean leaving out important, but secondary, aspects of a theory. If the design is successful, however, the simultaneous cognitive and experiential validation of a part of the theory will, through a halo effect, validate the rest of the theory for learners.

The following three examples based on theories and situations encountered in organization development suggest how such designs can be approached, if not achieved. Theory variations to the main designs are also suggested.

Impact of Assumptions on Organizational Behavior

Douglas McGregor (1960) was one of the first theorists to draw attention to the impact that assumptions about human behavior have on managerial and organizational behavior. His Theory X and Theory Y have become part of the everyday lexicon in many organizations, yet often prove difficult concepts to fully internalize and apply in real-life situations. The following design is intended to promote internalization by creating a structured situation in which participants experience the impact of assumptions about human nature on organizational behavior, while simultaneously performing a task that requires discussing and engaging McGregor's theory cognitively.

Design
Learners are divided into an even number of small (5–7 persons or less) work groups and one evaluation group. The work groups are all given the same assignment – to develop a plan and management structure for evaluating the validity of McGregor's theory – and are given a specified time frame to complete their work. Their plan must also address how they will assure a complete, quality work group product delivered within the specified time frame. Half the work groups are then told they must develop their plans consistent with Theory X assumptions about human behavior,

while the other half are to develop their plans consistent with Theory Y assumptions. The work groups are further informed that after a specified preparation period, they will present their plans to the evaluation group, who will decide which plan is most likely to deliver the best product.

While the work groups are developing their plans, the evaluation group is asked to develop the criteria and decision-making process they will use in determining the best plan. After the specified period has elapsed, the various plans are presented and evaluated. After the best plan is selected, the total experience is debriefed; for example: What happened? Why? How did you feel about that? How did the constraints of the beliefs you were working under impact how you and others acted? What are real-world implications?

Typically, Theory X group plans end up radically different, in predictable ways, from Theory Y group plans. All participants have engaged, in a cognitive way, the meaning and content of McGregor's theory. Simultaneously, they experienced the theory's implications in terms of the final product, as well as how individuals and their groups organized and managed their assignments.

Theory variations

Since McGregor many more theories and research about the impact of assumptions on organizational behavior have become prominent. Many of these relate to organizational and societal cultural assumptions (e.g., Schein, 2010). Modifying the above design to contrast the cultural dimensions and assumptions described by Hofstede (2001) or Trompenaars and Hampden-Turner (1998) might be one example. Another related variation would be to redesign the small groups around diversity-oriented dimensions. For example, one set of groups based on Gilligan's (1982) research about the socialization of boys (for example, define self through autonomy, competitive games, reliance on rules, fear of failure, and a morality of rights) as contrasted with girls (for example, define self through relationships, turn-taking games, reliance of preserving relationships, fear of competitive success at expense of others, and a morality of responsibilities). Since such theories, including Gilligan's, have been challenged or qualified, an additional variation is to use the assumptions without attribution until the exercise is almost over. This would be done to keep the focus on the power of assumptions on work behavior rather than whether or not a particular list of assumptions is true for any particular cultural or identity group.

Impact of Group Size on Group Behavior

There is a significant body of literature that discusses the various impacts that size has on such group dynamics as leadership, participation, motivation, cohesion, task performance, and satisfaction (Cartwright and Zander, 1968). This design is intended to highlight those impacts by creating a structured situation in which participants cognitively and experientially address the impacts of group size on group dynamics.

Design

Participants are divided into pairs and asked to discuss the impact of group size on group dynamics. If the learning situation includes pre-readings or lectures, participants can be requested to discuss a particular theorist or set of ideas.

After a short discussion period, participants are asked to reflect individually and take notes on the two-person group discussion experience in terms of such factors as leadership, participation, motivation, cohesion, satisfaction, task performance, and so forth.

Pairs are then joined to form quartets, who are asked to continue the discussion of the impact of group size on group dynamics or to discuss a different theorist's ideas. Again, after a short discussion period, participants individually reflect and take notes on the four-person group experience using the same set of factors.

This process of doubling the size of the group, followed by discussion and reflection, is continued until a total learner group is formed. The total group then discusses their earlier discussions, their reflections on what the different size groups were like in terms of the given aspects, and the large-group experience in which they are currently participating.

Theory variations

One type of variation to this design would be based on the principle of moving from one type of homogeneous group into a more heterogeneous group along one or more dimensions; for example, having groups of all men and all women discuss the impact of gender on leadership, participation, motivation, cohesion, satisfaction, task performance, and so forth. This composition would be followed by creating mixed groups of men and women. An additional variation would be after the initial homogeneous groups to create mixed groups (for example, 25 percent women, 50 percent women, 75 percent women). The effects of generational groupings could also be the focus of the exercise (boomers, X-ers, millennials, and so on) moving from homogeneous to various mixed groups based on some set of theory and research propositions. If working with an executive set of students, additional groupings could be based on organizational or professional roles (for example, executives, mid-managers, supervisors, human resources, sales, information technology, manufacturing) depending on the theories and research being highlighted about how such differences impact (or not) aspects of group dynamics.

Individual versus Organizational Needs

One of the foundational axioms underlying organization development is the belief that optimal organizational performance is achieved when organizational and individual needs are integrated (Argyris, 1957). While a worthy goal in theory, this has proven elusive in practice. The following design highlights and dramatizes the issues and complexities involved by creating a structured situation in which participants cognitively and experientially face the difficulties of creating such organizations.

Design
Learners are divided into several small (5–7 person) groups and asked to develop recommendations on how to create organizations that can meet organizational and individual needs simultaneously. The time period set to develop the recommendations is kept less than optimum – perhaps 45–60 minutes or so – to create a sense of urgency. After the allotted time period has expired, the groups are given further instructions and time, to: "Debrief how well your group met individual needs for participation, leadership, preferred methods of working together, engagement, and so forth, while simultaneously meeting the group's (organization's) overall need to develop a quality set of recommendations within the specified time period." Following that discussion, they are to review and either modify or confirm their original recommendations.

After the groups have "processed their process" and reviewed their recommendations, group presentations are given, and the whole experience is discussed and debriefed. Typically, the juxtaposition of the cognitive task with the process and emotions experienced in doing that task dramatically highlights the issues and dilemmas involved in integrating individual and organizational needs.

Theory variations
The emphasis of Argyris's seminal proposition was to highlight the impacts of policies and practices based mainly in the legacy of scientific management and bureaucratic organizations. Today there are a plethora of theories and research about new forms of organizations and how that might impact individual motivation; for example, how might one create an organization that is "built to change" (Lawler and Worley, 2006) while simultaneously engaging and motivating workers (Latham, 2007; Lawler, 1994), some of whom might prefer more certainty and stability. In this example, the dimensions of an organization "built to change" along with some current set of individual motivators would need to be provided, based on the various theories and research being covered in the course.

Debriefing Simultaneous Cognitive-Experiential Learning Events

If the simultaneous cognitive-experiential learning event is well designed it tends to highlight of its own accord the connections between conceptual abstraction and specifics. Thus, it lessens the need for the instructor to draw out these connections during post-experience debriefing and discussion, and gives more attention to other aspects of the learning process. As an example, one of those aspects is the communication of an understanding that theory and concepts are useful, practical tools. Other aspects which occur post-event are:

- Drawing out the feelings and emotions experienced by the learners during the event. This adds cohesion to the cognitive-experiential connections and aids internalization. Participants receive a conceptual overlay for a generic type of behavioral experience and identify the feelings and emotions associated with that experience. Understanding is reinforced, virtually simultaneously, at cognitive, process, and feeling levels.
- Modeling the usefulness of theories as practical tools through post hoc analysis of the event. This can be done, for example, by asking the question, "Before this exercise began, what would the theory have predicted would happen in such a situation?" This point can then be followed by, "What did happen?" If the concepts and design are good, predictive ability should be clearly demonstrated. Even in cases where this does not occur fully, the limitations of the theory or concepts will be identified. This may be as important as understanding how and when they apply.

While the simultaneous cognitive-experiential learning event has received the most attention in this discussion, it is not presented as the only way to learn theories and concepts. Learners benefit from a variety of stimuli, and any approach can be overdone. Instead, eclectic educational designs using combinations of various learning methods are recommended. However, one of the methods considered in developing the overall design should include the simultaneous cognitive-experiential learning event.

SUMMARY

This chapter is based on an important contention: learning by experience is an important aspect of understanding and applying abstract theories. In my experience, the idea that concepts can be learned, at least in part, experientially has been questioned by many of my colleagues. It is as if there is an unspoken assumption that theories can only be taught by assigning readings and then delivering a solid lecture, followed by discussion and an exam or paper. Learning experientially is acknowledged but implicitly relegated to application of practice such as how to handle conflict or what to do in an applied case study. This bias suggests that theory learning needs to be primarily cerebral and not include the messiness that comes with application in real life, nor the emotions and reactions that might arise during application. I have always thought differently, believing that theory learning should include more holistic learning experiences that ground abstract concepts in real-life-like applications, where people can "see" and "feel" the theory in action. So, to summarize, the main points of my beliefs follow briefly below.

Successful internalization and ability to use theories and concepts require more than acquiring cognitive knowledge of content. Instead, they need to be viewed as important tools for addressing and dealing with life in general, as well as specific situations such as managing organizational change. To help communicate and reinforce this understanding, learners should be presented with situations that permit application and experience of the theory or concepts in action. Experience-based methods therefore are an essential part of theory learning. They provide the bridge from abstraction to specifics necessary for internalization and use.

The link between the cognitive and experiential learning modes is an important aspect of the process, since the connection is one of the critical ingredients to internalization. One way to increase the likelihood of learners making desired connections successfully is by focusing explicitly on that aspect in learning design and methodology. The learning of theory and concepts through simultaneous cognitive-experiential learning events is offered as one way of doing this.

NOTE

* An earlier version of this chapter appeared as R.J. Marshak (1983). Cognitive and experiential approaches to conceptual learning. *Training and Development Journal*, 37(5): 72–79.

REFERENCES

Argyris, C. (1957). The individual and organization: Some problems of mutual adjustment. *Administrative Science Quarterly*, 2(1): 1–24.

Cartwright, D., and Zander, A. (eds) (1968). *Group Dynamics*, 3rd edition. New York: Harper & Row.

Gilligan, C. (1982). *In a Different Voice*. Cambridge, MA: Harvard University Press.

Hofstede, G. (2001). *Culture's Consequences*. Thousand Oaks, CA: SAGE.

Latham, G.P. (2007). *Work Motivation: History, Theory, Research and Practice*. Thousand Oaks, CA: SAGE.

Lawler, E.E. (1994). *Motivation in Work Organizations*. San Francisco, CA: Jossey-Bass.

Lawler, E.E., and Worley, C.W. (2006). *Built to Change*. San Francisco, CA: Jossey-Bass.

Lewin, K. (1947). Frontiers in group dynamics. *Human Relations*, 1: 2–38.

McGregor, D. (1960). *The Human Side of Enterprise*. New York: McGraw-Hill Book Company.

Trompenaars, F., and Hampden-Turner, C. (1998). *Riding the Waves of Culture*, 2nd edition. New York: McGraw-Hill.

Schein, E.H. (2010). *Organizational Culture and Leadership*, 4th edition. San Francisco, CA: Jossey-Bass, Wiley.

PART II

Self-learning and beyond through change exercises

5. Increasing managers' self-awareness through storytelling and mask-making

Philip H. Mirvis

There is increased emphasis today on self-awareness in leadership education and development (Toegel and Barsoux, 2012; Zes and Landis, 2013). This focus is amply evident in the wide-ranging use of self-assessment tools, the practice of self-reflection in personal and professional development, and experimentation with meditation, martial arts, yoga, and myriad forms of "soul work" among current and prospective executives (Mirvis, 1997; Quinn, 1996; Schön, 1983). The injunction to "know thyself" is received wisdom, once inscribed on the Temple of Apollo at Delphi and found in ancient spiritual and practical teachings in Asia.

Many branches of modern psychology see self-knowledge as integral to human development and essential to being a healthy, functioning adult. Not surprisingly, leadership development programs typically encourage people to cultivate this through personality assessments, 360-degree feedback, coaching, and the like. And, while these all have their place in personal development, I favor less structured, more timeless means to promote self-awareness among current and future leaders. One approach involves personal reflection and storytelling about one's life experiences and lessons (Mirvis and Ayas, 2003).

CULTIVATING SELF-AWARENESS THROUGH AUTOBIOGRAPHY

The preparation of an autobiography, familiar in consciousness-raising circles, is one tried-and-true method for increasing self-awareness (Bannan, 2005). A number of studies document how self-consciousness expands when people understand their familial roots and formative experiences, what moves and puts them off, as well as their highest hopes and deepest fears. These insights contribute to "emotional intelligence"

Leadership Journey Line

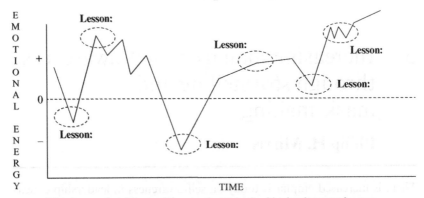

Plot the emotional ups and downs of your leadership development journey –
from birth to today. Label the critical events in your life and work that shaped
who you are as a leader. The ones that led to emotional peaks and valleys.

Figure 5.1   Know thyself: emotional lifelines

which means, among other things, being in touch with one's make-up and
proclivities, moods and emotions, and being able to recognize personal
strengths and weaknesses, as well as the impact a person has on others
(Goleman, 1995).

To begin the work of writing their autobiography, I often have people
individually prepare an "emotional lifeline" that charts their life's journey
from childhood to the present with careful consideration of emotional
highs and lows (see Figure 5.1 on doing a lifeline on "your leadership journey"). This technique, developed by organization development (OD) spe-
cialist Herb Shepard, then has them identify key experiences that shaped
their lives and the lessons learned (Shepard, 1984). These individuals then
share their insights with a colleague or fellow students in dyads and small
groups; in effect, transforming the chart and notes into a narrative and
conversation.

This medium has its authors delve into their formative experiences
and explore the roots of their identities. It is based generically on the
psychodynamic notion that people re-experience their lives when they
probe the most emotionally charged aspects of their past (Freud, 1965).
This process helps to surface unexamined and sometimes repressed feelings about one's life course and to lift them up for fresh consideration.
The approach is also integral to psychotherapy, where it strengthens the
"observing ego" and helps people to gain a clearer self-picture (Klein,
1959).

The "lifeline day" was powerful, and I think it allowed us to bond in a way that could not have happened without this.

Figure 5.2   A CEO shares his story with young managers

The "lifeline" methodology works well with adult learners of any age. I have used it with undergraduate students and MBAs in the classroom, with middle managers in training programs, and with executives at off-site retreats. Marker pens and flipcharts, or ideally poster-board pages, are the only supplies you need. With managers and executives, it can be helpful to have a senior leader from their company first present their own lifeline and key lessons. This role-modeling demonstrates the importance of self-awareness and legitimates self-disclosure among an otherwise skeptical audience. As an example, Figure 5.2 captures Lars Rabein, chief executive officer (CEO) of Novo Nordisk, telling his life story to a group of high-potential younger leaders. In the classroom, I sometimes prime the activity by showing a video or photos of executives preparing a lifeline and telling their stories. I have even shared my own lifeline with students.

In the college classroom or executive development programs, it is also useful to put some leadership theory behind this exercise in self-discovery and disclosure. Biographical studies by psychologist Howard Gardner (1995) underscore the relevance of the lifeline exercise for executive development by showing that formative experiences shape the beliefs and practices of leaders in almost every culture. He puts particular emphasis on "identity stories" as a means of connecting leaders and followers:

> Identity stories have their roots in the personal experiences of the leader in the course of his own development. But it is characteristic of the effective leader that his story can be transplanted to a larger canvas – that makes sense not only to members of his family and close circle, but to increasingly larger entities (Gardner, 1995, p. 25)

To get a feel for this, students can read or listen to excerpts of Gardner's work to savor the identity stories of Winston Churchill, Martin Luther King, Margaret Mead, Alfred Sloan, and others covered in his volume. Other leadership biographies can add local relevance and color. The real power, however, comes from presenting and listening to stories among a group of fellow students or managers. Such storytelling can be instructive for both the speaker and the listener. Here is one insight that emerged from a mid-manager's autobiography:

> Till now I had been trying to live up to this myth of invincibility even though I knew that I didn't have all the answers. I could not share my emotions and my fears with even my family as this, I thought, would be perceived as a sign of weakness. Now I realize how much more I could have done if only I had sought the emotional support that I knew was there all along.

On the overall process of writing his autobiography, another leader reflected, "It's like a surgery of the soul, you begin to see the roots and patterns, and you understand what truly moves you."

STORYTELLING AS A SHARED EXPERIENCE

Storytelling broadens consciousness of human experience. Gardner (1995, p. 43) documents the importance of this narrative approach: "The story is a basic human cognitive form; the artful creation and articulation of stories constitutes a fundamental part of the leader's vocation. Stories speak to both parts of the human mind – its reason and emotion."

My co-authored volume *To the Desert and Back* shows how storytelling can engage an entire organization (Mirvis et al., 2003). The company, the Dutch foods division of Unilever, had been through a difficult two-year turnaround and was then merged with another division. The integration of the companies had been technically efficient, but the human side of pulling people together had been neglected. To build person-to-person bonds, the

CEO, Tex Gunning, pulled together more than 250 managers, from all levels, in a leadership forum and went off site with them to a retreat in the Ardennes forest of Belgium. In a torch-lit cavern in an abandoned monastery, Gunning presented his lifeline to the managers. He talked hesitantly about his abusive stepfather, scraps with authority figures in childhood and military service, and assorted ups and downs over the life course. One young manager called out, "Thank you for sharing that Tex. Now we know you better and can forgive your anger." Subsequently, all the Dutch leaders prepared and shared lifelines with one another in small groups. In collective reflection thereafter, one recalled, "moments of silence became tangible." The combination of emotional openness and vulnerability seemed to touch people's hearts.

Two weeks later, in a large conference hall, all 2000 employees of the merged company prepared lifelines and shared their life stories with one another. As they found comfort and courage in each other's stories, the leaders were confronted with their sometimes hidden selves. As one of these individuals shared:

> Listening to other people's stories, you hear your own story. Other people's stories often clarify things in your own mind – what your past is and what drives you. I'm a 33-year-old guy, and I'm still trying to get recognition from my parents. That's not necessarily a bad thing, but having that self-awareness at least allows you to acknowledge and deal with that issue.

Still, in the competitive business culture it is difficult to "lower the guard," as one manager put it, when sharing life stories with peers. "The initial step of sharing personal information was difficult," he recalled, "but once you sense the value of truly connecting, building on it seemed relatively easy." Another participant noted:

> The important thing is to engage in the search and the inquiry into each other's cultures and mindsets, and into the relationship we have. To achieve this, one has to be open with oneself, understand one's own basic core values, and accept other people's differences "as is." This acceptance needs to be sincere and from the heart; without any prejudice, judgments and expectations.

Empathizing is central to what Erich Fromm (1956) calls the "art of loving." It too is integral to socialization and growth. Indeed, psychologists posit that just as seeing the world through another's perspective helps people to grow beyond egocentrism, so empathizing with another is the antidote to human selfishness. Alfie Kohn (1990), among others, suggests that empathy, more so than sympathy, is the basis for the "helping relationship." Certainly this is evident among the leaders who also reach out and offer support and comfort to each other: "With your help, not only I was able to [*sic*] get to know a great number of enlightened souls but I also discovered myself," reported one of them.

FINDING YOUR FUTURE SELF THROUGH MASKS

These kinds of conversations necessarily open up questions about personal identity, values, and priorities; in essence: Who am I? And even if feelings of anger, guilt, self-justification, and other kinds of defenses arise in such conversations, these are doors into deeper realms of self-consciousness.

In other education programs I have run, self-reflection has shifted from the past and present to the future. Within this context, leaders inquire: Who do I want to be? As an interesting and creative means to surface and convey visions of their future self, I have had leaders prepare a life-like "mask" of their face and decorate it with symbols of their life's intentions and aspirations. With the help of community artist Maggie Sherman, with whom I work, each leader's face is covered with gauze strips that, when dried, forms a three-dimensional plaster cast showing their facial features. Leaders are then asked to decorate these casts as they wish with paints, ready-made objects, cloth, feathers, pictures, or drawing to represent their future selves (see Figure 5.3 showing pictures of mask-making).

As Maggie points out, we typically see our face in two dimensions, like through a mirror. The three-dimensional mask allows us to see and convey our depth. The process of mask-making is easy but messy. It is a great way to build informal bonds among a group of students or managers as they typically put the plaster strips on one another, mold them, and joke along as a three-dimensional mask emerges. It is also a great activity for a special evening classroom session or off-site retreat. It can also be scaled: Maggie once involved a whole town of 10 000 people in mask-making. For a cleaner and quicker routine, she advises, make casts of people's hands. Gestures, cast in plaster, also have a story to tell.

Anthropologists have noted how tribal masks convey archetypal themes of human existence including unconscious fears and wishes (Levi-Strauss, 1982 [1979]). Often, the decorations on the leader's masks seem to communicate facets of their selves that are not conscious to them or have been "forgotten" in their busy lives and career pursuits. More than a few have commented how this "kid's craft activity" evoked images of their more playful selves and at the same time reminded them profoundly of their leadership role as parents and as stewards of the next generation.

After decorating their masks, leaders one by one are asked to describe for fellow leaders the personal meaning of their masks and who they aspire

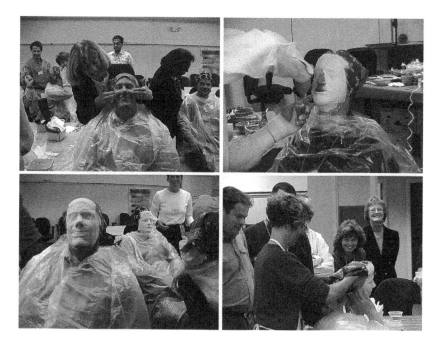

Figure 5.3   Mask-making

to be. This too is a form of storytelling and basis of interactive conversation with fellow leaders. In an executive development program at Ford Motor Company, I had managers prepare their lifelines to talk about their pasts, and later make masks to talk about their futures (see Figure 5.4 of a Ford manager talking about his future self). Many commented that mask-making was one of the high points of their development program. Much of the program stressed the analytic side of management. This exercise gave an opening to the emotive and aesthetic sides of human development.

CONCLUDING REFLECTIONS

Management educators have many frameworks and tools to draw on from the interrelated fields of action science, action inquiry, and action learning to help executives to know themselves more fully (Argyris et al., 1985; Revans, 1982; Torbert, 1978). Another set of frameworks and tools comes from the arts (Sutherland, 2013; Sutherland and Ladkin, 2013). On the use of aesthetics for learning, Taylor and Hansen (2005) differentiate "presentational knowing" from more formal propositional knowledge and

Figure 5.4   A Ford manager talking about his future self

colloquial know-how. They make the case that presentational forms of expression such as drawing, music, and drama are ideally suited to tapping into and representing people's tacit knowledge of themselves, other people, and the world around them. Gagliardi (1996) goes further and suggests that more rational representations of reality depend on and grow out of aesthetic experiences and understanding. That is the intent of these exercises in autobiography, storytelling, and mask-making.

How do these exercises fit into more comprehensive personal and organization development? Self-scanning can be a starting point for deeper "inner work" to, for instance, reflect on how you see yourself (self-image), how you value yourself (self-esteem), and how you compare yourself to who you would really like to be (ideal-self). This kind of self-examination is typically used in humanistic, Rogerian-type counseling, but it can also be taken up in the classroom and management development venues via journaling and structured exercises and can be assisted by peer-coaching sessions.

The deeper this self-reflection goes, the more attention you have to give to establishing ground rules that make participation voluntary, give people control over what they share with others, and sensitize all concerned to potential harms in giving and getting personal feedback. Some preparatory (and participatory) discussion about individual and cultural differences in people's openness to and comfort level with self-disclosure is important. It is also useful to give input on characteristics of helpful versus harmful feedback. As an educator it is your responsibility to ensure that this is a safe place for participants to learn about themselves and one another.

Work on self-awareness can also be a bridge to change: self and organizational. It is common for people to follow up self-reflection with action plans, whether for self-improvement or to adapt to new organizational requirements. See Schneider et al. (1996, p. 7) on this point:

> Changes in hierarchy, technology, communication networks, and so forth are effective only to the degree that these structural changes are associated with changes in the psychology of employees. Here is the central point: *organizations as we know them are the people in them; if the people do not change, there is no organizational change.*

Intentions toward self-improvement can also be joined up with broader aspirations to create, say, a better team, organization, or world as reflected in Gandhi's dictum: "be the change you wish to see in the world." On this count, I have worked with managers to traverse from discussions of personal values and examples of "when I was living my values" to work on collective values that might guide their management team or entire organization. Discussions of personal purpose can likewise be extended to bigger questions, such as: What is the purpose of our organization? And how can it reflect the guiding purposes of our own lives?

What does it take for a management educator to move from leading a few self-awareness exercises to engaging in full-blown personal or organization development? It takes some formal training, supervised guidance and practice in the early stages, and regular peer feedback and coaching. It is important to be self-aware about your own motivations for and skills at doing this kind of work, and to be prepared for push-back from students and managers (and their organizations) that it is "soft" and may not seem relevant for their "hard" world.

I have also found that working with a partner having complementary skills and temperament is useful. For example, I seem to be more of a "nurturer" when it comes to working with people on their personal development, so I turn to a fellow educator to dispense the "tough love." Somewhat paradoxically, I am more skilled at helping people to better "think" about themselves and their organization, so I like to partner with a "feeler" when it comes to providing them with more emotive guidance.

Finally, I recommend mixing modalities and methodologies in the classroom and management workshops: from individual to collective work, from logical-and-rational to aesthetic-and-playful, from inner issues to practical problems, indoors then outside, and so on. In that spirit, after reading this, draw your own lifeline or craft a mask.

REFERENCES

Argyris, C., Putnam, R., and Smith, D. (1985). *Action Science*. San Francisco, CA: Jossey-Bass.

Bannan, H.M. (2005). Writing and reading memoir as consciousness raising. *Feminist Collections*, 26 (2/3), 1–4.

Freud, S. (1965). *New Introductory Lectures on Psychoanalysis*. J. Strachey (ed.). New York: Norton.

Fromm, E. (1956). *The Art of Loving*. New York: Harper & Row.

Gagliardi, P. (1996). Exploring the aesthetic side of organizational life. In S.R. Clegg, C. Hardy, and W.R. Nord (eds), *Handbook of Organization Studies*, 169–184. London: SAGE.

Gardner, H. (1995). *Leading Minds*. New York: HarperCollins.

Goleman, D. (1995). *Emotional Intelligence*. New York: Bantam.

Klein, M. (1959). Our adult world and its roots in infancy. *Human Relations*, 12, 291–303.

Kohn, A. (1990). *The Brighter Side of Human Nature: Altruism and Empathy in Everyday Life*. New York: Basic Books.

Levi-Strauss, C. (1982 [1979]). *The Way of the Masks* (translated from *La Voie des Masques*, Paris, 1979 by S. Modelski). Seattle, WA: University of Washington Press.

Mirvis, P.H. (1997). "Soul work" in organizations. *Organization Science*, 8 (2), 193–206.

Mirvis, P.H. and Ayas, K. (2003). Reflective dialogue, life stories, and leadership development. *Reflections*, 4 (4), 39–48.

Mirvis, P.H., Ayas, K., and Roth, G. (2003). *To the Desert and Back: The Story of One of the Most Dramatic Business Transformations on Record*. San Francisco, CA: Jossey-Bass.

Quinn, R.E. (1996). *Deep Change: Discovering the Leader Within*. San Francisco, CA: Jossey-Bass.

Revans, R.W. (1982). *The Origins and Growth of Action Learning*. Bromley: Chartwell Bratt.

Schneider, B., Brief, A.P., and Guzzo, R.A. (1996). Creating a climate and culture for sustainable organizational change. *Organizational Dynamics*, 24 (4), 7–19.

Schön, D. (1983). *The Reflective Practitioner*. New York: Basic Books.

Shepard, H.A. (1984). On the realization of human potential: a path with a heart. In M.B. Arthur, L. Bailyn, D.J. Levinson, and H.A. Shepard (eds), *Working with Careers*, 25–46. New York: Grad School of Business, Columbia University.

Sutherland, I. (2013). Arts-based methods in leadership development: affording aesthetic workspaces, reflexivity and memories with momentum. *Management Learning*, 44, 25–43.

Sutherland, I. and Ladkin, D. (2013). Creating engaged executive learning spaces: the role of aesthetic agency. *Organizational Aesthetics*, 2, 105–124.

Taylor, S. and Hansen, H. (2005). Finding form: looking at the field of organizational aesthetics. *Journal of Management Studies*, 42 (6), 1211–1231.

Toegel, G. and Barsoux, J.L. (2012). How to become a better leader. *MIT Sloan Management Review*, 53 (3), 51–60.

Torbert, W. (1978). Empirical, behavioral, theoretical, and attentional skills necessary for collaborative inquiry. In R. Reason and P. Rowan (eds), *Human Inquiry: A Sourcebook of New Paradigm Research*, 437–446. London: Wiley.

Zes, D. and Landis, D. (2013). A better return on self-awareness. Korn Ferry Institute. https://www.kornferry.com/institute/better-return-self-awarenes (accessed March 15, 2017).

6. Exploring reactions to change: a card game simulation*

Susan M. Adams

Change often involves emotional and behavioral reactions. This exercise provides participants with the opportunity to explore such reactions when change is imposed on them, especially when new norms are not identified or fully understood. Participants go through several rounds of simulated organizational changes to experience their own reactions and observe reactions of others. By understanding reactions to change – from their own and others' perspectives – participants can become more aware of what is happening and can adapt change management accordingly. Numerous lessons from the change game simulation are possible for a wide variety of participants, from undergraduate students to top management teams of large business and nonprofit organizations.

As a general context for the exercise, people may enter change experiences predisposed to behave in ways that may hinder or support change (Lamm and Gordon, 2010). While recognizing and helping others to recognize resistance can be useful to reopen discussions about the situation that can lead to a common understanding of goals and engagement (Gardner, 2006), resistance can be costly by increasing time, resources, and success. This exercise is focused on making individuals aware of how reactions to change define the role one takes as supporter, bystander, or resister. During different steps in the change process, people may intensify or transform their perspective, with drastically different reactions such as changing from readiness to support change to resistance. The emotional intelligence literature suggests that awareness of one's reactions and identifying triggers enables us to better control our feelings and reactions (see Bar-On and Parker, 2000; Goleman et al., 2002; Nurick, 2011; Wong and Law, 2002).

By focusing on reactions to change, there are a number of potential uses of the game. The basic benefit from the exercise is increased awareness on multiple levels to form a better understanding of our own personal reaction to change, the different ways in which individuals react to change, group influences on reactions to change, and our own reactions to others' reactions to change. The exercise also provides an engaging forum for teaching aspects of change management, including, but not limited to, understanding types of change (for example, episodic and continuous change), the value of communication, ways to prepare for effective change, socialization of new group members, pacing change, and ways to manage reactions and resistance to change.

THE CHANGE GAME: THE CARD TOURNAMENT

Overview

The tournament simulates a business undergoing frequent reorganizations where people are moved to different groups (or business units). Participants start with a set of instructions – "game rules" – that simulate the organization's culture and the introduction of new policies and practices for everyone. Then the tournament begins with card game play; with instructions that, unbeknown to participants, are slightly different for each group. As play continues, the facilitator (or chief executive officer) announces a reorganization three to five times before ending the tournament.

The Game

Participants are divided into groups (typically 4–10 groups of 4–8 players depending on the number of people) for a card tournament. Basic instructions and a set of "game rules" are given to each group. See the Tournament Guide Sheet, Appendix 6.1. Each group receives the same Tournament Guide Sheet about how the game will be played, which is explained by the facilitator. This step simulates the organization's orientation program about new policies for employees.

What participants do not know is that in the next step, simulating practicing the new policies, each group is given slightly different rules as to how the game should be played (see Appendix 6.2). Participants then play a five-minute practice round of the card game in their groups.

Ten different rule configurations are provided in Appendix 6.2. As a way of tracking the different sheets, there is a series of card-like symbols at the bottom of each Game Rules Sheet:

① ace ♠ ④ ♦ ③ ♣ ⑦ ♥ ace ①
② ace ♠ ④ ♦ ③ ♣ ⑦ ♥ ②
③ ace ♠ ④ ♦ ⑤ ♣ ⑦ ♥ ③
④ ♦ ace ♠ ⑤ ♣ ⑦ ♥ ④
And so forth . . .

As you will notice, each set of symbols begins and ends with an identifying number: ①, ②, ③, ④, and so forth. Since participants only look at their group's Game Rules, they will not notice any differences, and the designators help you to easily keep track of the different rule configurations.

Once the game officially begins, the rules are taken away and no communication is allowed, including gestures and non-verbal communication. Each round lasts a few minutes: "winners" (those with most cards) move to the next "higher" level group; "losers" (with the least number of cards) move to the next "lower" group. When participants try to ask questions or look confused, they are reminded to do what they think is best as instructed by the initial "orientation" to company policies. In the next round, "winners" and "losers" unknowingly play under different sets of rules; the purpose of the exercise is to enable participants to examine how they and others act and feel when they are faced with situations where they do not fully know organizational rules or understand the norms. The longer the tournament lasts, the more participant reactions tend to change, which offers data for understanding what is triggering reactions. This information provides a foundation for self-management and overall change management.

Debriefing

Debriefing focuses on what participants experienced, for example, how they reacted to "new" rules, assumptions they made, whether they realized that the rules had changed, and what actions they took (for example, impose own rules, sit back and learn, try to negotiate the rules). Depending on time and emphasis, a range of other attitudes and behaviors can be explored (for example, effect of constrained communication, experience of winning and losing, personal behavior when confused, effect of various socialization efforts, how even small differences can lead to conflict and distrust). The debriefing should also focus on what can be done to recognize and manage problematic reactions to change. For example, value of communication discussion can include socialization of new group members and the power of culture. It is also interesting to discuss how behavior was related to what participants were focusing on. Some individuals will be group-focused while others will be focused on personal winning. A list of change management topics that can be discussed are mentioned above.

The following questions work well to begin the debriefing.

- What happened during the "tournament"? How did you react during the game?
- How did people discover they were not playing by the same rules?

- What did you do when you realized the rules were different? What options did you have?
- What are the strengths/weaknesses of these options (impose own rules; sit back and learn; try to negotiate new rules; withdraw/give up)?

Once the debriefing has helped participants to recognize what happened and why, the debriefing can turn to managing oneself, others, and the process.

Facilitating the Change Game

Preparation and play time
The facilitator:

- Determines the number of teams.
- Prepares a set of cards (with only ace through 7) for each group.
- Prepares a slide or copies of the Change Game Overview (Appendix 6.1). Note: a projected slide that remains visible throughout the tournament is suggested.
- Prepares copies of the group game play instructions (Appendix 6.2).
- Observes play, enforcing the "no talking" rule from beginning until debriefing time.
- Declares "time to reorganize" periodically, especially when groups are flustered or complacent.
- Ends the game when it appears that a significant number of participants are aware of different rules.

As the facilitator, it is important to enforce the "no talking, no notes, no signing" rule. It is also useful to have them keep score of each round in their heads; if you give them paper and pencil to track their scores, students tend to write notes to each other.

When taking the Game Rules away from the groups when the "tournament" begins, it is useful to tell them something like "You don't need these now, I need them for another class" to get them to stop thinking about why they do not have the rules during the game.

Variations

- For small classes or limited time, the simulation can be run with separate instructions randomly provided to all participants.
- Use full or larger decks of cards.

- Have students write their personal debriefings as an assignment.
- If the number of participants is too large, make some of them observers.

Concluding pointers

The game works best when groups are given enough time to get confused but most participants stay unaware that groups have different rules, before declaring organizational change or ending the game. It helps to display the location of the groups on a blackboard or flip chart so that winners and losers know where to go. Allow several minutes for a noisy room when game play is over before starting the debriefing. You will see and hear a wide range of reactions such as surprise, head-shaking, rolling eyes, and blaming self and others. These reactions also provide data for discussion. Debriefing becomes richer when the individual, group, organization, and societal levels of analysis are explored.

CONCLUDING THOUGHTS AND REFLECTIONS

What I enjoy most from using this exercise is its multifaceted lessons that are relatable for everyone. Participants can identify themselves or others in similar situations, whether it be at work, or in their personal lives such as moving or sending a child to college. Moreover, they can anticipate and identify reactions to change from themselves and others that can obstruct readiness for and engagement in change, so that they are prepared to manage and even leverage reactions. In essence, they are developing greater emotional intelligence with self-awareness, that leads to self-management and empathy with others, that leads to better, convincing communications. Consequently, participants reach and help others to reach change readiness. For example, recognizing and helping others to recognize resistance can be a tool used to reopen discussions about the situation that can lead to a common understanding of goals and engagement (Gardner, 2006).

Debriefings of this exercise often lead to new personal scripts for reducing resistance and managing personal reactions. A typical takeaway that participants mention is that they become more apt to share the history of common practices in their setting that new work group members or management may be unaware of. Such "blind spots" could inadvertently lead a new person to doing or saying something that upsets the group and/ or creates a negative image. In my sessions, I routinely end by saying, "This card game will continue to haunt you in many good ways for a long time if you let it."

NOTE

* The exercise is adapted from S. Thiagarajan (1990), *BARNGA: A Simulation Game on Cultural Clashes*. Yarmouth, ME: Intercultural Press.

REFERENCES

Bar-On, R. and Parker, J.D.A. (2000). *The Handbook of Emotional Intelligence: The Theory and Practice of Development, Evaluation, Education, and Application – at Home, School, and in the Workplace*. San Francisco, CA: Jossey-Bass.

Gardner, H. (2006). *Changing Minds: The Art and Science of Changing Our Own and Other People's Minds*. Boston, MA: Harvard Business Review Press.

Goleman, D., Boyatzis, R.E., and McKee, A. (2002). *Primal Leadership: Unleashing the Power of Emotional Intelligence*. Boston, MA: Harvard Business School Press.

Lamm, E. and Gordon, J.R. (2010). Empowerment, predisposition to resist change, and support for organizational change. *Journal of Leadership and Organizational Studies*, 17(4), 426–437.

Nurick, A.J. (2011). *The Good Enough Manager: The Making of a GEM*. New York: Routledge.

Wong, C.-S. and Law, M.N. (2002). The effects of leader and follower emotional intelligence on performance and attitude: an exploratory study. *Leadership Quarterly*, 13(3), 243–274.

APPENDIX 6.1:   GAME OVERVIEW

THE CARD GAME

Tournament Guide Sheet

- PREPARATION: You have 5 minutes to study the rules and practice playing the game. This period simulates a typical organizational orientation.
- GAME TIME:
  - Once the game (work) begins the rules will be taken away.
  - No verbal or non-verbal communication is allowed. During the game, NO WORDS, NO TALKING, NO SIGN LANGUAGE or other non-verbal communication. Just do your job.
  - ROUND 1: Begin the game at your Home Table. Keep playing until told to stop. Shuffle and deal cards again as necessary until told to stop.
- SCORING:
  - ROUND WINNER: Player winning the most games during the Round. Ties are resolved by alphabetical order of the group members' last name.
- MOVING (after each round):
  - Winner moves to next higher number table.
  - Loser moves to the next lower number table.
  - Others remain at the table.
- DETERMINE ANY OTHER RULES AS YOU GO (with no talking, etc.).

APPENDIX 6.2:   THE GAME RULES

(Note: When handing out the Game Rules, delete the Group 1, Group 2, Group 3, etc. indicators)

GROUP 1

The Game

CARDS: Only 28 cards are used: Ace, 2, 3, 4, 5, 6, and 7 in each suit. Ace is the
    lowest card.
PLAYERS: 4–6 (may vary depending on class size).
DEAL: Dealer shuffles the cards and deals them one at a time.
    Each player receives 4–7 cards (depending on number of players).
START: Player to the left of the dealer starts by playing a card of his/her choice.
    Other players take turns playing a card.
    The cards played (one from each player) constitute a TRICK.
    For the last TRICK, there may not be enough cards for everyone to play.
WINNING: When each player has played a card, the highest card wins the TRICK.
TRICKS: The TRICK winner collects the cards and puts them face down in a pile.
CONTINUATION: Winner of the TRICK leads the next round (see START).
    Procedure is repeated until all cards are played.
FOLLOWING: The first player in each round may play any suit; players must follow
    suit; if
SUIT: a player does not have a card of the lead suit, he/she may play any card.
TRUMP: Spades are trump. If you do not have a card of the played suit, you may
    "trump" with a spade, winning the trick. Highest trump card in a hand wins.
END/WIN: Game ends when all cards have been played. Player winning the most
    tricks is the winner.

① Ace ♠ ④ ♦ ③ ♣ ⑦ ♥ Ace ①

GROUP 2

The Game

CARDS: Only 28 cards are used: Ace, 2, 3, 4, 5, 6, and 7 in each suit. Ace is the lowest card.

PLAYERS: 4–6 (may vary depending on class size)

DEAL: Dealer shuffles the cards and deals them one at a time
    Each player receives 4–7 cards (depending on number of players)

START: Player to the left of the dealer starts by playing a card of his/her choice
    Other players take turns playing a card
    The cards played (one from each player) constitute a TRICK
    For the last TRICK, there may not be enough cards for everyone to play

WINNING: When each player has played a card, the highest card wins the TRICK.

TRICKS: The TRICK winner collects the cards and puts them face down in a pile

CONTINUATION: Winner of the TRICK leads the next round (see START)
    Procedure is repeated until all cards are played

FOLLOWING: The first player in each round may play any suit; players must follow suit; if

SUIT: a player does not have a card of the lead suit, he/she may play any card. The trick is won by the highest card of the original lead suit.

END/WIN: Game ends when all cards have been played. Player winning the most tricks is the winner

②Ace♠④♦③♣⑦♥②

GROUP 3

The Game

CARDS: Only 28 cards are used: Ace, 2, 3, 4, 5, 6, and 7 in each suit. Ace is the highest card.

PLAYERS: 4–6 (may vary depending on class size)

DEAL: Dealer shuffles the cards and deals them one at a time

Each player receives 4–7 cards (depending on number of players)

START: Player to the left of the dealer starts by playing a card of his/her choice

Other players take turns playing a card

The cards played (one from each player) constitute a TRICK

For the last TRICK, there may not be enough cards for everyone to play

WINNING: When each player has played a card, the highest card wins the TRICK.

TRICKS: The TRICK winner collects the cards and puts them face down in a pile

CONTINUATION: Winner of the TRICK leads the next round (see START)

Procedure is repeated until all cards are played

FOLLOWING: The first player in each round may play any suit; players must follow suit; if

SUIT: a player does not have a card of the lead suit, he/she may play any card

TRUMP: Spades are trump. If you do not have a card of the played suit, you may "trump" with a spade, winning the trick. Highest trump card in a hand wins.

END/WIN: Game ends when all cards have been played. Player winning the most tricks is the winner

③ Ace♠ ④♦ ⑤♣ ⑦♥ ③

GROUP 4

The Game

CARDS: Only 28 cards are used: Ace, 2, 3, 4, 5, 6, and 7 in each suit. Ace is the
highest card.
PLAYERS: 4–6 (may vary depending on class size)
DEAL: Dealer shuffles the cards and deals them one at a time
Each player receives 4–7 cards (depending on number of players)
START: Player to the left of the dealer starts by playing a card of his/her choice
Other players take turns playing a card
The cards played (one from each player) constitute a TRICK
For the last TRICK, there may not be enough cards for everyone to play
WINNING: When each player has played a card, the highest card wins the TRICK.
TRICKS: The TRICK winner collects the cards and puts them face down in a pile
CONTINUATION: Winner of the TRICK leads the next round (see START)
Procedure is repeated until all cards are played
FOLLOWING: The first player in each round may play any suit; players must follow
suit; if
SUIT: a player does not have a card of the lead suit, he/she may play any card
TRUMP: Spades are trump. You may play a spade any time – even if you have a
card of the first suit – "trumping" to win the hand. Highest trump card in a
hand wins.
END/WIN: Game ends when all cards have been played. Player winning the most
tricks is the winner

④♦Ace♠⑤♣⑦♥④

GROUP 5

The Game

CARDS: Only 28 cards are used: Ace, 2, 3, 4, 5, 6, and 7 in each suit. Ace is the lowest card.

PLAYERS: 4–6 (may vary depending on class size)

DEAL: Dealer shuffles the cards and deals them one at a time
Each player receives 4–7 cards (depending on number of players)

START: Player to the left of the dealer starts by playing a card of his/her choice
Other players take turns playing a card
The cards played (one from each player) constitute a TRICK
For the last TRICK, there may not be enough cards for everyone to play

WINNING: When each player has played a card, the highest card wins the TRICK.

TRICKS: The TRICK winner collects the cards and puts them face down in a pile

CONTINUATION: Winner of the TRICK leads the next round (see START)
Procedure is repeated until all cards are played

FOLLOWING: The first player in each round may play any suit; players must

SUIT: follow suit; if a player does not have a card of the lead suit, he/she may play any card

TRUMP: Spades are trump. If you do not have a card of the played suit, you may "trump" with a spade, winning the trick. Highest trump card in a hand wins.

END/WIN: Game ends when all cards have been played. Player winning the most tricks is the winner

⑤♦④Ace♠⑦♣♥⑤

GROUP 6

The Game

CARDS: Only 28 cards are used: Ace, 2, 3, 4, 5, 6, and 7 in each suit. Ace is the lowest card.

PLAYERS: 4–6 (may vary depending on class size)

DEAL: Dealer shuffles the cards and deals them one at a time
Each player receives 4–7 cards (depending on number of players)

START: Player to the left of the dealer starts by playing a card of his/her choice
Other players take turns playing a card
The cards played (one from each player) constitute a TRICK
For the last TRICK, there may not be enough cards for everyone to play

WINNING: When each player has played a card, the highest card wins the TRICK.

TRICKS: The TRICK winner collects the cards and puts them face down in a pile

CONTINUATION: Winner of the TRICK leads the next round (see START)
Procedure is repeated until all cards are played

FOLLOWING: The first player in each round may play any suit; players must follow
SUIT: if a player does not have a card of the lead suit, he/she may play
any card

TRUMP: Diamonds are trump. If you do not have a card of the played suit, you may
"trump" with a diamond, winning the trick. Highest trump card in a hand wins.

END/WIN: Game ends when all cards have been played. Player winning the most
tricks is the winner

⑥♦④♣Ace♠⑦♥⑥

GROUP 7

The Game

CARDS: Only 28 cards are used: Ace, 2, 3, 4, 5, 6, and 7 in each suit. Ace is the highest card.

PLAYERS: 4–6 (may vary depending on class size)

DEAL: Dealer shuffles the cards and deals them one at a time
Each player receives 4–7 cards (depending on number of players)

START: Player to the left of the dealer starts by playing a card of his/her choice
Other players take turns playing a card
The cards played (one from each player) constitute a TRICK
For the last TRICK, there may not be enough cards for everyone to play

WINNING: When each player has played a card, the highest card wins the TRICK.

TRICKS: The TRICK winner collects the cards and puts them face down in a pile

CONTINUATION: Winner of the TRICK leads the next round (see START)
Procedure is repeated until all cards are played

FOLLOWING: The first player in each round may play any suit; players must follow

SUIT: suit; if a player does not have a card of the lead suit, he/she may play any card

TRUMP: Diamonds are trump. You may play a diamond any time – even if you have a card of the first suit – "trumping" to win the hand. Highest trump card in a hand wins.

END/WIN: Game ends when all cards have been played. Player winning the most tricks is the winner

⑦♦④♣Ace♠⑥♥⑦

GROUP 8

The Game

CARDS: Only 28 cards are used: Ace, 2, 3, 4, 5, 6, and 7 in each suit. Ace is the highest card.

PLAYERS: 4–6 (may vary depending on class size)

DEAL: Dealer shuffles the cards and deals them one at a time
  Each player receives 4–7 cards (depending on number of players)

START: Player to the left of the dealer starts by playing a card of his/her choice
  Other players take turns playing a card
  The cards played (one from each player) constitute a TRICK
  For the last TRICK, there may not be enough cards for everyone to play

WINNING: When each player has played a card, the highest card wins the TRICK.

TRICKS: The TRICK winner collects the cards and puts them face down in a pile

CONTINUATION: Winner of the TRICK leads the next round (see START)
  Procedure is repeated until all cards are played

FOLLOWING: The first player in each round may play any suit; players must follow

SUIT: suit; if a player does not have a card of the lead suit, he/she may play
  any card

TRUMP: Diamonds are trump. You may play a diamond any time – even if you have a card of the first suit – "trumping" to win the hand. Highest trump card in a hand wins.

END/WIN: Game ends when all cards have been played. Player winning the most tricks is the winner

⑦♦④♣Ace♠⑥♥⑦

GROUP 9

The Game

CARDS: Only 28 cards are used: Ace, 2, 3, 4, 5, 6, and 7 in each suit. Ace is the
highest card.

PLAYERS: 4–6 (may vary depending on class size)

DEAL: Dealer shuffles the cards and deals them one at a time

Each player receives 4–7 cards (depending on number of players)

START: Player to the left of the dealer starts by playing a card of his/her choice

Other players take turns playing a card

The cards played (one from each player) constitute a TRICK

For the last TRICK, there may not be enough cards for everyone to play

WINNING: When each player has played a card, the highest card wins the TRICK.

TRICKS: The TRICK winner collects the cards and puts them face down in a pile

CONTINUATION: Winner of the TRICK leads the next round (see START)

Procedure is repeated until all cards are played

FOLLOWING: The first player in each round may play any suit; players must follow

SUIT: suit; if a player does not have a card of the lead suit, he/she may play
any card

END/WIN: Game ends when all cards have been played. Player winning the most
tricks is the winner

GROUP 10

The Game

CARDS: Only 28 cards are used: Ace, 2, 3, 4, 5, 6, and 7 in each suit. Ace is the lowest card.

PLAYERS: 4–6 (may vary depending on class size)

DEAL: Dealer shuffles the cards and deals them one at a time
Each player receives 4–7 cards (depending on number of players)

START: Player to the left of the dealer starts by playing a card of his/her choice
Other players take turns playing a card
The cards played (one from each player) constitute a TRICK
For the last TRICK, there may not be enough cards for everyone to play

WINNING: When each player has played a card, the highest card wins the TRICK.

TRICKS: The TRICK winner collects the cards and puts them face down in a pile

CONTINUATION: Winner of the TRICK leads the next round (see START)
Procedure is repeated until all cards are played

FOLLOWING: The first player in each round may play any suit; players must follow suit; if

SUIT: a player does not have a card of the lead suit, he/she may play any card

TRUMP: Diamonds are trump. You may play a diamond any time – even if you have a card of the first suit – "trumping" to win the hand. Highest trump card in a hand wins.

END/WIN: Game ends when all cards have been played. Player winning the most tricks is the winner

⑨♦④♣Ace♠⑥♥⑨

7. From both sides to all sides: creating common ground where there has been none before

Matt Minahan

One of the biggest challenges in any change effort is to align the beliefs and perceptions of the many parts in the system in order to take concerted action going forward. Whether it is a merger, acquisition, cross-departmental reorganization, change of strategy, or change of leadership, creating a commonly held narrative is vital to getting minds and hearts working together, aligned around a common set of facts and beliefs among organizational or community members. Successful organizational change – from mergers and acquisitions to internal reorganization – depends in large part on a clear vision of the desired future state, a common understanding of what brought the parties to this point, and their ability to be honest with themselves and each other about the beliefs and opinions they hold about each other. The two activities outlined in this chapter help to achieve the latter two.

Two good starting points for the change leader and/or facilitator are: (1) how to create conversations that help to build one common group among people who do not know each other and may in fact be threatened by each other; and (2) how to build the trust necessary to have that conversation. It is important to be deliberate about establishing a positive climate in which all can be honest with themselves and each other about assumptions, beliefs, projections, and generalizations about others engaged in the process. In some cases, this could be management versus staff. In others, it could be intra-departmental rivalries. In yet others, it could be the different entities involved in a merger or acquisition.

Given the high stakes in these conversations, it is helpful to use activities that enable honesty and truth-telling, and at the same time encourage a sense of humor and relief from the deadly serious tone that many such exercises require. It is also imperative to be intentional about creating the narrative for the change program, both about who we are and what has happened in the past, and who we want to be together in the future. Open, transparent, real-time activities that engage the whole system, as both of these activities do, go a long way toward creating the narrative that is required for a successful change effort.

The two activities outlined in this chapter – the "Argument of Obviousness" and "Dealing in Decades" – are designed to assist organizations in realizing and capitalizing on the complexity in the system. The route to complexity requires acknowledging that there are two underlying dimensions of organizational life, differentiation and integration, both of which must be dealt with, which might seem paradoxical. These two dialectically linked processes encourage us all and our organizations to reach their fullest potential and uniqueness (differentiation), while at the same time recognizing and committing to a whole that is larger than any one individual or entity (integration).

Given the significant differences that exist in organizations, the differentiation challenge is to better understand the ways in which the various entities come to a clear understanding of who they are. Integration reflects how these entities find common ground and help each other to reach common goals together. The both/and here dimensions are typically clear to participants. In an organization that is differentiated but not well integrated, there is individuality, freedom, and encouragement of differences, but not the kind of organizational discipline to make the entity much more than the sum of its parts. In an organization that is integrated but not well differentiated, policies and procedures are clear and compliance is required, often at the expense of individual commitment and creativity (Csikszentmihalyi, 2009).

Before introducing the two exercises, a few guiding thoughts are in order. First, revealing the perceptions that each entity holds of the other, which are often covert, is critical to any successful integration. Once at least a portion of these covert generalizations is made public and shared with each other, differentiation may continue (Marshak, 2006). Only when the parties know and understand each other better can integration truly continue on a solid footing of mutual respect and understanding.

A second key to successfully executing these activities is the participants' sense of free choice in what they say and how they show up. "Lewin's theory suggests that the choices an individual makes are not just the result of personal inside forces, but are affected by everyone in the group and the circumstances of the environment" (Smith and Leeming, 2011, p. 178). It follows that the full and free participation of all rests on their individual freedom to act on their own beliefs and feelings, unconstrained by requirements or expectations imposed from above or outside.

Finally, leaders and facilitators of these activities must feel free to amend or improvise along the way, based on the actions and reactions among participants. Redesign choices could include "adjusting the parameters of an activity, imposing time limits, allowing or disallowing certain activities, and placing limits on members of the group" (Smith and Leeming, 2011, p. 178). The time, setting, climate of the group, set-up in the room, and a dozen other factors can change the dynamics of the exercise, and it is up to the leader or facilitator to make those judgments in the moment.

THE ARGUMENT OF OBVIOUSNESS

The Argument of Obviousness is an experiential exercise exploring differentiation:

> Diagnose the differences that matter. In many cases, there are significant differences between the acquirer's culture and that of the acquired. But it can be difficult to pinpoint where, and how substantial, the differences are. (Stafford and Miles, 2013, Heading: "Next, diagnose the differences that matter," para 1)

The exercise encourages the separate parties in the merger, acquisition, or intra-organizational restructuring to give voice to the beliefs and assumptions that each side holds about the other by creating caricatures of each other. By responding to eight questions that are clearly generalizations and intended to elicit extreme perceptions of the other, the exercise helps to reveal the unspoken prejudices held by each side in a way that is both honest and humorous. The very act of generalizing and caricaturing the others help all sides to reveal the limitations of their own views, which can be useful in overcoming the stereotypes that underlie the caricatures.

These generalizations and stereotypes are often based on little information, often attached to the role, function, or job type, or even just the reputation of the other entity. Statements often heard are based on the jobs of the others, such as "We all know what accountants are like," or, "No one likes working for that organization," based on its reputation. The exercise is designed to assist in the differentiation between or among the various entities involved in the change project.

The goals of the Argument of Obviousness are to:

- help participants get in touch with their own prejudices and assumptions about others involved in the same change process;
- explore the different perceptions that each group has of the other(s);
- get out on the table and hopefully dispel some of the negative or unhelpful assumptions and beliefs that would limit the success of the change program; and

- lay the groundwork for building trust among the various parties and contribute to creating a narrative about the past that becomes the basis for the change program going forward.

The Argument of Obviousness can be used in the following ways:

- as part of a process of bringing together different elements of a community or organization;
- as a means of differentiating the different entities in a merger, acquisition, or organizational restructuring;
- as a light and humorous way to make explicit some of the stereotypes and prejudices that might be held by differing sides.

There are a number of advantages of this activity: (1) it is simple and easy to set up; (2) no specialized knowledge or tools are required, so everyone can easily contribute; (3) everyone has something to contribute; and (4) it is different from the kinds of activities that usually occur in these settings. At the same time, the exercise has an underlying disadvantage: if the differences between the groups are seriously felt and deeply held, the exercise could amplify those differences and make integration even harder.

The Exercise

- Intended audience: the separate parties of any organizational restructuring, merger, realignment, or acquisition.
- Duration: 40–60 minutes, depending upon how the debrief is structured.
- Exercise preparation (materials, room set-up, pre-work for participants, and so on): the activity requires participants to be seated at tables of six, eight, or ten, with tables grouped by organization, with the members of one organization sitting on one side of the room, and the members of the other organization sitting on the other side of the room. If there are three or more groups in the exercise, arrange the tables of each group together.

The Argument of Obviousness is comprised of the eight statements below. It is recommended to print one copy for each participant, and one for each table, so that each person can complete all eight and then discuss their results with others at their tables. A computer and projector are needed to project the questions during the work of the individuals and tables, and to record the results from all of the groups for all to see. It is helpful to leave enough room between statements to record the results from all of the tables. Before the event begins, it is helpful to recruit someone to record the tables' results into the document projected onto the screen.

The Argument of Obviousness statements are:

- Wouldn't it be cool if . . .
- And we didn't have to . . .
- And we could just . . .
- And then we could . . .
- All of {them} are {blank}
- None of {them} ever does {blank}
- The only way to motivate {them} is {blank}
- The only thing {they} are good at is {blank}

Each person receives a handout with the eight Argument of Obviousness statements, and each table receives one additional handout.

Instructions for facilitators
This activity is a high energy, fast paced way to get at the stereotypes that each side might hold of the other. It is important to keep things moving quickly so that participants do not overthink their answers. The following are general guidelines for conducting the exercise:

1. Briefly explain the purpose of the exercise. In this case, a lot of detail up front often limits the impact of the event. A brief statement along the following lines is sufficient: "Our goal is to get some perceptions of each other out in the open and on the table."
2. Distribute hard copies of the eight Argument of Obviousness statements to each table, and project these questions on the screen.
3. Outline the goals of the exercise (above) and that each table will come up with their own answers to the eight statements which will be shared with everyone in the room.
4. Ask each person to take just a minute to complete the eight statements in the handout, and encourage them to be provocative and outrageous if they want. Explain that they will share their answers with others at their table and that each table will have 7–8 minutes to develop a consensus set of answers to the questions, which will be shared with everyone in the room.
5. Task the individuals to complete the statements in approximately two minutes.
6. Task the table groups to discuss the individuals' responses to the statements and give them approximately 7–8 minutes to come up with the most interesting, or provocative, or funny responses on behalf of

the whole table. Explain that the purpose is not to have the best, well-formed consensus answers for each statement, but rather to come up with answers that seem true but may be provocative or funny.

7. After 7–8 minutes, and with a quick pace, ask each table to report its results. Make sure that they are being recorded by your volunteer properly on the master document on the computer for projection on the screen or a series of flipcharts. It is likely that the listeners in the other organization will want to question, respond, or argue with what is being said. Explain that there will be time for each side to respond once both sides are complete.

8. Once all of the tables have reported on both sides, display on the computer for projection on the screen or a series of flipcharts the results from all of the tables from the first group about the second group. Ask the members of the second group to call out their responses to what the first group has said about them. Hear them quickly; there is not normally a need to do any table work on this, or to record their responses, as that slows down the conversation and makes it a more rational and analytical exercise than is intended.

9. Then display the results from all of the tables from the second group about the first group. Ask the members of the first group to call out their responses to what the second group has said about them. Again hear them quickly; there is not normally a need to do any table work on this, or to record their responses, as that slows down the conversation.

10. Reconfigure the tables to maximize a mix of participants from both groups and as many functions as possible.

11. Task the groups to discuss the stereotypes that they have heard. Encourage all to listen carefully to what others are saying about their group, and to be open to the possibility that there is some truth in what is said.

Debrief for participants
Remembering that the goal of this exercise is to reveal biases and generalized prejudices on each side about the other(s), there are some questions to consider offering to the group once the activity is over, including, "In this exercise. . .":

- What did you learn about yourselves as a group?
- What did you learn about the people in the other group(s)?
- What about what they said about you did you find interesting? Funny? Accurate? Completely wrong?
- When you heard what they said about your group, how did you feel?

- When you heard what they said about your group, how did you feel about their group?
- When you heard what they said about your group, what did you want to say to them?

If time is short, these questions can be asked in plenary in 5–10 minutes. If there is more time, these questions can be worked at each table, and potentially in each group. The final question for the debrief is, "Now that you've done this, how will you behave differently in interacting with people from the other group(s)?"

Final Thoughts

This activity excels at getting participants from opposite sides of a system engaged in a simple but meaningful task, with very little explanation or time needed up front. It is excellent at exploring the differences among/between groups involved in the organizational change. It helps to accomplish the differentiation among/between groups that is necessary en route to the integration that is required for any successful merger, acquisition, or organizational integration. Even though the content of the exercise is about differences, it often has the desirable effect of bringing both/all sides of the change process together by exposing the very generalizations and projections that perpetuate and amplify our differences.

DEALING IN DECADES

Another challenge in organizational change is to create one whole perspective or aligned mindset among the multiple people and individual parts of a system. Where the preceding exercise emphasized differentiation, this is a natural follow-up emphasizing integration. It is particularly useful after the differences have been explored and the components have been united into the same organization.

There are many ways to do this, but Dealing in Decades is intentionally designed to flatten the hierarchy, give all voices equal weight, and to engage the whole system including all of its subsidiary components all at once in creating the history and current perspective on the organization. This is an important factor in a system in which people with titles or roles have undue influence and where there are concerns about bringing forth voices of those who have previously been marginalized. As noted by Roberts (2012, p.15):

While it is certainly the case in the twenty-first century that notions of experience from women, African Americans, Native Americans, and other marginalized groups both in the West and in the developing world are rising in attention and prominence, more work needs to be done in exploring the intersections between these so-called marginalized or subaltern voices and present-day experiential education.

This exercise enables voices from all corners of the organization to be heard fully and to contribute to the joint creation of the organization's history, thereby creating an inclusive environment for marginalized people to come forward, be heard, and fully contribute.

Dealing in Decades is a small, simple, experiential activity that achieves large-scale results. The goals of the activity are to:

- engage the whole system in a fun, interesting, and highly participative activity;
- complement the organization's efforts to integrate different components into one coherent whole;
- establish a narrative around a commonly held set of facts about the history of the organization, including key leaders, pivotal events, and how the organization has navigated its outside environment;
- lay the groundwork for understanding the organization as it exists today, and the organization's past as its prologue and the necessary precursor to creating a narrative for the future;
- flatten the hierarchy and equalize all voices in the room.

Dealing in Decades can be used in the following ways:

- to create a shared sense of history among members of a community or organization;
- to provide context and set the scene for decisions or actions to be undertaken in the future;
- to contribute to the creation of the narrative for change in an interesting and often fun event in real time;
- to illustrate the separate and shared histories of entities during a merger or acquisition;
- to reframe current events within the community or organization in light of past events;
- to expand the frame of reference of an organization or community to include larger, societal factors that have impacted the organization;
- to integrate members who are new to the community or organization by including participants who have longer standing in the system;

- to help build trust among all participants by conducting the event openly, transparently, and in real time for all to observe and contribute to.

Similar to the Argument of Obviousness exercise, there are a number of advantages with this activity: (1) it is simple and easy to set up; (2) it relies upon pairs and trios to do the work; (3) no specialized knowledge or tools are required, so everyone can readily contribute; (4) everyone has something to contribute; (5) there are no group reports; and (6) the group often surprises itself with its output and results. Given the pull of this activity, a drawback is that the room typically gets noisy when pairs are talking.

The Exercise

- Intended audience: anyone/everyone in an organization or event where a shared understanding of the history and context, built from the bottom up, is important.
- Duration: 40–90 minutes, depending upon the number of decades and the number of participants.
- Exercise preparation (materials, room set-up, pre-work for participants, and so on): this activity requires one page of chart paper for each decade under discussion, markers to write on the chart paper, and enough flipchart stands or wall space to accommodate the hanging of the chart pages. Participants can be seated at tables or theater style.

Instructions for facilitators
This activity is a high energy, fast paced way to get all voices into the room. Instructions for facilitators are:

1. Select the decades to explore, and write each decade on a separate piece of chart paper. At a recent session on the field of organization development (OD), for example, charts were created for 1890, 1900, 1910 . . . through 2010. The selection of the decades should be a reflection of the history of the organization and the political, economic, social, and technical factors that might have preceded the establishment of the organization.
2. Once a chart page is created for each decade, post the decade chart papers on the walls in sequence from earliest to latest.
3. Recruit volunteer scribes to chart each decade.
4. Recruit a volunteer scribe to record on a projected computer screen the themes that emerge from the review of the decades.

5. Briefly explain the purpose of the exercise. Much of the benefit comes from the group's surprise at what they have developed, so overexplaining what you hope to accomplish will short-change that benefit.
6. Keep the instructions brief; get participants into the conversation quickly; collect their comments for the decade pages and plenary discussion quickly; keep the energy level and pace high.

Exercise description and instructions for participants

Participants are directed to notice the decade pages on the walls, and told that they will generate the content for each. In the first round, participants are invited to speak with a partner, together selecting a decade in which they have a mutual interest, and identifying a few key facts or events that occurred during that decade. After 5–6 minutes, scribes are asked to stand near their decade page. One at a time, participants are invited to call out their decade and event(s), which are quickly written down. Most of the content will likely focus on the more recent decades. Duration: 10–15 minutes.

In the second round, participants are still in plenary. Starting with the earliest decade, the volunteers who have recorded the items call out to the room what is recorded on their flipchart. Once the content of each flipchart has been reviewed, ask all participants to call out additional facts or events that occurred during that decade, for recording on the flipcharts. Most times, participants will identify events or factors from history that have been overlooked. It also is helpful if the facilitator has a few key facts or events relevant to the organization or the historical period to add for each decade, in case they are not mentioned by the participants. It is important to keep the pace and energy level high. Duration: depending upon the number of decades and people, this can take 10–30 minutes.

In the third round, once the charts are full or time has expired, invite the participants to review all of the content, either from their seats or via a gallery walk among the decade charts, and to look for themes. A common question is, "Are there any topics or themes that carry over across decades that stand out for you?" Still in plenary, participants call out themes that they have identified, which are recorded on a computer and projected to the full room. Typically, these themes are longer, more textual and contextual than can easily fit onto a chart page, and occasionally are the source of next-steps actions, so having them recorded in a document makes them easy to act upon. Duration: 15–20 minutes.

The wrap-up: once the themes are identified, it is often helpful to have someone in leadership, possibly someone who has been around a longer time, summarize the main messages that they take out of the exercise, and how this effort will feed into another phase of the organizational change.

The objectives of this activity are to engage the whole system, to complement other components of the change effort, and to establish a commonly held set of facts for moving forward. Even though this event may be central to an overall change program in the organization, its purpose and intention go more toward community-building than project management, so there are often few if any direct, actionable tasks that come out of it; but if there are, it is helpful to call out specific actions that will occur as a result.

Debrief for participants
Remembering that the goal of this exercise is to have a light, fun way to build community and a common world view about the organization by sharing key facts and events in the organization's history, there are some questions to consider offering to the group once the activity is over, including, "In this exercise, . . .":

- What key or pivotal events that were discussed here stand out or made a significant impression on you, and why?
- Watching the organization participate in this process, does the organization appear in a different light to you? If so, how?
- What did you learn about the people or groups in the organization that you didn't already know?
- Was there anything you heard that was particularly interesting?
- What about what you heard did you find particularly interesting? Funny? Accurate? Completely wrong?

If time is short, these questions can be asked in plenary in 5–10 minutes. If there is more time, these questions can be worked at each table, and potentially in each group.

Variations and Other Advice on Running the Exercise

During the first round, an option is to have participants write down their contributions on index cards instead of speaking with a partner. Once they have written their contributions on index cards, they would walk up to the decades poster and tape the cards directly onto the poster. Similar to the Argument of Obviousness exercise, this variation creates a need for a gallery walk, or some method for all in the room to see and understand the content of all of the decade posters, before moving on in the exercise. In the second round, it is an option to have the facilitator call out the content on each flipchart rather than the individual chart recorders. In the third round, an option is to return participants to pairs to identify cross-cutting themes and call them out. Finally, in the wrap-up phase, a new member of the organization could also have a unique perspective on the data generated in this exercise, with the potential of offering an alternative view about the meaning of the themes and the potential actions the themes might suggest.

Final Thoughts

This activity excels at getting all participants engaged in a simple but meaningful task, with very little explanation or time needed up front. It helps to generate a jointly held, shared narrative with key highlights from the history of the community or organization. It highlights key factors in the external environment, such as political, economic, societal, and techno-logical factors that were and may still be a force in effecting the work of the community or organization. It is also an excellent method for integrating new members into the system and acculturating them quickly around the key events and personalities that have preceded them. A common perspective on the organization and the world is a valuable prerequisite to successful joint action. Dealing in Decades helps to achieve that in real time in front of, and by, all concerned.

CONCLUDING REFLECTIONS

In a merger, acquisition, or internal reorganization, it is not the lines and boxes on the organization chart that are the hardest obstacles to success; it is winning the hearts and minds of those affected and gaining their trust, which is often the hardest part of successful change programs. In different and complementary ways, these two activities help to do that.

The Argument of Obviousness relies upon the myths and stereotypes that we create and carry about "the other," particularly when we are chal-lenged or threatened by organizational change. It explores those myths and stereotypes, and invites them into full view in a light and entertaining way, poking fun at "the other" and at the owners for creating them. By getting these beliefs and assumptions out on the table, both sides can see and make light of what they are saying about each other as a first step toward moving into a cooperative and collaborative stance together.

Dealing in Decades helps to build the common ground and shared perspective among those affected that is necessary for organizational align-ment and concerted action. It intervenes on that most challenging variable, the narrative. Change agents work tirelessly on how to create the narrative that will persuade people to enroll in the desired change, with posters, signs, messages, and presentations drafted for senior management, focus groups, training sessions, and so on. Dealing in Decades complements all of those activities by bringing together some or all parts of the system to create jointly the pivot point between a past that is now better understood by all, and the new future the change is intended to achieve.

Finally, the keystone of any successful organization undergoing change, or even in steady state, is trust, and the ability of those in the system to accept and believe what others say and commit to. Both of these activities, by virtue of their here-and-now designs and inclusive approaches, contribute to the difficult conversations that so often prevent the common understanding, shared perspective, and actionable trust required for human beings to work together.

REFERENCES

Csikszentmihalyi, M. (2009). *Flow: The Psychology of Optimal Experience*, Kindle edition. New York: Harper Collins.

Marshak, R.J. (2006). *Covert Processes at Work: Managing the Five Hidden Dimensions of Organizational Change*. San Francisco, CA: Berrett-Koehler.

Roberts, J.W. (2012). *Beyond Learning by Doing: Theoretical Currents in Experiential Education*. New York: Routledge.

Smith, T.E. and Leeming, C.S. (2011). Kurt Lewin: another Kurt for experiential educators to know. In T.E. Smith and C.E. Knapp (eds), *Sourcebook of Experiential Education*. New York: Routledge, pp. 173–180.

Stafford, D. and Miles, L. (2013). Integrating cultures after a merger. Retrieved from http://www.bain.com/publications/articles/integrating-cultures-after-a-merger.aspx on May 29, 2018.

8. Eliciting group affect and emotive tone: the Mads, Glads, and Sads exercise

Michael R. Manning and Melissa Norcross

The "Mads, Glads, and Sads" exercise is a way of unearthing the feelings and thoughts within a group of individuals. The exercise creates the context for groups of all sizes to reflect on their personal organizing experiences – both emotionally as well as cognitively – so that participant engagement and commitment to change is enhanced. Recent research on emotions and change suggest that group affect and emotive tone play critical roles in the change process and are essential elements in achieving sustainable organization change (Barsade, 2002; Barsade and Gibson, 2007; Tobey and Manning, 2009). The Mads, Glads, and Sads exercise was originally designed as one aspect of large-scale change initiatives, which focused on getting the whole system in the room to engage in system-wide action planning. The exercise dates back to the work of Ron Lippitt (1958, 1959), which has been further developed using more recent large-group intervention processes (Dannemiller et al., 1999; Weisbord and Janoff, 2010). Most recently, the exercise has increasingly been used as an approach deployed during agile scrum retrospectives. Related, but slightly modified versions of this approach are also in use today, including "Prouds and Sorries" and "Successes and Frustrations."

EXERCISE BACKGROUND

The origination of this exercise is not well documented. What is known, however, is that Ron Lippitt, a disciple of Kurt Lewin and co-developer of the National Training Laboratories for Applied Behavioral Science (NTL), co-inventor of the T-Group, and the subsequent field of group dynamics (for examples of Lippitt's work, see Lewin et al., 1939; Lippitt, 1958, 1959), employed various versions of this exercise with his work in community development and organization change from the 1940s to the 1980s. One of his former students, Kathie Dannemiller, furthered this approach in her large-scale change work, initially at Ford Motor Company. These large-group approaches emerged to address the shortcomings of traditional top-down interventions, which typically failed to produce sustainable long-term changes and the hoped-for results (Bunker and Alban, 1997). Large-group initiatives engaged a wider cross-section of the organization at all levels, involved outside stakeholders, and overcame several of the fundamental challenges with the traditional approaches: (1) the marathon effect, whereby only the few involved at the very beginning understand what is truly happening; (2) the lack of engagement by those beyond the core leadership team; and (3) the lack of buy-in to the change initiative.

By the 1980s, large-scale change initiatives such as Future Search and Whole-Scale Change were being leveraged as a way to drive sustainable change (Bunker and Alban, 1997; Dannemiller et al., 1999; Weisbord, 1987). These approaches were participative in nature, sometimes involving hundreds of individuals who engaged in every step of the process, from developing the change agenda to executing the change initiatives, thereby enhancing engagement and buy-in at all levels during the planning phases (Arena, 2009). Such methods employ various types of participative activities, data collection, and analysis that the participants engage in to establish a common understanding of their present situation. These large-group initiatives allow participants to co-create their desired future (Arena, 2009; Bunker and Alban, 1997; Weisbord, 1992). The Mads, Glads, and Sads exercise is one of these participative and data-driven exercises.

How the Exercise Works

Individuals often have different perceptions and experiences when faced with a similar situation and must actively listen and experience it from other perspectives in order for the group to establish a shared and complete understanding (Weisbord, 1987). This includes not only thoughts and perceptions about a situation, but feelings and emotions as well. Thus, the first portion of each of the meetings, which are at the heart of these approaches, consists of a set of exercises and activities that aim to establish a collective understanding of the current situation and allow for open and candid conversations. Lippitt's (1958, 1959) work focused on exercises that simultaneously engaged people on both cognitive and emotional levels, all with the objective of getting participants to curate their own experience so that they would be able to process it for themselves and then share it with others.

In the Mads, Glads, and Sads exercise, participants are asked to describe their experiences to one another by distilling them down into things that they would categorize as certain types of feelings, such as being mad, sad, happy, sorry, proud, and so forth (Arena, 2009; Bunker and Alban, 1997; Lippitt, 1959). This process allows participants to easily transfer a rich set of information about their experiences to others in an efficient manner, without removing the necessary emotional context from them. Versions of these exercises have been used in large-scale change initiatives, and while not exactly the same, their purpose and results are similar. For example, Whole-Scale Change utilizes "Mads, Sads and Glads" (Dannemiller et al., 1999), and Future Search utilizes "Prouds and Sorries" (Weisbord, 1987), yet both approaches create an efficient way for groups to explore affective dimensions of their realities. In these instances, expression of emotions is key as they convey an important aspect of a person's ideas and thoughts about their organization. These emotions are data and vital input to the change process. The emotion (mad, glad, sad, and so on) attached to organizational experiences is shared in a way that it is constructively recognized and validated, creating intense personal investment and commitment to achieving organizational change. The use of this exercise creates a safe context where others can support and buy in to the emotional experience of other individuals. Our observations, supported by research (Barsade, 2002), suggest that a common group emotive tone results, aided by processes of emotional contagion, and this emotional attunement is a necessary condition for a group to endorse sustainable organization change (Tobey and Manning, 2009). Hence, the exercise exposes group-level feelings that are identified in alignment to organizational experiences. This emotive state compels a group with action, in a way that has a higher likelihood of sustainability.

This approach, which has proven valuable in large-scale change initiatives, is also useful as a tool for teams, both large and small, in a variety of contexts and smaller initiatives. It is a helpful approach when establishing a shared team vision (McCarthy and McCarthy, 2002), a framework used in agile development retrospective meetings (Derby et al., 2006), and a tool for surfacing opportunities for growth and improved performance particularly during debriefing (Eddy et al., 2013; Fanning and Gaba, 2007). It can be implemented and works well in groups as small as 12–15 or groups as large as 1000.

Philosophy Underlying the Exercise

Although there are multiple reasons that many initiatives, particularly large-scale change initiatives, end in failure (Kotter, 1995; Kotter and Cohen, 2002), one important contributing factor is that the majority of change efforts begin and end with centralized, cognitive approaches (Arena, 2009; Kotter and Cohen, 2002). Unfortunately, the systems that must be changed are rooted in human behavior and have an emotional dimension that must also be addressed (Tobey and Manning, 2009). Research on group dynamics suggests that affect and emotions play a significant role in individual decisions, and have the power to impact group processes (Argyris, 1982, 1991; Barsade and Gibson, 2007). Therefore releasing, immobilizing, and incorporating the emotive tone of stakeholders is key to any change effort (Kotter and Cohen, 2002), a conclusion supported by the processes put forward by Tobey and Manning (2009) based on studies of multiple change initiatives.

Managing and influencing change has long been a challenge for practitioners, and academics have attempted to create a more scientific approach to enhancing it, including developing formulas to explain the underlying behavior (Cady et al., 2014). Today, one of the most recognized and applied change models in use to explain behavior was published by Beckhard and Harris (1987) and further explained by Dannemiller and Jacobs (1992). The model is expressed as:

$$D \times V \times F > R$$

where (D) is the dissatisfaction with the current state of affairs, (V) is the vision of an alternate possible future, (F) is the first steps necessary to initiate a change, and (R) is the resistance to change. While several refinements to the core formula above have been proposed (Cady et al., 2014), this model is still widely accepted, and the formula continues to impact much of the work on change initiatives.

The above equation explains the dynamics in two parallel levels: the personal or individual level, and the group/organizational or system level (Beckhard and Harris, 1987), making it critical to engage at both levels. Furthermore, engaging at both of these levels from merely a cognitive perspective is insufficient to initiate change, as both (D) and (V) are primarily based on emotional elements, suggesting that stakeholders must be engaged at that expressive level (Beckhard and Harris, 1987; Tobey and Manning, 2009). This approach is supported by cognitive and social psychology, which suggest that effective change is emotion-driven, and that emotional engagement precedes cognitive engagement (Tobey and Manning, 2009). So, if we are to truly affect change, we must engage stakeholders to mobilize their emotional states in terms of their own internal change process and that of the group/organization. As mentioned previously, this approach assumes that emotions are essential to the change process and a key aspect of one's experience. Emotions, along with cognitions, provide critical data to drive sustainable organization change.

Based on the foregoing logic, the exercise asks participants to reflect upon and share their experiences and observations with the wider group in a way that surfaces both facts and feelings. Individuals share what they are "mad" about, what they are "sad" about, and what they are "glad" about with respect to the change target. These lists are then shared across groups so that, very quickly, participants can understand not only others' cognitive perspectives, but also the deeper, emotional experiences attached to their experiences. It creates a common database for the group as they work on a particular organizational process, allowing participants to quickly express values, beliefs, attitudes, and emotions. By enabling the group to openly discuss how they feel about their experiences in a safe way, this Mads, Glads, and Sads intervention often creates a common group affective tone, very important in creating impetus for and immobilizing sustainable change (Tobey and Manning, 2009).

THE MADS, GLADS, AND SADS EXERCISE

The Mads, Glads, and Sads is a high impact exercise that creates a common database to collaboratively address the target of a change project (organizational redesign, organization vision and mission, leadership development, strategic planning, quality improvement, enhanced inclusion, and so on). The exercise allows participants to quickly express values, beliefs, and emotions using an action research diagnostic method where the group collects, synthesizes, and analyzes their own data. The exercise works best with multi-stakeholder audiences and can be administered in as little as 1.5–2 hours depending on group size.

Typically, this exercise is effective for enhancing organizational processes (for example, communication, decision-making, planning, resource allocation, visions, and so on) that require the involvement and support of heterogeneous stakeholders. In addition, it is useful for post hoc debriefing of projects, which has made it very popular for agile project retrospectives (Derby et al., 2006). The Mads, Glads, and Sads exercise has a wide range of use whenever an intervention can benefit from unleashing and connecting the emotive tone of a group with their change objectives.

This exercise works well in a variety of contexts. It can be used within smaller groups of a dozen or so members as the primary source of data collection. The exercise, however, is most often used with larger groups comprised of as many as 1000 or more individuals, as one part of a larger group meeting in which various sources of data are produced by the group and initiatives are developed for design improvement opportunities or change initiatives. The purpose of the exercise is to tap into the collective experience of the gathered participants by analyzing some of the basic issues each individual has observed.

Conducting the Mads, Glads, and Sads exercise involves dividing the participant group into subgroups of no more than eight and allowing them to focus on a single predetermined question or topic. In parallel, each subgroup then discusses their assigned topic or question, and captures a list of what they are mad, glad, or sad about based on their brainstorming session. The wider group then reconvenes, where each subgroup shares their captured mads, glads, and sads. The exercise typically is accomplished in 1.5–2 hours, depending upon the size of the group.

Preparation and Planning

Advanced planning is similar to any organization development (OD) intervention and should include:

- identifying and communicating the purpose of the meeting;
- planning the rest of the meeting, inserting this activity after at least one warm-up or introductory activity;
- sharing with participants the focus of the meeting (for example, identifying cost savings opportunities, figuring out how to speed up production, improving customer satisfaction, evaluating how to improve the next agile sprint); and
- developing a list of topics for this activity based on the change target or focus of the meeting (for example, if the focus was improving customer satisfaction, topics might include product features, service and support, product reliability, and/or purchase experience).

The detailed step-by-step directions for the activity follow. Timing for the exercise depends on group size, so it can vary from approximately 1.5 to two hours.

Setup (Typically 5–10 Minutes)

1. Form the participants into groups of approximately eight people, ensuring the group is heterogeneous with respect to stakeholder groupings and hierarchy. For example, if there were 96 participants, the facilitator should divide them into 12 heterogeneous groups of eight. Groups should be as representative as possible of the wider group, ensuring there is a good distribution of level, function, role, tenure, and all other factors. For example, groups should not be formed based on individuals who represent the same function, business unit, seniority, geography, background, and so on.

2. Assign each group a specific topic or organizational process related to the change target that will be the focus of their group work. If, as per the above example on improving customer satisfaction, four topics were identified (product features, service and support, product reliability, and/or purchase experience), then each of the four topics will be assigned to three groups (4 topics x 3 groups each = 12 groups). If 12 topics were identified, each group would focus on a unique topic. If only one topic was identified, then each group would have the same topic.

3. Within each group, have them self-identify a group facilitator, a recorder, a timekeeper, and a reporter. The group facilitator ensures that all members have an opportunity to participate in the performance of the team task. The recorder ensures that the group's deliberations are recorded on flipchart paper and visible to all. The timekeeper monitors the group progress in a timely manner and makes sure the task is completed on time. The reporter shares the group's product with the other groups during the debriefing period.

4. Remind each group of the general rules of brainstorming and post them on the wall or hand them out to each group facilitator. Brainstorming within the (eight-person) group (typically 45 minutes). Some basic brainstorming guidelines that have proven useful with this exercise are:
   a. Piggybacking is okay.
   b. Add to the list whatever anyone says, no evaluating.
   c. It is okay to repeat.
   d. No discussion.
   e. Silence is OK.
   f. Someone can be glad about something while someone else can be mad or sad about the same thing; that's okay, it gets recorded in both places.

5. Instruct each group to briefly agree on a working definition of the topic assigned to them to ensure everyone at the table is talking about the same thing (ten minutes).

6. Brainstorm the following about your topic (30 minutes). The recorder should record it on a chart in the following format:

Topic: _____		
MAD Personal:	GLAD Personal:	SAD Personal:
Organization:	Organization:	Organization:

    a.   What am I mad about? Personal/Organization.
    b.   What am I glad about? Personal/Organization.
    c.   What am I sad about? Personal/Organization.

It is important that the data collected are on both the individual/ personal and group/organizational levels. The data are collected by all group members in a brainstorming fashion. We encourage groups not to hold back; to be honest in order to have a complete assessment.

During the discussion, the facilitator will ensure that the group stays on task, and that all members contribute. Meanwhile, the recorder will be capturing the input on the chart. It is important that the data recorded within the groups are at both the individual/personal and group/organizational levels.

Voting Within the (Eight-Person) Group (Typically Ten Minutes)

1.   Post the brainstorming chart output.
2.   Give each group member six dot stickers to place as votes on their group's output.
3.   Each group member should place a single dot on their:
    a.   Two "maddest glads."
    b.   Two "gladdest sads."
    c.   Two "saddest mads."
4.   The group reporter will then tally the votes, circling the top 2–3 in each category (Mad, Glad, Sad).

Discussion and Debriefing (15–45 Minutes, Depending upon the Number of Groups)

1.   If the same topic was given to more than one group, the facilitator should prepare a chart for each topic to capture the mad, glad, and sad items from each group. If only one group worked on a topic, their chart can be used by the facilitator to summarize the findings.
2.   Reporters in each group then share their group's top 2–3 items in each category while the entire meeting listens. If more than one group worked on a topic, the facilitator will capture their items on a single new chart. Then, when other groups with the same topic report their results, the facilitator will add them to the list. If an item is repeated, it is up to the group sharing their item to determine whether it is the same as a prior item or not. If it is a new item, the facilitator will add it to the chart.
3.   This process is repeated until reporters from all groups have shared their findings.

Close-Out (Typically 15 Minutes)

The facilitator then asks participants for any observations they made during the debriefing, and also determines whether there are additional items to be captured. The conversation then shifts to how these findings inform the gathered participants about the challenge they have been brought together to address. In most cases, the output will remain on the wall of the room for the remainder of their time together and act as a foundation for the activities to follow.

Transition to the Next Activity

If the Mads, Glads, and Sads exercise is part of a larger intervention, then the facilitator transitions to the next activity. The potential options for the next activity are numerous and should take advantage of the rich data this exercise provides. The specific choice, however, should depend upon the objectives of the meeting as a whole and the structure of the remainder of the agenda. For a meeting focused on:

- creating a detailed plan of action going forward, it would be appropriate to conduct an exercise in which the learnings from the Mads, Glads, and Sads exercise are used to create a list of the potential initiatives to be part of such a plan and then prioritize them;
- better understanding how to integrate with other parts of the organization, the list of mads, glads, and sads could be used to map to a list of stakeholders who are affected by them, and action plans could then be developed;
- creating a new product, the list generated during the Mads, Glads, and Sads exercise could be used as a starting point for groups to develop future product features or prototype products.

Benefits of the Exercise

This exercise allows facilitators and participants to delve deeply into the team experience very quickly and uncover strengths and issues within the team. Often, it enables participants to think about their experiences in a way that allows them to organize and process both their individual and collective experiences, to then share them with other individuals. This exercise structures an activity around the emotions that play a central role in not only managing, but also activating change. Emotions can mobilize action, but can also help to ground a large group in a shared reality. Furthermore, it is a way to engage the emotional commitment of the group and engender greater individual and shared commitment to change. All of these aspects benefit the change process and those associated with it, increasing the odds that the change will be sustainable.

Variations

Other versions of this activity include "Prouds and Sorries" and "Successes and Frustrations," which can be equally effective. Any of these versions are implemented in a manner similar to the exercise detailed here. Deciding on the words that frame the exercise is something the facilitator would do early on, and in consultation with the client. The exercise, outcome, and focus are similar regardless of the categories used. However, the language, style, or culture of a given organization, or focus of the topic, should drive the choice of the optimal version to be used. For example, certain organizations find it more culturally acceptable to discuss successes and frustrations rather than what individuals may be mad, glad, or sad about. Conversely, it may be necessary to use emotional terms as a way to "shock" an organization that finds it difficult to acknowledge its own shortcomings and whose members fail to fully engage in team-building exercises. The key to the activity, however, is to be sensitive to the organizational context, while encouraging the emotional connections to be a part of the exercise. Depending on the language or culture of a given organization, one particular version may be more appropriate than another. The key to the activity, however, is to allow the emotional connections to be a part of the exercise; therefore, changing the categories to something that robs it of any emotional attribute (such as "1s" and "10s") would not maintain the integrity of the approach.

CONCLUDING REFLECTIONS

This exercise is useful in creating a context from which driving sustainable change is possible. It surfaces the full range of experiences from all participants in a way that enables them to be articulated and understood across the group. The exercise enables the group to identify common ground at both emotive and cognitive levels. Additionally, it allows issues and opportunities to be recognized, that otherwise are often not surfaced. Once there is a collective deeper understanding of past experiences, action may then be taken by all participants in a way that focuses the collective effort in a consistent direction which then facilitates organization change.

Since emotions play a central role in managing change, such sustainable change requires both emotive and cognitive reflection and expression.

Interventions that include exercises such as the Mads, Glads, and Sads help to synchronize individual feelings and thought. This synchronization is accomplished via a group's emotional arousal and becomes the motivating mechanism of change. Hence, intervention processes that elicit a group's affect and emotive tone at the collective level create the common ground required for mobilizing participative change. Employing intervention processes that surface both emotion and cognition at this group level are necessary if we want to increase the odds of sustainable change in organizations.

REFERENCES

Arena, M.J. (2009). Understanding large group intervention processes: A complexity theory perspective. *Organization Development Journal*, 27(1), 49–65.

Argyris, C. (1982). *Reasoning, Learning, and Action: Individual and Organizational*. San Francisco, CA: Jossey-Bass.

Argyris, C. (1991). Teaching smart people how to learn. *Harvard Business Review*, 69(3), 99–109.

Barsade, S.G. (2002). The ripple effect: Emotional contagion and its influence on group behavior. *Administrative Science Quarterly*, 47(4), 644–675.

Barsade, S.G., and Gibson, D.E. (2007). Why does affect matter in organizations? *Academy of Management Perspective*, 21(1), 36–59.

Beckhard, R., and Harris, R. (1987). *Organizational Transitions: Managing Complex Change*. Reading, MA: Addison-Wesley.

Bunker, B.B., and Alban, B.T. (1997). *Large Group Interventions: Engaging the Whole System for Rapid Change*. San Francisco, CA: Jossey-Bass.

Cady, S.H., Jacobs, R., Koller, R., and Spalding, J. (2014). The change formula: Myth, legend, or lore. *OD Practitioner*, 46(3), 32–39.

Dannemiller, K.D., and Jacobs, R.W. (1992). Changing the way organizations change: A revolution of common sense. *Journal of Applied Behavioral Science*, 28(4), 480–498.

Dannemiller, K.D., James, S.L., and Tolchinsky, P.D. (1999). Whole-scale change. In Holman, P. and Devane, T. (eds), *The Change Handbook: Group Methods for Shaping the Future*. San Francisco, CA: Berrett-Koehler: 201–216.

Derby, E., Larsen, D., and Schwaber, K. (2006). *Agile Retrospectives: Making Good Teams Great*. Dallas, TX: Pragmatic Bookshelf.

Eddy, E.R., Tannenbaum, S.I., and Mathieu, J.E. (2013). Helping teams to help themselves: Comparing two team-led debriefing methods. *Personnel Psychology*, 66(4), 975–1008.

Fanning, R.M., and Gaba, D.M. (2007). The role of debriefing in simulation-based learning. *Simulation in Healthcare*, 2(2), 115–125.

Kotter, J.P. (1995) Leading change: Why transformation efforts fail. *Harvard Business Review*, May–June, 59–67.

Kotter, J.P., and Cohen, D.S. (2002). *The Heart of Change: Real-Life Stories of How People Change Their Organizations*. Boston, MA: Harvard Business Press.

Lewin, K., Lippitt, R., and White, R.K. (1939). Patterns of aggressive behavior in experimentally created "social climates." *Journal of Social Psychology*, 10, 269–299.

Lippitt, R. (1958). *The Dynamics of Planned Change: A Comparative Study of Principles and Techniques.* New York: Harcourt, Brace.

Lippitt, R. (1959). Dimensions of the consultant's job. *Journal of Social Issues*, 15(2), 5–12.

McCarthy, J., and McCarthy, M. (2002). *Software for Your Head: Core Protocols for Creating and Maintaining Shared Vision.* Reading, MA: Addison-Wesley Professional.

Tobey, D.H., and Manning, M.R. (2009). Melting the glacier: Activating neural mechanisms to create rapid large-scale organizational change. In Woodman, R.W., Pasmore, W.A., and Shani, R. (eds), *Research in Organizational Change and Development* (Vol. 17). Bingley: Emerald Group Publishing: 175–209.

Weisbord, M.R. (1987). *Productive Workplaces: Organizing and Managing for Dignity, Meaning and Community.* San Francisco, CA: Jossey-Bass.

Weisbord, M.R. (1992). *Discovering Common Ground.* San Francisco, CA: Berrett-Koehler Publishers.

Weisbord, M.R. and Janoff, S. (2010). *Future Search: Getting the Whole System in the Room for Vision, Commitment, and Action* (3rd edition). San Francisco, CA: Berrett-Koehler Publishers.

PART III

Communicating change

9. Symbols: creating meaning from the change message*

Richard Dunford

It is always risky to describe an exercise as foolproof, but this is an exercise that has been successfully used in hundreds of situations with, in total, thousands of participants. This exercise has many great qualities:

- it is engaging for participants;
- what occurs during the exercise can be linked to a range of different change topics, which enhances the debriefing opportunities for the facilitator;
- it involves a task where there is little basis for disagreement regarding whether it has been achieved or not achieved;
- the success of the exercise is not dependent on a particular outcome being achieved in the sense that, regardless of whether or not the task at the center of the exercise is achieved, participants and/or the facilitator can derive lessons for various aspects of communication in the context of organizational change.

COMMUNICATING CHANGE: EXERCISE BACKGROUND

This exercise can be used to illustrate several phenomena of relevance to organizational change, particularly in regard to communication. The learning objectives associated with the use of this exercise can include one or more of the following:

- recognizing the importance of clearly communicating to people the objective of the activities in which they are engaged;
- understanding the behavioral and organizational effects of miscommunication, including misunderstanding (management's objectives), frustration (even anger), demotivation, and underperformance against objectives;

- understanding how inadequate communication can lead to the (mis)attribution of meaning to specific activities by organizational members, and its impact;
- experiencing the role of clear communication in achieving "emotional buy-in" by organizational members;
- seeing the impact of data overload on behavior;
- experiencing and understanding aspects of intra-team and inter-team dynamics.

Intended Audience

This team-based exercise has been successfully used with a wide range of participants including those in undergraduate degrees, postgraduate degrees (including full-time and executive MBAs), open executive programs, and corporate executive programs (those provided for a specific organization). In general, the more experienced the participants, the more likely they are to successfully accomplish the task and to do so quickly. "Experience" in this sense is having worked in roles within organizations where task achievement has required input from multiple parties within the organization (with an associated need for clarity in communications). In debriefing such a group, emphasis can be given to:

- identifying what it was about how the task was undertaken that contributed most to the successful outcome (and even more so if the task is achieved very quickly); and
- drawing on the participants' organizational and management experience to identify communication factors that have been associated with unsuccessful (or excessively slow) task achievement.

Undergraduates are the most likely to get into a tangle and have difficulty in achieving the task. Experiencing this outcome coupled with good debriefing can produce a valuable learning experience.

Time Requirement

The total time to run the exercise, including introduction, instructions, seating, carrying out the task at the core of the exercise, and the debrief, is 30–60 minutes. A typical total time is about 45 minutes (for a longer, more challenging version see Appendix 9.1).

The task at the core of the exercise typically takes 20–30 minutes and involves participants being put in one of five teams. The task has been accomplished in less than ten minutes, but this is rare. Occasionally the participants do not accomplish the task. In my experience, if the task is going to be completed this will almost always occur within 30 minutes. If the task is not achieved after the teams have worked on it for 30 minutes, it is usually advisable to call a halt to the task component at that point – for reasons explained below – and to move to the debrief.

Exercise Preparation

There is no specific pre-work or preparation required to be done by the participants. The facilitator prints the instructions sheets (see Appendix 9.2) for Teams A, B, C, D, and E, ensuring that there is at least one copy of the relevant sheet for each team. You may wish to give a copy of the relevant team instructions sheet to each team member, but we have found that it is sufficient to have just one instructions sheet per group. Optional materials include one flipchart (with a flipchart stand) and a set of color marker pens for each team.

The room set-up can vary according to the nature of the available space and your preference. This exercise has been successfully carried out in rooms with and without desks, and with or without flipcharts. It has also been carried out using one room or multiple rooms (see the "Advice for Facilitators" subsection for more detail).

Advice for Facilitators

In the exercise, each of the five teams is given an instructions sheet which contains an organization chart, a set of rules, and five symbols:

- Each team gets its own instructions sheet and each sheet is identified as such, for example, "Instructions – Team A," "Instructions – Team B," and so forth.
- The five symbols are drawn from a pool of six symbols; only one symbol is common to all five teams.
- The information on each team sheet is the same, except for one very important difference: only Team A's instructions sheet contains a statement identifying the task at the core of the exercise.
- The task is to find out which of the six symbols is held in common by all five teams.
- All teams must follow the rules given on their instructions sheet; the rules include the specification of which team(s) each team can communicate with and the only allowed form of communication (written).

A variation of the exercise is to place some of the participants in the role of Observers. This option is especially useful in large classes as an alternative to having larger teams. For example, instead of teams of seven, construct teams of six plus one Observer (of team dynamics).

- Having Observers also gives you some extra "eyes and ears" to note intra-team and inter-team behavior which can add to the range and richness of the material to discuss during the debrief.
- A team's Observer is allowed to see the team's instructions sheet.
- Observers must not share information on their team's instructions sheet with anyone outside their team (including other Observers).
- The Observers' job is to watch and listen to how the team operates so that during the debrief they can provide comments on such things as: In what ways did the team seem to work well? Did the team seem to be having any difficulties? Did any team members show signs of frustration? What was said about the symbols? Did anyone break the rules?, and so on.

A key element of the exercise is that comments by, and conversations between, members of a team must be kept confidential. That is, they must not be overheard by any other team. Confidentiality is much more likely to be achieved if there is sufficient physical separation between teams to make it unlikely that intra-team conversations can be overheard by other teams.

The Symbols exercise can be carried out in a single room, and regardless of whether that room is big or small. However, very small rooms add substantially to the challenge of having intra-team conversations take place without being overheard:

- This exercise is one where participants sometimes become quite animated which can produce a situation where, despite the best of intentions, intra-team talk exceeds the volume needed to prevent its being overheard.
- Where facilities allow, an effective means of minimizing the chance of intra-team conversations being overheard is to locate some of the teams in rooms adjacent to (or at least close-by) the main room. Syndicate or break-out rooms are ideal for this purpose.
- If only one room is used, along with flipcharts, extra care needs to be taken to ensure that what is written on a flipchart is not visible to other teams.
- If only one team is to be located in a room by itself, it is best that it be Team A, as this is the team whose conversation, if overheard, has the

greatest potential to undermine the exercise (because it is only Team A that has the task listed on its instructions sheet).

The Facilitator usually, but not necessarily, takes on the role of the Courier of the messages between teams. In the Courier role, you are able to both observe intra-team and inter-team dynamics while also ensuring that the exchange of notes between teams is in accordance with the specified rules.

The Courier can become very busy, especially towards the end of the exercise, making it a challenging role, so if a participant is selected to take on the Courier role, it is best that the Courier concentrates just on maintaining the flow of messages and leaves the observation of group dynamics to the Facilitator and/or the Observer(s).

It is important to note that at times the participants will have difficulty with the task. In most instances it is optimal to call the task component of the exercise to a halt after about 30 minutes even if the task has not been accomplished. The reason for suggesting this time limit is that giving the teams more time will often take them further away from, not closer to, successful completion:

- Additional time may not be helpful because, as time goes by, data overload is likely to become a problem for Team A and/or Team B. Also, misinformation can be a significant problem in that it can lead teams in unhelpful directions.
- Where teams are getting further from, rather than closer to, identifying the outcome that completes the task, giving the teams more time will often cause them to end up in even more of a mess.

One of the characteristics of the Symbols exercise that makes it attractive to use is that regardless of whether or not the task is accomplished, the dynamics of what occur during the exercise provide a good basis for discussion (see more detail in the "Debriefing the Exercise" section). Because the exercise involves both intra-team and inter-team dynamics, it is most effective where the total number of participants is less than about 50. Above this number, team size makes effective intra-team discussion difficult to achieve.

CARRYING OUT THE EXERCISE

In starting the exercise:

1. Put each participant into one of five groups (teams) of equal or roughly equal size.
2. Physically separate the teams so that they cannot hear each other's comments and conversations.
3. Give each team the instructions sheet for that team. When doing so, stress that it is critical that all team members familiarize themselves with, and act in accordance with, the rules listed in their team's instructions.
4. Tell the participants that if, once they have seen the instructions, they think that they are familiar with the exercise they should inform you of this (and also not say anything to fellow participants about the exercise). Teams do not have to stop acting on their instructions while this contact is occurring.
5. Participants who you decide know (or correctly suspect) key aspects of the exercise should not rejoin their team but can still play a key role in the exercise as Observers. Participants who you decide are incorrect in regard to what they "know" (or suspect) about key elements of the exercise may rejoin their team (although you might still decide to use them as Observers).
6. If you are going to use one or more Observers, select them by this point and brief them on their role.
7. Take note of the start time.
8. The task part of the exercise finishes as soon as a team tells you the correct answer (that is, the identity of the common symbol). The team that does this will almost always be Team A, but the exercise does not preclude another team being the one to provide the correct answer.
9. Take note of how long (minutes) the task has taken to complete.
10. Once a team has given you the correct answer – or you call a halt to the exercise – you should ask all participants to return to their pre-exercise seating. This action is particularly important if not all teams have been located in one room for the period of the task part of the exercise. It is important at this point that you ask the participants not to say anything to each other about the exercise until you ask them to do so.

DEBRIEFING THE EXERCISE

The Facilitator announces that the task has been successfully completed (or if not completed, that the time for the exercise has finished). Use the latter wording where the exercise has been called to a halt without the common symbol having been identified.

A good starting point is to ask the participants to raise their hands if they know what the organization (the five teams) was trying to achieve (that is, the task at the core of the exercise). An alternative version of this step is to ask the teams in turn what they thought the organization was trying to accomplish. If this version is used, it is important to first ask Team E and to finish with Team A because the latter alone has this information in their instructions sheet.

Even where the task has been achieved, one or more teams may still be unaware of the nature of the task. If this is the case, ask someone in Team A to read aloud the bullet point on their instructions sheet that specifies the task (that is, "Your job is to find out which of the six symbols is held in common"). One of the advantages of having the task read out at this point is that if the task was not completed it draws participants' attention to the potential simplicity of the task. This helps participants see that: (1) even if the task was accomplished, it could have been accomplished more quickly; or (2) if the task was not accomplished, it becomes apparent that the failure was not due to the task being either unknown (at least to Team A) or inordinately complex.

Where the task was accomplished, begin by getting views from the teams on such matters as:

- What helped the task be successfully accomplished? Typical factors include clarity of the communication (a simple and clear message).
- What would have helped the task be accomplished more quickly? Typical factors include better (for example, clearer) inter-team communication and better intra-team communication.

In those situations where not all teams were aware of the task, this may be due to various options including:

- Team A did not communicate the task information to Team B.
- Team B received the task information from Team A but did not pass it on to one or more of Teams C, D, E.
- One or more of Teams B, C, D, and E received a message identifying the task but the information was "lost" or its importance was not recognized.

If Team A is required to read the task aloud – because one or more teams are unaware of the task – the situation is sometimes rather confrontational for the members of some teams (most commonly Team A) because participants realize that Team A, and perhaps others, were provided with the information that identified the task that the organization was required to undertake. Participants who consider themselves to have a consultative style can be quite taken aback if they realize that they have been part of a team which has been issuing directives without also communicating the point of the designated activities. This reaction is also more likely if some members of Teams B, C, D, or E complain about being "kept in the dark."

An alternative dynamic that sometimes causes the lack of knowledge of the task is where the problem has arisen not from the failure of the information to be sent, but from the failure of the information to be absorbed. In some instances, teams have been sent the task details but, due to information overload, or some other glitch in the intra-team handling of information, this piece of information is misplaced or its significance is not realized by the receiving team.

Another factor that can cause difficulties is when a message requesting information is sent from a team but without adequate identification of the sender. That is, the recipient team may well be happy to provide requested information but not know which team has requested the information (for example, although messages to Team A must come via Team B, the message could originate in any of Teams B, C, D, or E).

If the task has been achieved but some teams were unaware of the purpose of the activity in which they were engaged, it is often quite instructive to ask members of the latter teams how pleased they are that the organization has achieved the task. It is common for the members of these teams to express little satisfaction at the outcome. Their reaction often highlights the contrast between the satisfaction of the "top management team" (Team A) at having accomplished organizational objectives, and the lack of emotional buy-in by the others. Not knowing the purpose of the task in which they were involved seems to take away a lot of the satisfaction people could otherwise feel at its completion.

At this point in the exercise, if some participants acted as Observers, invite them to comment on the behavior and comments that they observed or heard. Observers often report behavior and comments that produce "laughter of recognition" from the participants and teams concerned, because they recognize it as a description of what happened in their team.

One phenomenon that has been observed on a number of occasions is that if the task is not clearly communicated, teams will often construct their own meaning for the activity in which they are engaged:

- One common form that meaning construction takes is for one or more teams to conclude that the task is a competitive activity. This conclusion can have unfortunate implications for task achievement. For example, teams have been observed refusing to provide requested information unless the "requesting team" first provides some information of its own (that is, information becomes something to be traded, not given away).
- Teams have also been observed deciding that the task is competitive and, subsequently, intentionally providing incorrect information to other teams because of a belief that such action will make it less likely that another team will "win." ("We don't know the purpose of the exercise, but we're not going to come last!")
- Observers will sometimes report behavior such as that cited above. If they do not, ask team members whether any such responses occurred.
- Where these (or similar) responses occur, they provide you with a good opportunity to make, and illustrate, the point that people do not like operating in a "meaning vacuum" and that in such a situation people will often fill the vacuum by attributing a meaning to the activity in which they are involved (even if the attributed meaning is wildly wrong).

At this point in the exercise, the Facilitator should give participants the opportunity to make further comment on their task experience. Some participants may comment that the exercise was unrealistic in terms of the rules around communication. Acknowledge that while any exercise is necessarily a simplification of a complex reality, organizational structures and associated expectations about both who reports to whom and expected forms of communication are normal features of most organizations.

As with all experiential exercises, it is important to bring the exercise to completion by linking the debrief on the exercise back to organizational change themes such as those listed previously in the introductory section of this chapter. Where several, if not all, of the participants have had significant work experience, this is a good time to invite them to contribute to the debriefing discussion their own experiences of communication issues in the context of organizational change.

CONCLUDING REFLECTIONS

The Symbols exercise can be used to highlight many aspects of organizational change that are linked, in particular, to the role that the quality of communication plays in enabling groups of people to work towards a common goal. It is not a simple exercise, in the sense that a range of different outcomes can emerge rather than one highly predictable and consistent outcome. That is, in part, the beauty of this exercise: different groups of different experience, capability, and internal dynamics can produce different outcomes. However, one of the great strengths of this exercise is that every outcome can be used to make a point about the dynamics of communication in the context of organizational change.

Symbols might be described as a "facilitator's exercise" in that its full value comes when a skillful facilitator can link the various outcomes of any specific application of the exercise to key organizational change issues. It is an exercise that is great for students because it is a vehicle that enables good facilitators to link the student or participant experience in the exercise to a range of organizational change issues. Specifically these issues include: recognizing the importance of clearly communicating to people the objective of the activities in which they are engaged; understanding the behavioral and organizational effects of miscommunication, including misunderstanding (management's objectives), frustration (even anger), demotivation, and underperformance against objectives; understanding how inadequate communication can lead to the (mis)attribution of meaning to specific activities by organizational members, and its impact; experiencing the role of clear communication in achieving "emotional buy-in" by organizational members; seeing the impact of data overload on behavior; and experiencing and understanding aspects of intra-team and inter-team dynamics.

NOTE

* This exercise dates from at least the early 1980s. I have been unable to identify its original source, something that I would like to know in order to be able to acknowledge its creator. This chapter is based primarily on a version of the exercise that was adapted by my colleague Ian Palmer and me. It reflects our collective experience of using this exercise with more than 1000 students and executives over many years.

APPENDIX 9.1:   A MORE CHALLENGING VERSION OF THE SYMBOLS EXERCISE

The Symbols exercise can be made more challenging by making one altera-tion: not telling the groups the location of each group. In this case, groups have to work out the location of the team(s) with which they are able to exchange notes.

If using this version of the exercise:

- Allow ten minutes longer for the exercise.
- Make sure that the Courier knows "which group is which" and where they are physically located.
- Inform the groups that the Courier is bound by the rules as to which group can communicate with which group(s).
- If one or more groups are located out of the sight of other group, inform all groups where groups are located, but without identifying which group is at which site.

The first time that the Courier is asked to deliver a note to a named team (for example, "Take this note to Team C"), the Courier should ask the sending team to identify the physical location to which it would like the note taken (that is, like any Courier, they need to be given an "address," not just a company name):

- If the identified location is inhabited by a team with which the send-ing team is allowed to communicate, the Courier should deliver the note as requested.
- If the identified location is inhabited by a team with which the sender is not allowed to directly communicate, the Courier should tell the sender that he/sheis not able to deliver the note. If queried, the Courier should tell the (would-be) sender that he/she is not allowed to make that delivery. If the sender team has understood its instructions it will soon realize that the Courier's refusal must mean that it is asking the Courier to make a delivery which is in conflict with the instructions rules. By a process of elimination the sender can soon identify the location of the team(s) with which it can directly exchange notes.

APPENDIX 9.2:   INSTRUCTIONS FOR TEAMS A, B, C, D, AND E

INSTRUCTIONS — TEAM A

The structure of your organization is:

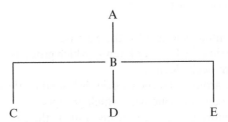

Rules:

- Team B reports to you; three teams (C, D, E) report to Team B.
- Teams A and B may exchange notes.
- Teams C, D, and E may exchange notes with Team B only.
- Notes must be exchanged via the Courier.
- Notes are the only permitted form of communication.
- You must not give or show your instructions sheet to any other team.
- If you have any questions about process, or need the Courier's services, raise your hand.
- The Courier cannot deliver notes between teams that are not allowed to exchange notes.
- Each team has five symbols printed on its instructions sheet. There are a total of six symbols used in the exercise. Your job is to find out which of the six symbols is held in common.
- When you have determined the common symbol, raise your hand. (Do not call out the answer.)

$$\div \; \Omega \; \Psi \; 6 \; \text{ß}$$

INSTRUCTIONS — TEAM B

The structure of your organization is:

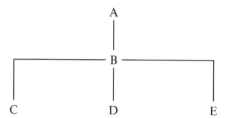

Rules:

- Teams A and B may exchange notes.
- Teams C, D, and E may exchange notes with Team B only.
- Notes must be exchanged via the Courier.
- Notes are the only permitted form of communication.
- You must not give or show your instructions sheet to any other team.
- If you have any questions about process, or need the Courier's services, raise your hand.
- The Courier cannot deliver notes between teams that are not allowed to exchange notes.

$$\Omega \div \Psi = 6$$

INSTRUCTIONS — TEAM C

The structure of your organization is:

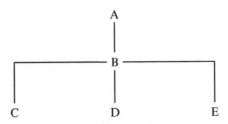

Rules:

- Teams A and B may exchange notes.
- Teams C, D, and E may exchange notes with Team B only.
- Notes must be exchanged via the Courier.
- Notes are the only permitted form of communication.
- You must not give or show your instructions sheet to any other team.
- If you have any questions about process, or need the Courier's services, raise your hand.
- The Courier cannot deliver notes between teams that are not allowed to exchange notes.

$$\Psi \div \Omega \, \text{ß} =$$

INSTRUCTIONS — TEAM D

The structure of your organization is:

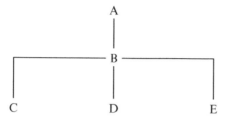

Rules:

- Teams A and B may exchange notes.
- Teams C, D, and E may exchange notes with Team B only.
- Notes must be exchanged via the Courier.
- Notes are the only permitted form of communication.
- You must not give or show your instructions sheet to any other team.
- If you have any questions about process, or need the Courier's services, raise your hand.
- The Courier cannot deliver notes between teams that are not allowed to exchange notes.

$$\Psi \div 6 = \text{\ss}$$

INSTRUCTIONS — TEAM E

The structure of your organization is:

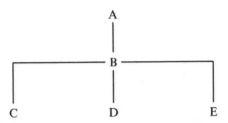

Rules:

- Teams A and B may exchange notes.
- Teams C, D, and E may exchange notes with Team B only.
- Notes are the only permitted form of communication.
- Notes must be exchanged via the Courier.
- You must not give or show your instructions sheet to any other team.
- If you have any questions about process, or need the Courier's services, raise your hand.
- The Courier cannot deliver notes between teams that are not allowed to exchange notes.

$$ß \div 6 = \Omega$$

10. The Ball Game: teaching organizational change and communication

Cynthia A. Martinez

> When current theoretical models of organizational change are reviewed, it is clear that the communication process is certainly more than a variable, it is the process within which change is conceived, constructed, delivered, implemented, and many times denied. (Avanzino, 1997, pp. 3–4)

Communication, in essence the transference of meaning and understanding from one person to another (Robbins, 2005; Keyton, 2011), plays a critical role in implementing organizational change (Lewis, 2011). Communication processes are central to the success and failure of organizational change (Avanzino, 1997; Lewis, 1999), through implementers' interactions with stakeholders as well as stakeholder interactions with each other (Lewis, 2011). Communication processes shape the ways stakeholders understand and interpret change.

The communication process begins with a message to be conveyed; for example, an announcement of a reorganization communicated between boss and subordinate. In this case, the boss is the sender and the subordinate is the receiver. The message of the reorganization is encoded and passed to the subordinate through a channel, whether verbal, non-verbal, or written, to the receiver who decodes the message of the reorganization initiated by the sender. The result of the communication process is the transfer of information and how meaning is formed from sender and receiver (Robbins, 2005). Noise in the communication process reflects the barriers that may distort the clarity of the message, which can be anything from language (word meaning differing due to age, education, and cultural background), how information is perceived, to senders purposely manipulating information. The final link in the communication process is the feedback loop (Robbins, 2005), which determines whether the message was understood (see Figure 10.1).

There are, of course, a variety of communication methods that capture the ways in which individuals and groups transfer meaning between and

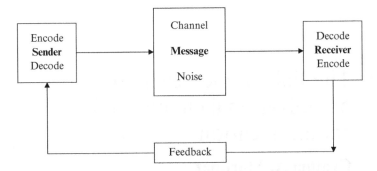

Figure 10.1   The communication process

among each other. Three basic communication methods consist of oral communication (for example, speeches, formal one-on-one and group discussions, and the informal grapevine), written communication (for example, memos, letters, electronic mail, instant messaging, notices on bulletin boards), and non-verbal communication (for example, body movements, facial expressions, physical distance between sender and receiver). Each approach has advantages and disadvantages. The advantage of oral communication is that a message can be conveyed in a minimal amount of time. A major disadvantage, in contrast, is that the message can be distorted as it is passed through several people. People often choose written communication because it is tangible and verifiable, yet a drawback is that is that it can be time-consuming. Non-verbal communication often complicates verbal communication. For example, body language can give fuller meaning to a sender's message. Thus senders and receivers should be aware of the ways in which non-verbal cues may cause contradictions to what is being expressed verbally.

Elements in the communication process and selection of a particular communication method determine the quality of communication (Lunenburg, 2010). A problem in any of the elements of the communication process can reduce communication effectiveness (Keyton, 2011). In other words, effective communication is a two-way process with both the sender and receiver of the message.

The chapter focuses on enhancing our understanding of the critical role the communication process plays during organizational change. To put such complex issues into context, educators are looking to experiential learning exercises to demonstrate key learning concepts (Kolb, 1984). This chapter presents an experiential learning exercise that helps to illustrate the key concepts behind organizational change and communication. The classic "Ball Game" exercise demonstrates how organizational change and communication can differ from the traditional approach of creating a learning process, from such simple tasks as learning someone's name to more compelling challenges as creative team-building. Through the experiential learning exercise participants are able to experience what it feels like to encounter change and work through the communication process.

THE BALL GAME EXERCISE

In my graduate course that I teach on communicating strategy and change, students are asked to share an event in their life that has caused some type of change. It can be something that happened at work, or it might be a political or personal event that affected them. Responses usually vary from mergers, reorganizations, and acquisitions to change in marital status and relocations to new states or countries. When discussing what was changing, who was involved, who oversaw the change, and their role in the change process, communication-related problems were identified as a significant reason why the change did not work out as they hoped it would.

No doubt, change is messy. In the middle of a change effort it frequently seems as though everything is up in the air. Feelings of fear, stress, confusion, frustration, and chaos occur when change is not being properly communicated. There is often a sense of not being in control. When there is a lack of communication regarding the change effort, we can also jump to conclusions and make assumptions.

The Ball Game is best used at the beginning of a class lecture on communicating change, or a first consulting meeting to introduce how to communicate and implement change. The balls in this exercise symbolize change in a team or organization. The exercise places participants in several teams and has them develop a pattern by tossing a ball back and forth to each other. The exercise not only breaks the ice, but it helps participants to experience the chaos of change, how they approach actual change implementation, and the need to create strategies and action for implementation and evaluation; and the difficulty of "keeping an eye on the ball." The activity gets people up and moving, and keeps them laughing.

Exercise Set-Up and Materials

The suggested time needed to run the activity is approximately 15–20 minutes, but there is a lot of flexibility with this exercise depending on the number of rounds with variations you would like to administer. Preparation is simple: all you need are participants, tennis (or similar) balls, and a large enough space to conduct the exercise. You will need at least two balls per person. For a group of 20 people, 40–50 balls are needed. The size of the space needed depends on the number of people participating in the exercise.

Process

To begin, the facilitator holds up a ball and asks the participants if they would like to "play ball." The facilitator might say, "Before we begin, let's play a game which will help us understand what it feels like to be involved in change." As the facilitator of the exercise, separate the participants into groups of 5–10 people. This exercise can be done with as little as 5–6 people and as many as 100 people. Once the groups have formed, the facilitator tells participants to stand in a circle, and then hands each group a ball.

The rules for the exercise are as follows:

1. Create a process for giving and receiving the ball in your group.
2. Establish a pattern where one person consistently sends the ball to the same person.
3. You cannot pass the ball to the person next to you.
4. The ball must return to the person who started with it.
5. The ball must travel through the air.
6. The ball cannot be rolled across surfaces (floors, walls, tables, chairs).
7. If you drop the ball, you must start all over again to create the pattern.

After reading the rules, the facilitator says that they will be walking around and will give the group additional instructions at the end of each round. Next, allow the group to get their ("communication") pattern going.

The amount of time for each group to develop a pattern varies, and depends on the number of people in the group. Typically, a group of five people can establish a pattern in under two minutes. Larger groups of ten can take 3–5 minutes. Once a pattern is established, the facilitator hands each group another ball and tells them to keep the pattern going. Sometimes the groups simplify their pattern, which is fine and usually makes for a great discussion (for example, the impact of simplifying work processes). This issue is discussed in the debrief and discussion section.

The classic ball game exercise has traditionally been used by adding additional balls in each round, for three to four rounds, while maintaining a pattern. For each round, the facilitator can continue adding balls until each group has four to five balls in the air. However, to incorporate the foundations of communication and organizational change models in the debrief it is important to explain each change intervention. There are a variety of ways you can move people around in the groups to symbolize change and dissatisfaction in organizations. For example, after two rounds of adding additional balls, the facilitator can announce that they have just been given information about the organization's competitive environment. To symbolize this new incorporated dissatisfaction, have someone turn their back to the group and instruct the group to keep the pattern going.

In another round, announce to the groups that each group received feedback from their 360-degree evaluation that their team does not feel supported or valued. Have the participants move back five steps and ask them to continue to keep the pattern going. Other variations include: moving people from group to group; adding a time limit; varying the size and shape of the balls to include footballs, sponge balls, or Koosh® balls; or telling the participants they cannot verbally communicate with one another. As a final alternative, the facilitator can ask a person to move to the center of the group and continue to keep the pattern going. With all the variations to symbolize change, it is important to tell the groups to continue the pattern, no matter what new instructions they receive. With each instruction, the facilitator can get creative with the change and dissatisfaction injected into the group; for example, informing the groups that they are having an open forum to discuss issues occurring in the organization, or the boss has just announced a set of high but realistic expectations.

It is important to note that since the facilitator will need people standing and throwing balls, they should be aware of the audience and determine whether any adjustments need to be made due to physical disabilities. For example, if someone is in a wheelchair or cannot stand for long periods of time, they can ask participants to sit on chairs in a circle instead of standing.

DEBRIEFING THE EXERCISE

The key learning objective of this exercise is not only to give participants the opportunity to experience change and chaos, but also to experience how they communicate with one another during each phase of the change process. If the group is larger than 20, ask the groups to start debriefing in smaller groups, and ask for one representative from each group to report back to the larger group. If the group is less than 20 people, you can debrief as one large group. The amount of time needed to debrief the exercise can be 15–30 minutes, depending on how long the facilitator gives participants to answer each question and discuss.

Debriefing can focus on various aspects of the communication process, from the basic functions of communication, the communication process itself, various communication modes, and its link with organizational change. Because the ball in the exercise is used as a metaphor for real change that may occur in their organization or team, it is important for the participants to begin by discussing the work process they created. When discussing the work process, participants should begin by focusing on how the formal structures (authority hierarchies and formal guidelines) and informal structures (work groups or individual members) affected communication behavior (see the Appendix for a list of sample questions).

The facilitator should remind participants that the communication process begins with a message to be conveyed. In this experiential learning exercise, the message was the pattern created with balls. During the debrief participants should identify the sender and receivers in each group and determine whether or not their communication was effective. It is also important to discuss that in verbal communication settings, listening plays just as important a role. Listening is hearing attentively, verifying instructions, and acting and responding appropriately.

Sometimes when conducting the exercise people assume that you cannot talk during the exercise, even though this is not stated in the rules. Be observant and discuss why they assumed they could not talk if you did not tell them they could not verbally communicate. Ask the groups to discuss any additional communication barriers observed through the exercise.

Effective communication is when the message is clearly transferred and understood as intended. For example, some of the groups may have been able to demonstrate effective communication when only one ball was being passed around, but not when two or three balls were passed around. Effective communication begins by understanding the functions of communication, with the realization that each function is equally important. It is through the communication process that messages sometimes get lost, resulting in miscommunication. Choosing the correct channel and method of communication on both sending and receiving the message is the foundation for effective communication.

If groups were split up into smaller groups, you can ask one representative from each group to report back on what they discussed in the small groups. It is also helpful to have some additional questions available for the larger group, if time permits. (See the Appendix for sample questions.)

After about 5–10 minutes, ask the groups to summarize the lessons learned. Examples of previous responses have included, but are not limited to: attention to the communication process helps to implement change; knowing your job or role in the process is important; listening to ideas and being willing to experiment eases the chaos; and, having a positive attitude makes the activity fun.

ADAPTATION FOR ONLINE LEARNING

Online learning is up and coming and there is a growing trend to offer online courses and training workshops. However, there are challenges in translating in-person experiential exercises used in a classroom or workshop to an online environment. Although the Ball Game exercise could not be replicated exactly for the online environment, since you could not provide tennis balls to people across different countries or have participants together in groups, a task was created for an online environment to demonstrate change and chaos.

Online platforms such as Adobe Connect 8 Pro work well because the program allows for breakout rooms just like a regular classroom. Participants can speak to one another and use the chat box to communicate. Adobe Connect 8 Pro allows for 200 participants spread across 20 breakout rooms.

Create a task which would require group collaboration. Building a dream house is easy to explain and demonstrate. Tell the class (before they go into their breakout rooms) that they need to work with their assigned group to build their collective dream house with the tools provided with the software. Groups will be assigned breakout rooms in the Adobe software. You can spend 3–5 minutes demonstrating the drawing tools to create lines, circles, paint, and so on. Tell the groups they will have ten minutes to illustrate their home in whatever way they choose, and you will select the best house to win.

As the facilitator, you will need to rotate from room to room once everyone is in their groups. Mark up the houses as people begin to draw out their dream home. Draw on them, remove windows, doors, and so forth. There is often so much going on in the breakout room that they cannot tell who went in and removed a window or door. You do not need to stay and hear people complain or ask who removed the door, because that will come up again in the large-group discussion. Sometimes groups spend too much time planning out their dream home, so that they only get a basic framework with no windows and doors and you completely wipe out their drawing, with no dream home to show when they return to the group.

After the ten minutes are up, have everyone return to the large group for discussion. Just like the ball exercise, you can debrief the foundations of communication and approaches to managing change. In an online environment, since balls are not directly touching each person, it is interesting to hear who was shut out or did not participate once they felt as though their contribution was erased or not valued. The debriefing questions are applicable to the ball exercise and to adaptation for online learning (see the Appendix).

FINAL THOUGHTS

We study change because it is rapid and continuous. Managers, students, practitioners, and consultants are called upon every day to communicate changes in strategy, focus, and intent. Change is an ambiguous process and communication is vital in planning, implementing, and evaluating change. The basic foundations of communication help people to understand the functions of communication, the communication process, and communication methods.

Communicative processes and practices are a prominent part of change and often mediate other organizational issues (Jones et al., 2004). Therefore, it is imperative that when discussing organizational change the communication process is also discussed (Lewis and Seibold, 1998). It is through the communicative process that individual and group activity can move the organization to where it wants and needs to be (Gardner et al., 2001), by coordinating shared meaning and action (Avanzino, 1997). During times of organizational change, we should not work in silos and communication needs to flow across and between groups. Awareness of relationships between stakeholders, and the motivation of people to perform and address organizational goals, is imperative to the change process (Jones et al., 2004).

In summary, taking a communication perspective allows for a more human-centered, meaning-focused, multiple-participant, and dynamic-interaction orientation to be applied to the current organizational experience with change (Smith, 1990). The Ball Game puts participants in several teams and has them develop a pattern by tossing a ball back and forth to each other. Variations to the conditions stimulate additional discussion to experience how change can be communicated through the communicative process. The Ball Game gives us an understanding of how interactions and relations drive our behavior as it relates to change.

REFERENCES

Avanzino, S.C. (1997). Communication practices and organizational change: The structuring of process improvement experiences. Doctoral dissertation. Retrieved from ProQuest. UMI No. 9835054.

Gardner, S., Paulsen, N., Gallois, C., Callan, V., and Monaghan, P. (2001). An intergroup perspective on communication in organisations. In H. Giles and W.P. Robinson (eds), *The New Handbook of Language and Social Psychology* (pp. 561–584). Chichester: Wiley.

Jones, E., Watson, B., Gardner, J., and Galloic, C. (2004). Organizational communication: Challenges for the new century. *Journal of Communication*, 54(4), 722–750.

Keyton, J. (2011). *Communication and Organizational Culture: A Key to Understanding Work Experience*. Thousand Oaks, CA: SAGE.

Kolb, D. (1984). *Experiential Learning: Experience as a Source of Learning and Development*. Englewood Cliffs, NJ: Prentice Hall.

Lewis, L.K. (1999). Disseminating information and soliciting input during planned organisational change: Implementers' targets, sources, and channels for communicating. *Management Communication Quarterly*, 13(1), 43–75.

Lewis, L.K. (2011). *Organizational Change: Creating Change through Strategic Communication*. Chichester, UK and Malden, MA, USA: Wiley-Blackwell.

Lewis, L., and Seibold, D. (1998). Reconceptualizing organizational change implementation as a communication problem: A review of literature and research agenda. *Annals of the International Communication Association*, 21(1), 93–152.

Lunenburg, F.C. (2010). Communication: The process, barriers, and improving effectiveness. *Schooling*, 1(1), 1–11.

Robbins, S.P. (2005). *Organizational Behavior*. Upper Saddle River, NJ: Prentice Hall.

Smith, R.C. (1990). In pursuit of synthesis: Activity as a primary framework for organizational communication. Doctoral dissertation, University of Southern California.

APPENDIX: DEBRIEFING SUMMARY

Functions of Communication

1. How did the formal guidelines set at the beginning of the experiential learning activity control behavior?
2. How did individuals handle each variation in structure? Did culture, hierarchy and/or power come into play?
3. If a time limit was added to create a pattern, how did the time constraint impact the work process?
4. Did the time limit cause additional chaos and stress to the work process?
5. Did the competition prevent or motivate a work process?
6. Regardless of time constraints or competition, were there any informal structures created?
7. Were there individual members in the groups who stepped into a leadership role to communicate the pattern?
8. How did individuals handle each variation in structure?
9. Was there a member of the group reminding the group of the task at hand?
10. In the initial round, was it one individual?
11. As the groups changed, did the individual group members giving feedback change?
12. How did the group respond to those communicating the goals and pattern for the group?
13. What were the emotions expressed when the pattern worked or did not work?
14. How did communication (or lack of communication) facilitate decision-making in the group?
15. Was there anyone in the group who resisted the pattern created because they were not part of the process?
16. How was information shared when new members joined the group?

The Communication Process

1. How was the message (pattern) communicated to each group member?
2. If it was only one person communicating the pattern, what were the attitudes and behaviors of the receivers?
3. What was the impact of simplifying work processes?
4. What was the impact of having more than one sender and receiver at one time?

5. When discussing the channels of communication, were there any groups making assumptions about the rules and that did not verbally communicate through the exercise?
6. Were there any language barriers that stifled the communication process?
7. If a new change intervention was added in each round, how did each intervention impact the communication process?
8. How did the groups adjust through each variation?
9. How do the groups know whether or not the communication process was successful?
10. How was feedback used in the communication process to determine whether or not the message (pattern) was understood?
11. Ask the participants to discuss the communication and feedback loop at each variation.

Communication Methods

1. Were the instructions clear from the sender?
2. Did everyone in the group listen?
3. At any time, did the pattern fail? Was the failed pattern a result of failing to listen?
4. Did the incorporation of new balls distract from listening and acting out the pattern? Why, or why not?
5. What was the impact of being moved away from the original circle? Was it harder to communicate and receive instructions?
6. After two rounds of adding additional balls, what changed for the group when the facilitator had someone turn their back to the group and instructed the group to keep the pattern going?
7. Did anyone feel isolated?
8. Discuss any additional communication barriers observed through the exercise.

Planning for Change

1. Was there any resistance when participants were asked to move groups or turn away from the group?
2. How was the approach to the change implemented?
3. Were there any specific strategies and actions for implementation?
4. Who were the change agents?
5. Were there any variables or circumstances affecting the change process?

Implementing and Evaluating Change

1. When the facilitator announced that they had just been given information about the organization's competitive environment, did this create a sense of urgency for the group?
2. When some of the participants were asked to turn their back, who helped to keep the pattern going?
3. When participants experienced change in their work process, did they create a new strategy to keep the pattern going?

Sample Questions for the Larger Discussion

1. Why would we do this activity in a class (or training) about change?
2. What was your experience like?
3. What seemed to make you more effective?
4. Explain the communication process that occurred in each group.
5. Did anyone assume a leadership role?
6. What was it like when someone new was added to the group?
7. If you were added to a new group, what was it like, how did you know what to do, how were you integrated?
8. Did anyone feel left out or ignored? Why?

PART IV

The human side of change: strategy, culture, and change recipients

11. Applying Lewin's Force Field Theory to facilitate SWOT analysis: an effective and efficient approach

Mary M. Nash, Michael R. Manning, and E. John Heiser

One purpose of strategic planning is to better ensure the success of organization change efforts. A form of analysis frequently used to inform strategic planning processes is the SWOT analysis – an assessment of strengths, weaknesses, opportunities, and threats. Sometimes considered confusing and overly time-consuming by participants and even organization development (OD) professionals, this chapter presents a method for SWOT based on Lewinian theory and practice, which has proven understandable, effective, efficient, and surprisingly enjoyable. This methodology may be useful for leaders, members, and stakeholders of organizations involved in strategic planning processes, as well as facilitators (internal or external) of such initiatives. The methodology will also prove useful while planning for change: the outcome can inform preparations for change and is beneficial to revisit during the implementation of organization change.

CONCEPTUAL BACKGROUND

The SWOT acronym was developed in the 1960s and gained popularity during the 1990s. While there is no definitive documented history of the origins of SWOT analysis, in the early 1960s Albert Humphrey developed a SOFT analysis at the Stanford Research Institute during a research project to determine reasons for failure of corporate planning (Hindle, 2008). SOFT represented: "what is good in the present is Satisfactory, good in the future is an Opportunity; bad in the present is a Fault and bad in the future is a Threat" (Morrison, 2016). In 1964, Urick and Orr at a Long Range Planning seminar in Zurich (Thakur, 2010) changed the F to a W (for "weakness") and the S to indicate "strength," and the acronym SWOT stuck (Morrison, 2016).

While the exact developmental process of the SWOT analysis is undocu-
mented and therefore unknown, it seems to have conceptual underpinnings
from Lewin's theoretical and practical work. Several decades prior to
the development of the SWOT analysis, beginning in the 1930s, Lewin
developed Force Field Theory (Lewin, 1939), and the related Force
Field Analysis (Lewin, 1951). Force Field Theory can be expressed as a
formula, $B = f(p,e)$, indicating that human behavior (B) is a function of an
individual's personality (p) and their environment (e). Grounded in social
psychology and originally developed for application with individuals,
the theory and resulting Force Field Analysis have gained broad use and
applicability for organizations as well.

Development of Force Field Analysis

The equilibrium or steady state of an organization or initiative may be
graphically represented by indicating forces for or driving the state, and
forces against or resisting the state (Figure 11.1). Conducting an analysis
of those forces for and against the status quo enables strategy development
to move the state or facilitate a desired change. In order to effect movement
or change, forces for the status quo need to be bolstered, and forces against
it must be alleviated or ameliorated. These simple Force Field Analysis
concepts emerged into a three-stage model of change characterized by an
unfreezing stage, followed by a change stage, and solidified with the final
refreezing stage. Most practical models of change adhere to these general
three stages and have evolved from this model.

Development of SWOT analysis

The SWOT analysis is typically considered fundamental to the strategic
planning process. The four components are represented as quadrants of
a four-quadrant framework (see Figure 11.2). Positive aspects (strengths

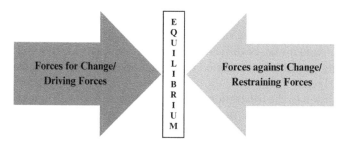

Figure 11.1   Force Field Analysis

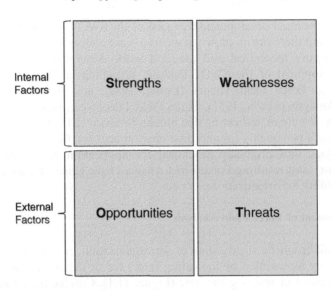

Figure 11.2   SWOT analysis

and opportunities) are represented on the left, and challenges (weaknesses and threats) are indicated on the right. Strengths and weaknesses (the top two quadrants) are internal to the organization, and opportunities and threats (the lower two quadrants) are external to the organization. One challenge with conducting SWOT analysis in a traditional manner is it can be difficult for participants (and facilitators) to grasp the framework, and to understand what falls within each quadrant. This confusion can lead to a very time-consuming and inefficient process, resulting in a less than positive start to the strategic planning process.

While it may be tempting, and is often recommended, to "go in order," filling out the matrix one quadrant at a time beginning with strengths, this may lead to some of the frustrations common with using this tool. Strengths and opportunities are often confused, as are weaknesses and threats. It is common for planners or strategic planning teams to get stuck, frustrated, and conflicted in attempting to determine what goes in which quadrant, and it may be difficult to focus on one quadrant at a time. While discussing one quadrant, related items that belong in other quadrants are often surfaced.

In addition to the frustration sometimes experienced with clarity around what belongs in which quadrant, there is also sometimes frustration around the amount of time a SWOT analysis can take to conduct. SWOT analyses can be considerably time-consuming; some propose as much as a five-day process. We believe that the exercise we offer here minimizes the above frustrations and allows the analysis to be efficiently conducted in a timely manner: as brief as two hours. The key is the use of Force Field Analysis concepts together with a SWOT analysis procedure.

THE EXERCISE

In order to clarify the process and conduct it efficiently and effectively, we present a procedure which can be completed effectively in two hours, resulting in an analysis that can be as beneficial as one developed over a week or longer. One of the keys to conducting the SWOT in this manner is ensuring that the right people participate. It is important to include experts and leaders from various levels of the organization, and key stakeholders from each division or part of the organization, so that as much as possible all perspectives and positions can be represented. We have conducted this process with as many as 50 participants, and with appropriate facilitation many more could actively participate and contribute.

The goal of strategic planning is to advance the organization in achieving its mission, and then progressing toward its vision. A clear, compelling vision is a critical foundational aspect of any effective strategic planning process. Sometimes, an organization may not yet have a vision statement, or the vision statement is not clear or compelling, or may more resemble a mission or values statement. Or, the strategic planning process may be focused on a portion of the organization or its mission, and therefore the overall organizational vision may not be most relevant to the strategic planning process. Therefore, a helpful way to begin the strategic planning process is to clarify these different statements, develop a desired future state, and clarify or reaffirm the vision.

An organization's mission statement indicates the day-to-day work of the organization (its purpose); and the vision statement is an aspirational statement of where the organization is headed or what the organization would like to achieve in the future. For example, a healthcare organization may have a mission to provide high-quality healthcare to the residents of a certain community; and the vision may be to improve the overall health of the region. When conducting strategic planning and prioritization, referring back to these two statements guides every decision; for example, Does this strategy support us in striving toward our vision? Does this priority or this one better support achievement of our mission? In addition, values statements indicate the core beliefs of the organization, and perhaps give an indication of its priorities.

While all of these statements inform strategic planning processes, a clear, compelling vision statement is perhaps most critical. Alternatively, a "desired future state" is another way to articulate the organizational aspirations that strategic planning is setting out to address. For example, perhaps the desired future state of the example healthcare organization is to provide expanded care to more patients in the region. This example is between the mission and vision of the organization, and is a helpful statement to guide a strategic planning process. Use of a desired future state can feel more concrete to participants than a vision statement, and in our experience coming to consensus on the desired future state can be a valuable first step in the process. The facilitator of the strategic planning process can support the participants to develop this statement as an initial step in the strategic planning process. There are many methodologies, such as appreciative inquiry, that can help to facilitate the determination of the desired future state. Once the right people are in the room, and the desired future state has been articulated and agreed upon, the first step toward development of the SWOT can be conducted.

Preparation

A smooth blank wall or large window surface will be helpful, as will painter's (masking) tape, 3 x 3 inch sticky notes in light green and red, fine-tipped black marker pens (one per participant), and chart paper. You may also wish to have a camera to photograph the process and finished product, to aid in documentation and transcription. Place a vertical line of painter's tape at the halfway mark of the wall or window, allowing equal space to the left and right. Ideally, a space of at least 4 x 4 feet is available to each side of the vertical tape line. This forms the space for conducting and documenting a Force Field Analysis. Utilizing chart paper, make and place large labels for "Driving Forces" above the left space, and "Restraining Forces" over the right-hand space. If for any reason sticky notes cannot be placed on the wall, or there is a desire to preserve and be able to move the actual product of the work intact for further refinement, then chart paper (or other large paper) may be temporarily affixed to the wall, and sticky notes can be tacked to the paper.

It may be helpful to brainstorm or otherwise discuss a few forces as a group before having individuals come up with their own individual ideas. The facilitator will use a question such as: "What are the forces that support the change that we wish to see?" or "What may get in the way of us achieving the desired future state?" Participants then write driving or restraining forces on sticky notes, one per note, and stick them to the wall on the appropriate side of the model (driving on the left, restraining on the right). We find it works well to write forces for on green notes, and forces against on light red or orange notes (dark red can make writing less visible).

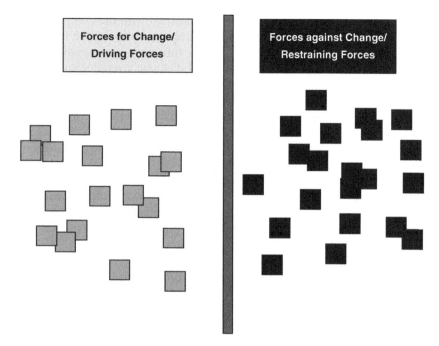

Figure 11.3   Exercise example: Force Field Analysis

Allowing individuals to write their ideas and post them promotes feelings of inclusion, safety and anonymity, and helps to surface as many diverse ideas and perspectives as possible. Plan to allow 15 minutes for this portion of the exercise. The recommended format is illustrated in Figure 11.3.

When all ideas have been exhausted and posted on the wall, the participants conduct a "gallery walk," reviewing the analysis and reflecting as a group. At this point, the facilitator encourages questions and any additions to the Force Field Analysis. It is interesting for the participants to note the frequency with which certain driving and restraining forces are noted, and as they participate in grouping the duplicates, which typically prompts beneficial dialogue about the nuances in meaning of what individuals have written. The facilitator should support this clarifying dialogue and ensure mutual respect for differing perspectives. For example, if two or more forces for seem similar, the facilitator can ask questions to clarify whether they are indeed referring to the same thing, and ask permission to combine them; or if not, to clarify the differences and indicate the distinctions on the notes. Sticky notes can be added or clarified as needed at this point. Plan to allow 20 minutes for this grouping of duplicates, dialogue, and additions to the wall.

Once participants (and facilitator) are satisfied with the completeness of the resulting Force Field Analysis, participants focus on the left side, and separate the forces for into strengths (internal), and opportunities (external). There may be disagreement and dialogue around what constitutes internal or external to the organization. Such divergence is further complicated when planning for a portion of the organization; for example, is "internal" in relation to the department, or the organization? In our experience, while still complex, this activity is more manageable while considering two quadrants at a time rather than all four. We also suggest beginning with opportunities, as the initial focus on external and out-of-control factors helps to determine what actual (internal) strengths are. Opportunities sticky notes are then shifted to the lower left quadrant, and strengths are shifted to a newly created upper quadrant. With everyone participating, and the facilitator facilitating productive dialogue, plan for 30 minutes on determining strengths and opportunities.

Once satisfied with the strengths and opportunities quadrants, attention is focused on the right side of the analysis. Forces against are divided into internal weaknesses (upper right quadrant), and external threats (shifted to bottom right). Again, focusing first on external, out-of-control threats may be helpful in later determining internal weaknesses. Plan for another 30 minutes on this side, and then ten minutes for a summary wrap-up discussion, for an overall total exercise time of approximately two hours (see Figure 11.4).

Once complete, the SWOT analysis may be photographed to aid with documentation and transcription. The resulting SWOT analysis is typically found to be less confusing and difficult to develop, and every bit as thorough and useful, as one completed more traditionally and taking exponentially more time to develop. The SWOT analysis provides a solid foundation and will be utilized to determine priorities to be addressed through the strategic planning process.

Two Case Examples

One application of this methodology was conducted with the national Engineering Services division of the Federal Aviation Administration (FAA) (Nash and Manning, 2014). The 17-member strategic planning team, comprised of union and management leaders, collaboratively and successfully developed their first ever strategic plan utilizing this SWOT methodology as the foundation. The SWOT was conducted utilizing this procedure early in their strategic planning process (as is typical), while they were still firmly within the "forming" and "storming" stages of team development. The union leaders and management representatives were broken

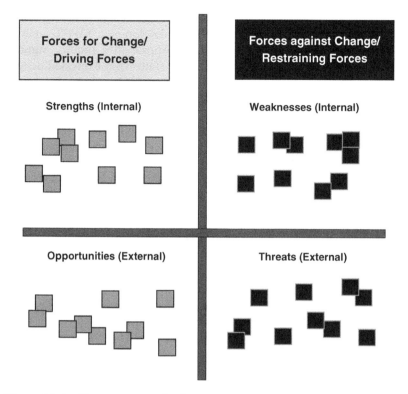

Figure 11.4   Exercise example: SWOT analysis

out separately to develop desired future states, and then came together to discuss their assessments. They were surprised and gratified that their future states were very similar and aligned, which helped to facilitate a productive SWOT analysis process.

Despite the very different perspectives and positions of the various participants, this methodology enabled all to participate and "feel heard." The active, experiential nature of the exercise, as well as the visual, graphic representation, supported the successful outcome. The early realization of the shared desired future state and goals was surprising (to the group) and helped to begin to forge a strong bond among the participants, who had previously been staunchly on separate sides of the table.

In a very different group – leaders of Magnetrol International, Incorporated, a middle-market, privately held, international technology/engineering/manufacturing company that innovates level controls and flow controls – this methodology was also used to great success. A global group of 14 senior and executive leaders participated in a strategic planning summit for which the SWOT analysis provided the foundation (Magnetrol, 2013). They utilized this methodology for developing a SWOT analysis that was then incorporated into a global Appreciative Inquiry Summit to develop and articulate the desired future state. They expressed delight with the process and outcome, and found it much less time-consuming, and every bit as effective, as previous, more traditionally developed SWOT analyses. The process itself proved to be supportive of relationship-building in this case as well, as leaders learned more about each other's expertise, perspectives, concerns, and desires for the future. The participatory and inclusive nature, combined with the efficiency, effectiveness, and enjoyable nature of the process, made this a memorable experience that the participants appreciated – and talked about – for years to come.

Limitations

Limitations of this model include that this methodology will almost certainly result in a product that is not as completely comprehensive as a more traditionally conducted (and more time-consuming) SWOT analysis. In our experience, the quality of the outcome balanced with the engagement of participants and the motivating factors of efficiency and effectiveness have proven more than sufficient. It is necessary to have a clear vision or desired future state before embarking upon the process.

CONCLUDING THOUGHTS

This exercise is intended to facilitate a SWOT analysis in a more efficient, effective, and enjoyable way, resulting in a useful foundation for prioritizing strategic planning. The combination of Force Field Analysis and SWOT analysis simplifies the process and lessens confusion, clarifies what belongs in each of the SWOT quadrants, and can help to ameliorate frustration. Considered "elegantly simple" by participants, it is an example of making the complex simple. This process can be facilitated with groups of any size, in any type or portion of organization engaging in strategic planning. The exercise is quick, can be completed in approximately two hours, and with minimal materials and space requirements. The resulting analysis provides a foundation that can be followed up with in-depth prioritization and planning.

This SWOT methodology was an innovation that was initially created in the moment, when a client organization was struggling getting started with its strategic planning process. Each time we use it, we are amazed at how easily it flows, and the overwhelmingly positive response that clients give to the exercise. In hindsight, it was not something that perhaps we could have planned a priori; given the needs of the moment it worked out, and it is now a frequently used tool in our toolbox to quick-start effective strategic planning processes. When we return to client organizations, even years later, we are delighted and gratified at the number of times this exercise is remembered and mentioned, and more importantly at learning that the results of the planning are implemented and achieved.

REFERENCES

Hindle, T. (2008). *A Guide to Management Ideas and Gurus*. London: Profile Books.

Lewin, K. (1939). Field theory and experiment in social psychology: Concepts and methods. *American Journal of Sociology*, 44(6): 868–896.

Lewin, K. (1951). *Field Theory in Social Science*. New York: Harper & Row.

Magnetrol International, Inc. (2013). *Magnetrol Strategic Plan: 2014–2017*. Aurora, IL: Magnetrol International, Inc.

Morrison, M. (2016). SWOT analysis made simple: History, definition, tools, templates & worksheets. https://rapidbi.com/swotanalysis/ (accessed February 2, 2018).

Nash, M.M. and Manning, M.R. (2014). Collaborative strategic planning: Labor and management partner for success. In G. Sardana and T. Thatchenkery (eds), *Understanding Work Experiences from Multiple Perspectives: New Paradigms for Organizational Excellence* (pp. 313–323). New Delhi: Bloomsbury Publishing.

Thakur, S. (2010). History of the SWOT analysis. https://www.brighthubpm.com/methods-strategies/99629-history-of-the-swot-analysis/ (accessed February 2, 2018).

12. Diminishing resources: building strategy for change

Ann E. Feyerherm

Organizations often have to manage resource constraints, especially in entrepreneurial firms, those undergoing significant change, and during economically challenging times. Resource constraints can lead to high levels of frustration, lack of motivation, feelings of helplessness, and even fraud. However, creativity, innovation, and adaptation can be antidotes to these undesirable outcomes (An et al., 2018; Dopfer et al., 2017; Rivera and Casias, 2001).

This exercise gives participants the opportunity and challenge of physically dealing with diminishing resources, in the form of paper squares on the floor with the task of finding creative solutions to the problem presented when squares are removed. While simple (and somewhat reminiscent of the children's game of Musical Chairs) it can add profound meaning and a springboard to innovatively dealing with change. There is also the opportunity to bring to life the phrase "Necessity is the mother of invention" in a very real way. Such rather colloquial phrases and examples illustrate fundamental underlying dynamics that surround many changes in personal and organizational life that are highlighted by this exercise.

The learning goals for this exercise are that participants: (1) make the visceral and theoretical connection between resource constraints and innovation; (2) can articulate their own reactions to change; and (3) bear witness to and can describe an organization's response to a changing environment. Two principles are intended to be made visible to participants: (1) that personal and organizational reactions to a changing environment are normally denial or resistance; and (2) that innovation can emerge in the face of resource constraints.

The intended audience for this exercise is wide-ranging. It could be used in undergraduate classes in organization behavior, management, or strategy. Graduate courses in organization development and change management are also appropriate audiences (in fact have been most often successfully used by this author). The exercise could also be used in an organization as an exercise to illustrate change management and readiness for change. The caveat is that there must be at least 15 people to successfully illustrate the dynamics of change and innovation upon which this exercise is based. This makes it appropriate for a classroom setting or corporate group training.

GETTING STARTED

The main resources needed for this exercise are large squares of sheets of paper (2 ft x 2 ft or 2.5 ft x 2.5 ft). The facilitator should position two to three people to initially be standing on the pieces of paper. Depending on the size of the group, 5–12 pieces of paper will be needed. Flipchart paper or newspapers work well for this exercise. The room set-up is a large flat space of at least 15 ft by 15 ft. Again, a larger group will need a larger space. It is not necessary to have a square room, but it is important that all of the pieces of paper can be laid out with at least 2.5 ft between them. It cannot be done in a classroom where the chairs are bolted to the floor. If that is the only type of classroom available, you may have to sequester the hallway. This exercise may be performed with just one instructor, but if there is access to a colleague or graduate assistant, all the better for an extra person to remove the pieces of paper.

There is no specific pre-reading required for the exercise, but it is useful to place the exercise in context: for example, change management, innovation, or environmental scanning. My experience suggests that the exercise is more powerful when related to course or workshop readings. As examples, useful readings would be along the lines of Kotter's (2016) *Our Iceberg is Melting* for change management, von Oech's (2008) *A Whack on the Side of the Head* for innovation, or Teece's (2012) article on dynamic capabilities for environmental scanning.

THE EXERCISE

Exercise Description and Instructions for Participants

Square pieces of paper are placed in front of the participants, laid about the room like stepping stones in a garden. After greeting them to the exercise, the participants are instructed that they are to find a place where their feet are in a square. The facilitator will go to the nearest piece of paper and stand in the square to demonstrate. The participants are told that they may share the squares with others. Once everyone is on a square, the facilitator tells participants (or uses a bell) that they are to move to another square. In other words, they may not be in the same square after they are instructed to move. Participants should be encouraged to pay attention to their strategy and to how they are thinking and feeling during the exercise.

The rules of the exercise are simple: (1) both feet need to be in a square; (2) when instructed (or the bell sounds), they must move to another square; (3) the group does not continue the exercise until everyone has both feet in a square; and (4) square-sharing is allowed. It is important to do this rapidly and to ensure that everyone is involved. The rules may be placed on a flipchart or board where all may see them.

Instructions for Facilitation

The exercise is set up to position the "resource" as represented by the square pieces of paper that are strewn about the floor. Since everyone must have both feet in a square, the pieces of paper represent this resource at the beginning and throughout most of the exercise. The participants move from paper to paper as rapidly as possible. This continues for two rounds (a round is when people start on a square; the facilitator instructs or rings a bell to signal a move to another square, and the round ends when everyone has their feet in a new square). At round three, immediately after the bell rings, the facilitator removes one of the square pieces of paper. While a little flummoxed, people usually adjust fairly quickly and jump to another square. An interesting thing to note is whether people who notice the change say anything to the whole group. At round four, remove another piece of paper. You have to be quick as a facilitator. At round five, remove another piece of paper.

Participants will have caught on by now and will be trying to maneuver to step on the piece of paper before you can remove it. Some may start yelling at you to stop doing that. They may get frustrated. Your job as a facilitator is to remain calm, ask if everyone's feet are in a square, and do not move on until they are. There will typically be someone wandering around without their feet in a square; your response is, "We can't move on until everyone's feet are in a square." At some point, it is useful to reinforce the exercise objective – everyone must be involved – so it is not just the poor person who is left without their feet in a square. Inevitably someone will say something, or just move, so that there are four people standing together, with all of their feet forming a newly defined "square." They make a square pattern, with two feet on a side. The other option is that the whole group forms a square. At the point in time that no paper squares are needed, this is when the exercise is complete, since a new "resource" has been found: the players' own physical positioning in a square. The physical portion of the exercise usually takes about 20–25 minutes to complete.

The Debrief

Generally, there is a fun "buzz" in the room after the participants have successfully landed their feet in a newly defined "square." There are several directions for the debrief. The first starts with a personal one. Ask people to reflect on what they were thinking and feeling throughout the exercise. Also ask participants to reflect on when they first noticed that the paper squares were disappearing, and their honest thinking. Was it a strategy to jump harder and faster to the next square? Was it to think about how to find a new type of square? Was it that of despair? Anger? You are looking for some initial thoughts about them managing change on a personal level. After having time for individual reflection based on your seeded questions, give some time for group sharing. There is then the option to characterize various responses to change: resistance, fear, an attempt to ignore it, complacency, a chance for innovation, and so forth.

The next area for debrief is at the group level, focusing on sensing a shift in the environment. You can keep track of the rounds of "play" and when you took the first sheet away, the second, and so forth. Ask people to recall when and how they noticed. Did someone visually see it first? Did they hear it from others? This can be related to how changes in the environment are captured in an organization. The ones "closest" to the changes are normally the first to notice. What might this be in an organization? Sales? Customer Service? How much are those people listened to? What happens with the information? Are systems set up to gather external information? And, did people just get mad at the instructor and accuse them of changing the rules? Think of how often we blame the customer or trends first, before looking at our own processes and adaptability.

It is also instructive to look at any innovations that emerged. It is interesting to trace the origin of the innovation. Who first challenged the assumption of what "feet in a square" meant in practice? Did the innovative idea spread? If so, how? Was it tested (for example, a small group of people standing with their feet "in a square" physically)? Was there questioning of authority?

Finally, it is useful to apply this exercise to something going on in their own organization or life. The group could brainstorm times when this happens; for example, rising customer complaints, falling market share, or loss of funding, are all possibilities. Your group will come up with more. Then ask for how they could apply the lessons of individual reaction, environmental scanning, and innovation to the issues. The debrief portion can take between 20 and 45 minutes, depending on the number of participants and how much application discussion is done.

Variations and Other Advice for Running the Exercise

An additional perspective could be added by having a couple other students (or participants, for corporate groups) observe the behaviors of their classmates or peers. They could be prompted to look for specific issues: for example, when did they notice alternative views of "what is a square" and if and how they were adopted (or not) by the other participants? They could also look for resistance to moving to a new way and how that manifested.

If there is a large class, the class or group could be divided into two groups, each with their own facilitator. This could turn into a timed exercise, with the facilitators timing to see how quickly each group shifted into a new paradigm and what caused the shift. You would then have an interesting case comparison.

Another variation is to add the element of "no talking" among the participants. How would the idea of forming a "human square" be adopted? Would it take longer? What would this represent when applied to an organization, and trying to make change and get attention to the alternatives?

It is important when running the exercise is to be very clear to always say "your feet in a square" not "you are in a square" or "your feet are on a square." While setting up the exercise, it is already seeded in the minds of the participants that they should have their feet "on" a square, so it is critical that you, as the facilitator always say feet "in" a square. It is also good to have a loud voice or use a device (for example, a bell) to signal the switch.

CONCLUDING REFLECTIONS

This exercise is intended to take participants out of their "normal" world to experience something that easily has parallels in their own world of work. Since the mode has been changed to physical from cognitive, it allows for a more visceral and outward expression of what might be going on in a person's mind. The exercise demands action and movement. It is in the debrief that cognitive connections to their own situations are captured, where one hopes insights are derived that can be applied to the real issues the participants face.

One of the overarching themes for this exercise is that organizations normally take time for changes in the environment to be noticed, and then some additional time for adaptation to occur. People get busy trying to maximize their own actions (jumping to the next "square") and fail to notice changes (paper being removed). There is also the possibility of denial: the instructor will not really take another square from the floor, will she? And, potentially, anger: generally at the instructor who is removing the squares. These are all illustrations of reactions to change.

There are a few who take the creative challenge, which leads to the next theme. Even with resource constraints, innovation can emerge, if personal resistance and organizational inertia are overcome. A typical reaction is for people to "freeze" a bit and keep doing what they were doing. Yet, when someone finally discovers another solution set, they are not always heard. This is also illustrative of the normal reticence towards change. However, with the breakthrough that normally comes when someone discovers a new solution, the whole group generally rallies behind the new method. The exercise can provide a lovely illustration of what is possible with creativity and innovation. While the exercise can be fun and challenging, the real learning comes from application to the participants' own situation, which comes through the debrief. In summary, this is a fun exercise to illustrate individual reactions to change, the influence of the environment on a system, and the process of challenging assumptions and the resulting innovation that emerges.

REFERENCES

An, W., Xu, Y., and Zhang, J. (2018). Resource constraints, innovation capability and corporate financial fraud in entrepreneurial firms. *Chinese Management Studies*, 12(1), 2–18. doi:10.1108/CMS-02-2017-0024.

Dopfer, M., Fallahi, S., Kirchberger, M., and Gassmann, O. (2017). Adapt and strive: How ventures under resource constraints create value through business model adaptations. *Creativity and Innovation Management*, 26(3), 233–246. doi:10.1111/caim.12218.

Kotter, J. (2016). *Our Iceberg Is Melting: Changing and Succeeding Under Any Conditions*. New York: Penguin Random House.

Rivera, M.A., and Casias, R.A. (2001). Resource constraints in information systems development: A land management case study. *International Journal of Public Administration*, 24(6), 521–547.

Teece, D. (2012). Dynamic capabilities: Routines versus entrepreneurial action. *Journal of Management Studies*, 49(8), 1395–1401.

von Oech, R. (2008). *A Whack on the Side of the Head: How You Can Be More Creative*. New York: Grand Central Publishing.

13. Exploring the dynamics of organizational culture and change: developing skills and strategies to navigate change in a complex world

David W. Jamieson, Jackie M. Milbrandt, and Nicole M. Zwieg Daly

In today's rapidly changing global economy, organizations are fraught with an increasingly complex, and volatile, unpredictable, chaotic, and ambiguous (VUCA) business environment (Horney et al., 2010). Given these forces, interest in the dynamics between culture and organizational change (which began in the 1990s) have persisted and increased. As a result, thinking and practices related to how cultural dynamics impact organizations have never been more important (see Hofstede, 2001; Ang et al., 2007; Meyer, 2014; Kirkman and Shapiro, 1997; Schein, 1983, 1990). This chapter addresses the expressed need to develop the awareness, skills, and strategy needed to navigate relationships between organizational culture and change in a rapidly changing world.

In this chapter we invite change practitioners, leaders, and learners across a variety of professional fields to explore the dynamics of culture and organizational change through an experiential learning activity with guided reflection. Below we offer a general introduction to the topic followed by a detailed description of the activity which includes facilitation notes, critical reflection questions, and suggested uses in organizations. We also provide an original conceptual framework of organizational culture that can be used along with the activity or as a stand-alone tool when designing and preparing for organizational change. Finally, we conclude with a discussion exploring common outcomes and insights gained using the activity with different groups, and ways the activity may be modified or adapted for use in various contexts (for example, organizations, classrooms, or among professional networks).

THE ESSENCE OF ORGANIZATIONAL CULTURE

In the most basic sense, culture is made up of the core values, assumptions, and norms that drive and maintain group behavior. The extent to which we are aware of, understand, and identify cultural dynamics will play an important role in our overall experience of work-life and our ability to manage change. In this chapter, we define cultural dynamics as a combination of values, assumptions, and beliefs that regulate (1) what is valued and valuable; (2) what is right and good; and (3) the practices or behaviors that reinforce these things (Schein, 1983, 1990). Essentially, values act as a "glue" that bonds and bridges relationships within and across organizations. Whether in small groups, larger divisions, or as part of cross-functional teams, understanding cultural dynamics can play a central role in organizational outcomes.

Adding to cultural dynamics are the feelings associated with individual experiences of culture (for example, belonging, satisfaction, "fit" with personal preferences). These individual experiences, described as "climate" (Hofstede, 2001), will color organizational experiences with either positive and/or negative affect, and in turn readily contribute to the overall outcomes of any effort in the organization. Considering that organizational climate and culture can be as varied and complex as the organization itself, the extent to which leaders, teams, and individuals understand how to observe, articulate, and manage these dynamics will be critical to success or failure of organizational change efforts. Therefore, in an era of unprecedented change, the need for change leaders and participants to develop skills and strategy to do so has never been greater.

Dynamics of Organizational Culture

Because values drive how we think, feel, and act, they are core to understanding organizational norms, practices, and behaviors. Values impact how people work together, make decisions, organize, and exchange perspectives. While there is a vast body of scholarship on values and behavior, one widely cited conceptual framework in the context of organizations is Hofstede's (2001) "Big Five":

- long versus short term orientation;
- individualism versus collectivism;
- high versus low power distance;
- high versus low uncertainty avoidance;
- masculine (competing) versus feminine (collaborating) orientation.

Accordingly, organizational values are expressed as norms, practices, and logics that drive behavior, and may also be indicators of why change efforts in an organization ultimately succeed or fail. If a change in strategy, process, or staff introduces a change in the operating values, for example, more time, energy, and efforts may be need to implement change.

Using Hofstede's framework, organizations that hold a value of long term orientation are more likely to be strategically conservative and risk-adverse, using "patient capital" with long term (5–10 years) expectations of gains. In contrast, organizations that hold a short term value orientation are more likely to be strategically aggressive, pursuing short term (quarterly to annual) expectations of gains. While this is just one example, it effectively illustrates the impact organizational values have on culture and consequently behavior, which can be helpful in understanding or anticipating how to manage the relationship between culture and change.

The underlying concept of system alignment during change is examined in greater depth in the following section, "Intersections of Culture and Change." As the reader will see, an organizational culture is embedded as a central element within an interdependent organizational system. As such, based on alignment, the cultural dynamics affect all changes within the system, acting as either a help or hindrance to the intended change. Planning for organizational change entails understanding not only values, but also the implications they have in the organization (practices, norms, behaviors) and at the level of work groups. Meyer's (2014) work on organizational culture adds these additional layers to Hofstede's cultural values framework.

In Meyer's "Culture Map," cultural dynamics are depicted on paradoxical continuums that include:

- Communication: a continuum related to assumptions of norms as explicit (low context) to implicit (high context).
- Feedback/evaluation: a continuum related to feedback on performance as either direct or indirect (especially on negative aspects of employee/leader performance).
- Influence/persuasion: a continuum related to motivation as either principle (why) versus application (how).
- Decision-making: a continuum related to decision-making processes; consensual versus top down.
- Trusting: a continuum related to task-based versus relationship-based trust.
- Conflict: a continuum related to confronting versus avoiding differences.

● Timing: a continuum related to linear (direct, rigid) versus non-linear (indirect, flexible).

When change efforts violate or clash with established culture values, norms, or assumptions, misalignment can result. And when misalignment occurs, an experience often described as "resistance to change" is usually eminent.

Change in this chapter is focused on organizational change, including such core elements as structure, systems, processes, and behaviors. Culture in this chapter is focused on the norms, values, and assumptions operating within and across the organization, with sensitivity to implications of national culture(s) in which the organization, or the teams within the organization are embedded. Given that cultural dynamics can affect both the process and outcomes in change, understanding these dynamics and what an individual, group, or team can do to develop awareness and skills in navigating these dynamics is of the utmost importance. When attempting to launch any change initiative, having an intended awareness of ways to consider culture and the alignment between existing culture with the desired change is a critical first step. The primary contribution this chapter makes is found in the tools and frameworks that may be used by change leaders and change agents toward this end.

Intersections of Culture and Change

The Organizational Systems Alignment Model (Jamieson, 2017; and see Figure 13.1) shows how the elements of the organization relate to one another and illustrates how organization culture (which is context-specific and developed over the life cycle of the organization) is a central element that influences all the other elements in both organization design and change. The basic premises of this model are threefold:

● strategy as the driver of the organization's other choices;
● structure, culture, and systems/processes (the middle) as the core of organization's design; and
● behavior as influenced by all the elements above.

In general, this model is useful when designing organizations or planning change. Elements and aspects included in the organizational system model may help to inform desired behaviors, and a systems view of the organization that can help to raise questions that may be used to understand how the organizational aspects and elements relate to other elements (especially culture) during change. Such questions may include:

Figure 13.1   Organizational Systems Alignment Model

- At what level of the system is the change happening? What elements will be affected?
- What are the implicit values, norms, and assumptions that are currently driving how things are done?
- How will the desired change align with the culture, or differ, and in what ways?

From a complexity perspective, which views the organization as a complex adaptive system (Meadows, 2008; Stacey, 2001), change would not only be influenced by cultural dynamics at the level of the change (for example, organization, unit, team) but also at the levels above and below the change (see also Olson and Eoyang, 2001; Eoyang and Holliday, 2013).

For example, change in an organization division (for example, an internal merger between two work teams) would be highly influenced by cultural norms, values, and assumptions operating within the larger organization (above) and those operating within the various teams involved (below). Moreover, cultural implications may extend beyond the organization itself (as depicted by "environment") to norms, values, and assumptions that are dominant in the national culture (country where the organizations or divisions are based) or differences of national culture that may result from today's increasingly global and multinational workforce. Therefore, depending on the type and frequency of change in an organization, there are some key relationships within and across the organization where alignment becomes critical.

Aligning the Organization System with Change

First, consider the relationships between strategy and the three elements illustrated in the center of the model in Figure 13.1: structure, culture, and systems/processes. These particular elements are often referred to as organizational design elements. They frame the shape of the organization and contribute to social interactions within and outside of the organization. In particular, organizational structure provides close or distant contact with others, and creates boundaries and efficiencies needed in work relationships. The organization's systems and processes establish how work flows, how people work with each other, and the steps or sequences of desired ways of working. And the culture establishes the values and norms guiding behavior and influencing all other system elements. When any strategy calls for particular behaviors, these design elements, working together, will help to shape how people behave in the organization, when well managed by the leaders.

When organizational elements are not in alignment with change strategy, there are often differing logics, more conflict, and/or more inefficiencies that result in confusion, poor functioning, and less than effective results. For example, in an organization characterized by low employee participation, outcomes in planning and implementing change will be affected. In low participation cultures important values, structures, and processes that encourage participation may be underdeveloped or missing. In such cases important perspectives could be left out, including those from key groups and people who will be involved in implementing the change and committing to making the change work. So what might change leaders or participants do to align elements and effect positive outcomes?

- From a values perspective, change leaders and participants can evaluate whether participation is being encouraged and valued at various levels across the organization, or whether there are marginalized units, divisions, or staff.
- From a structural perspective, they may need to consider what types of communication structures and systems are in place (vertically and laterally across the organization).

- From a process perspective, change leaders and participants can consider how to develop, use, or create alignment between current practices, and identify what will be needed to achieve the desired future state.

When leaders, teams, and individuals understand how cultural dynamics at various levels of the system are operating, tangible strategies can be developed to navigate culture's seemingly invisible but potent effect on organizational change.

EXPERIENCING THE DYNAMICS OF CULTURE AND CHANGE

Since culture has a strong role in everything an organization does, it becomes important to know how to understand and navigate the cultural dynamics. When doing organizational tasks or any change work, the operating culture will influence how the work gets done, how people feel doing it, and what results will occur. In this section we offer an overview of the experiential activity, the "Culture and Change Challenge," followed by design and facilitation notes.

Following experiential learning theory (Kolb, 1984), the instructions and narrative below provide specific notes and comments mirroring the experiential learning cycle:

1. Experiential activity: set-up, timing, and facilitation of the activity.
2. Participant reflections: suggested questions for small and large groups.
3. Conceptual underpinnings: ways to deepen activity learning, connecting it to conceptual frameworks (for example, Hofstede's Big Five, Meyer's Culture Map, Jamieson's Organizational Systems Alignment Model).
4. Experimenting with new knowledge (next steps): suggestions on how to apply and experiment with new knowledge.

A General Note on Learning Groups and Spaces

In general, we developed the Culture and Change Challenge as an adaptable learning activity that can be used with small or large groups. The narrative below is based on facilitation for smaller groups (12–36 participants). In order to facilitate the activity in larger groups (those greater than 36 participants) you may need additional facilitators to subdivide the large group into smaller groups to maintain the proposed timeline. If this is not possible, we offer some suggestions to modify later in the chapter.

As for the types of groups that may benefit from this activity, we have identified (and created learning spaces with) a broad set of participants ranging from traditional classroom learners, to organizational managers and leaders, to a network of development and change practitioners (see Milbrandt and Zwieg-Daly, 2016). The version published in the chapter has evolved over time and is the best representation of what has been effective in creating an experiential learning space across a variety of learners. While objectives may be modified or altered to best meet group learning needs, three are primary to the activity design:

1. raise awareness of how culture (at various levels of the organization) impacts group behavior and outcomes;
2. develop strategies to prepare for the impact of cultural dynamics on organizational change; and
3. identify new ways to experiment with new knowledge on culture and change, and apply learning to real-life change efforts.

The Culture and Change Challenge

The underlying purpose of using the Culture and Change Challenge as an experiential activity is to provide participants with an experience of how cultural dynamics may interact with organizational life and organizational change. In this activity we have constructed two opposing sets of "culture norms" to guide work groups in their task completion. For most, Part I of this activity will be a familiar and accelerated experience of assimilating into a new work group, followed by Part II which may also be a familiar experience of a culture clash. Here is how it works. In Part I each group is given an activity card (see Box 13.A1 and 13A.2) with a description of the task and their group culture norms. After successfully completing Part I, participants are regrouped with others into mixed culture groups to perform another task. Easy, right? Hold on! In Part II, participants must blindly navigate culture norms as they also manage increasing complexity of their task with less time to complete it.

Each part of the activity will take approximately 30 minutes with time for a large-group discussion following the activity. The overall time suggested is between 90 and 120 minutes to adequately allow for completion of Part I and Part II and the concluding large-group discussion. We have found that 90 minutes is the minimum amount of time to complete with a small group (10–15 participants). Larger groups may require up to 120 minutes to accommodate the extra time needed for the small-group reports or to plan next steps which may be used with "intact" teams.

As previously mentioned, there are two sets of culture norms included in the activity cards. From here on we will refer to these as culture A and B, or the A and B groups. In Part I, these culture norms (behavior guidelines) are explicit and used to inform various decisions related to the group norms and the group structure, process, and systems. At this stage, observing or following culture values and norms is as important as completing the task. Each of the groups will use the values and norms on the instruction card to guide their team approach.

In Part II, the explicit norms groups are not reassigned; rather, participants from culture A and culture B are mixed. This creates an experience of navigating different and opposing cultures in teams. In Part II, participants are told to use what they learned in Part I to inform their approach in the new group. After each part of the experiential activity, participants will engage in individual and small-group reflection on the experience. What each participant notices, experiences, and feels as a result of adhering to the culture norms will be part of the reflection process. Outcomes of the group experience (for example, the process they used to complete the task, how decisions were made, and what happened) will also be part of a small- and larger-group discussion. Below we offer a brief facilitation guide, followed by more detailed instructions on how to run the activity (see Table 13.1).

Part I: Experiencing the Dynamics of Culture in Work Teams

In Part I, the espoused goal of the activity is twofold: (1) learn your shared culture norms; and (2) complete the task while observing your experience of your unique culture norm. In the most basic sense, this is an assimilation experience. Individually and as a group the team will try to adhere to the culture norms and complete a simple task. In a deeper way this experience may trigger individual responses to group climate, how they feel about working with their assigned culture norms, as well as noticing how the culture seems to either support or hinder group process.

Notes on activity sequence and facilitation (approximately ten minutes)
Step 1: Group configuration Begin by establishing small groups (5–8 members for each group). To save time you may have activity cards ready at predetermined group work stations. Depending on the number of participants, the size of the small groups will vary. For example, 24 participants may be divided into four groups of six; 20 participants may be divided into four groups of five; with as few as 16 participants you may opt for only two groups (one A and one B) with eight members, or three groups of six and so on. Additional set-up may include strategically alternating group A and group B culture types throughout the room in order to facilitate mixing the groups in Part II of the activity (see Figure 13.2 and Figure 13.3).

Table 13.1 Activity summary

Activity sequence	Description	Approximate timing	Chapter resources
Part I (30 minutes)	Step 1: Group configuration (participant groups of 5–8 people)	2 minutes	(see Figure 13.2)
	Step 2: Facilitate Part I of the work task activity	8 minutes	Part I activity cards (see Boxes 13A.1 and 13A.2)
	Step 3: Post-activity reflections using reflection worksheet	2 minutes	Part I reflection worksheets (see Box 13A.3)
	Step 4: Small-group discussion	10 minutes	
	Step 5: Synthesis of group discussion on flipchart	8 minutes	
Part II (25 minutes)	Step 1: Reconfigure groups (mixing A and B cultures)	2 minutes	(see Figure 13.3)
	Step 2: Facilitate Part II of the work task activity	6 minutes	Part II activity cards (see Box 13A.4)
	Step 3: Post-activity reflections using reflection worksheet	2 minutes	Part II reflection worksheets (see Box 13A.5)
	Step 4: Small-group discussion/synthesis of group discussion on flipchart	15 minutes	
Large-group discussion (45–60 minutes)	Step 1: Facilitate Part II post-activity reflections for A groups	8 minutes	(see Figure 13.4)
	Step 2: Facilitate Part II post-activity reflections for B groups	8 minutes	
	Step 3: Facilitate Part II post-activity reflections for mixed groups	15 minutes	Part II reflection worksheets (see Box 13A.5)
	Step 4: Facilitate large-group discussion	15 minutes	
Next steps (5 minutes)	Participants identify simple next steps to apply what they have learned.	5 minutes	

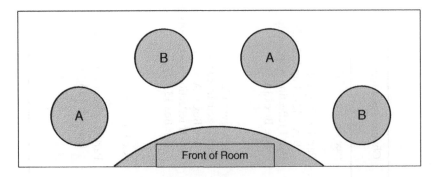

Figure 13.2   Part I: normed culture groups

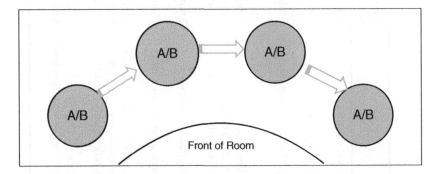

Figure 13.3   Part II: mixed culture groups

Step 2: Facilitate groups   Facilitate the activity as a supportive observer. If groups have questions, we recommend using as little influence as possible while remaining supportive. Provide time prompts at five minutes and at seven minutes to warn of closure of the activity. Ensure a hard stop at eight minutes. Groups that complete ahead of schedule can begin their individual reflections on the experience.

Ensure each group has the following materials prior to beginning the actual task:

- Part I activity instructions for culture A (see Box 13A.1) and culture B (see Box 13A.2);
- Part I reflection worksheet (see Box 13A.3);
- standard deck of playing cards;
- flipchart or notepads for reflection writing;
- markers and/or individual writing utensils.

Post-activity reflections (approximately 20 minutes)
Step 1: Individual reflections (2–3 minutes)   Once time is up for the activity, have group members individually reflect on their experience during Part I by answering the following questions:

- How well did the assigned group behaviors fit with your personal work preferences?
- How did you feel as an individual?
- What was confirming or distancing?
- What surprised or confused you?
- What seemed to help or hinder the process?
- Based on the outcomes and your reflections what, if anything, would you do the same? Differently?

Step 2: Small-group discussion (16–18 minutes)   When the facilitator feels individuals have had enough time to individually reflect, ask groups to come back together to collectively share their personal experiences and reflections. Then ask the group to discuss and take notes on the following recommended questions:

- What common or unique themes emerged related to the experience of your group culture in this activity (for example surprises, confusion, confirmation)?
- What seemed to help or hinder the group process?
- What strategy did the group use to complete the task?
- What was the process for completing the task?
- What was the end result? (What did you do?)
- What, if any, questions did this experience raise for you?

Part II: Dealing with Differences, Disorientation, and Disconfirmation

In Part II, the goal of the activity itself is similar to Part I, except that in this version the norms, assumptions, and behaviors are not explicitly known or discussed. In the most basic sense, this is an immersion and norming exercise. Participants will need to detect and understand differences between the cultures, manage their own confusion about these differences, and decide and try strategies to navigate the new cultural dynamics in this intentionally culturally mixed work team.

Activity sequence (approximately ten minutes)
Step 1: Mix groups   In Part II, the original groups will be recast, intentionally mixing members from culture A and B into new groups. If

you followed the A, B, A, B group configuration suggested in Part I, this should simplify mixing the groups (see Figure 13.3).

Simple steps we have used include asking half of the original A and B group members to stand up, followed by asking those standing to move clockwise or counterclockwise (depending on your preference) to the next group. Once new groups are formed make sure each group has approximately the same number of A and B group members in their new configurations. Then hand out facilitation cards and the additional group reflection and the Part II Worksheet (see Boxes 13A.4 and 13A.5).

Step 2: Facilitate Part II of the activity   Prior to beginning the task for Part II make sure you have handed out additional materials:

- Part II activity instructions;
- Part II reflection worksheet;
- an additional deck of playing cards;
- more flipcharts or notepads for reflection writing;
- markers and/or individual writing utensils.

Post-activity reflections (approximately 15 minutes)
Step 1: Individual reflections (2–3 minutes)   Once time is up for the activity, have group members individually reflect on their experiences as they did earlier in Part I:

- How did you feel as an individual?
- How did you fit your "new" group's behaviors?
- What aspects of what you learned in Part I helped or hindered your group two process?
- What surprised or confused you?
- What did you learn? Based on the outcomes and your reflections what, if anything, would you do the same? Differently?

Step 2: Small-group discussion (10–12 minutes)   When the facilitator feels individuals have had enough time to reflect individually, ask groups to come back together to collectively share their personal experiences from Part II. Following individual reflection group sharing, ask each group to reflect and discuss the Part II experience as a group by answering the following questions:

- What did you find in common or different about individual experiences during Part II of this activity?

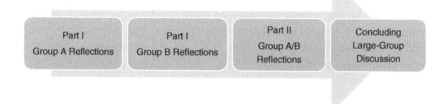

Figure 13.4   Suggested small-group reporting sequence

- What parts were challenging or surprising about repeating this task?
- What strategy did the group use to complete the task?
- What was the process for completing the task?
- What was the end result? (What did you do?)
- What, if any, new questions did this experience raise for you?

Part III: Harvesting Collaborative Knowledge (Approximately 30–45 minutes)

This part of the activity always wants more time. In our experience the most daunting task for the facilitator is to maintain the time limits. We recommend a structured report out for debriefing on small-group discussions (see Figure 13.4) followed by a more generalized large-group open discussion at the end. In addition to keeping time limits facilitators may also consider modifying small-group reports if the number of groups is time prohibiting.

Step 1: Small-group reports (about two minutes per group)   The small-group reports can take up a lot of time, but hold important information. In this facilitation guide we allocate approximately 20 minutes for small-group reports. This goes quickly, considering that these are reports on Part I and Part II of the activity, and depending on how many groups you are working with can be extremely restrictive.

To help move the harvest along we found it helpful to have a group member selected to make the report. We also found it useful from a logistics point of view to have all the A groups report followed by B groups. This encouraged discussion on similarities between groups that later contributed to discussion of differences. Finally, we have also found it helpful to emphasize that reports be concise, highlighting common themes, insights gained, emerging questions.

Most of the groups we have facilitated have been small groups of 15–30 people; and most groups have succeeded in staying within the suggested time limits. Modifications that may be considered to save time if needed include use of large-scale technologies (Bunker and Alban, 1997), or gallery walks of small-group work that can be incorporated into the large-group discussion.

Step 2: Large-group discussion (15 minutes)   Based on reflections from the small groups, the following questions have been useful to synthesize learning and begin to think about the next steps in using what was learned:

● What was different/similar between group experiences (for example, from Part I to Part II; between groups)?
● What aspects of culture seemed to help or hinder group processes?
● What have you learned about culture that you can apply to your work in organizational change?

There are a number of common themes that we have found emerge from these discussions, regardless of setting or demographic population. Below we explore and share these experiences and thoughts.

Final Observations

Since developing this activity, which has been used in the classroom, at conferences, and in workshops, we see a variety of applications. We have seen that it has enormous potential to help individuals and teams working on strategies related to cultural dynamics and change.

As facilitators of the activity, we have learned alongside participants as they explored and discovered how changes that appear to be simple may have more complex implications when considering culture and change. And we have learned through observations that there are consistent outcomes that culture values and norms engender which are helpful to consider when attempting to align culture with planned change.

For example, reoccurring patterns discovered in Part I of the activity, coupled with the conceptual framework may be used by a group to identify and create new and intentional culture norms. Sensitizing recognition of patterns in the activity may lead to recognition of unconscious or existing patterns in group or organizational life. After experiencing some culture values in the activity – such as Hofstede's Big Five value schema and others from Meyer's continuum scale – participants will have a better understanding of how organizational values that impact behavior may help or hinder desired change. We summarize the main differences between

Table 13.2   Culture values and norms

Culture A Values-in-Use	Culture B Values-in-Use
• High power distance	• Low power distance
• Top-down decision-making	• Consensus-driven decision-making
• High-uncertainty avoidance	• Low-uncertainty avoidance
• Task-based trust	• Relationship-based trust

the two groups (selected as opposing values and norms for each group) in Table 13.2.

Essentially, we have found that groups using overt values and norms in the activity have led to some predictable outcomes. For example, participants in group A typically completed the task with one solution and finished ahead of schedule. A familiar organizational benchmark that could be linked to this culture norm is efficiency, which is bad not in and of itself. However, there were other reoccurring effects reported by participants, including feeling bored and disconnected. As well as one incident where a late-comer who was assigned to the group described his experience as simply "weird." According to that participant, no one in the group acknowledged that he had joined or bothered to invite explanation as to what they were doing. They simply continued toward completion. While this response completely fits the norms of the group, it raises a moment to reflect on and beg the question, "How might this experience be reflected in organizations that adhere to norms similar to those we constructed?"

Similarly, we found patterns that were typical of participants in the B group which, not unlike the participants in A, had interesting real-world implications. For example, participants in group B typically took longer to complete, but also generated multiple solutions. We observed participants being highly engaged, and participants often described their experience as a creative and collaborative one in which they felt engaged and connected. Again, taking a reflective pause, we may ask, "How might this experience be reflected in organizations that adhere to similar norms to those we constructed?"

Finally, reoccurring patterns we observed from Part II of the activity related to group climate. While most groups completed the task and often had multiple solutions to the problem posed, the experience was consistently described as difficult, tense, confusing, and frustrating. One participant said that it took her group nearly till halfway through the exercise to stop and ask others in the group, "What norms are you following?" This was a breakthrough for them. And yet, other groups that never directly asked this question but used various strategies to surface conflicts, including negotiation over process and creating rules as they progressed, also had breakthroughs. For most, the uneasiness they linked to being unsure about what was the "right" or "accepted" norm was combated by creating agreements along the way. Participants found this strategy to be highly relevant to experiences in organizations when forming new or project-based work teams. One participant commented that this experience was how they felt "all the time" in their organization: feeling that they had to be on guard, and trying to fit in to a culture they did not completely understand. We feel that having these two experiences back to back was extremely helpful in creating new insights in the post-activity reflections, and thinking about ways to experiment with new knowledge.

CONCLUSION

Although we have only had a handful of experiences thus far using the Culture and Change Challenge with groups, the consistency with which observations of learning and outcomes emerged leaves us hopeful. While simulated, these are accelerated learning experiences that have real-world implications for change leaders and managers. And there may be a variety of ways to build upon the initial learnings this experiential activity offers. We offer some suggestions toward this end below.

Continued Learning

If you are lucky enough to be working with a group that you will see again, such as an academic class or ongoing organizational client, this exercise may lend itself to creating possible follow-up activities to exploit or expand the new knowledge in the group. In our introduction, we offered several conceptual culture frames (for example, Hofstede's Big Five values and Meyer's Culture Map) and a model showing culture as part of the organization system (Jamieson's Alignment Model). Taking a deeper dive into all or any of these frameworks to further reflect on the experience may be used to deepen reflective and connective dialogue. Some suggestions toward doing this include:

- Using parts of Hofstede's or Meyer's conceptual frameworks, new culture types could be created for further simulation activities and used for "what if" discussions.
- Real "home cultures" of participants could be used as a cultural lens to analyze and fuel discussions about how they individually navigate cultural dynamics at work or in their organization.

- Real-time change situations could be analyzed with the Organizational System Alignment Model (Jamieson, 2017) to better understand, in particular, how cultural dynamics interact with all organization elements, helping or hindering the desired change.
- A general discussion could be facilitated to help participants better understand how what they have learned could be applied to cross-cultural (national-level) work and mixed teams.

Expanding and building upon learning in these ways may offer participants a chance to build understanding and awareness of how culture norms, values, and assumptions influence not only change outcomes, but also the overall processes, systems, and behavior in their organization or work context. It may also offer a unique perspective on what may happen when culture is ignored, especially when two or more different cultures are embedded in a work team or group.

Learning from this experiential activity makes it possible to develop the awareness and skills needed to anticipate, observe, and leverage culture in organizational change. As participants explore the dynamics of culture and change in this way, we are confident that they are building cultural awareness, thinking, and strategies needed to plan for, respond to, and successfully manage change in a complex world.

Final Thoughts

As we stated in the introduction, the existing culture in any organization can either help or hinder the work process, the satisfaction of the participants, and the outcomes. Our hope is that readers will take aspects of the conceptual frames we offered and think about how to:

- align the organization (strategy, structure, culture, systems/processes, or behaviors);
- navigate change with existing culture (which is intended to keep the organization's social system in line with certain norms and "rules" of engagement); and
- anticipate how change will affect how work gets done and what happens.

By considering these things before launching into tasks of change or other work, change leaders and others can recognize their own views and develop greater skill and efficacy in navigating cultural dynamics at work and within their organizations.

As the world continues toward the trend of growing complexity and globalization, change efforts will continue to bump or fall into different culture quagmires. At small and larger scales, organizations will require new and improved skills in understanding the dynamics between change and culture and the implications of both of these in organizations. It is our hope that the Change and Culture Challenge (when used with other tools) will significantly improve how this knowledge can be developed and used by organizations to successfully navigate the dynamics of culture and change in an increasingly complex world.

REFERENCES

Ang, S., Van Dyne, L., Koh, C.K.S., Ng, K.Y., Templer, K.J., Tay, C., and Chandrasekar, N.A. (2007). Cultural intelligence: Its measurement and effects on cultural judgment and decision making, cultural adaptation, and task performance. *Management and Organization Review*, 3, 335–371.

Bunker, B.B. and Alban, B.T. (1997). *Large Group Interventions: Engaging the Whole System for Rapid Change*. San Francisco, CA: Jossey-Bass.

Eoyang, G. and Holliday, R. (2013). *Adaptive Action: Leveraging Uncertainty in Your Organization*. Palo Alto, CA: Stanford University Press.

Hofstede, G. (2001). *Cultures Consequences* (2nd edition). Thousand Oaks, CA: SAGE.

Horney, N., Pasmore, B., and O'Shea, T. (2010). Leadership agility: A business imperative for a VUCA world. *People and Strategy*, 33 (4), 32–38.

Jamieson, D. (2017). Strategic organization design and change. Presentation for PhD in Organization Development and Change Degree. Radnor, PA: Cabrini University.

Kirkman, B.L. and Shapiro, D.L. (1997). The impact of cultural values on employee resistance to teams: Toward a model of globalized self-managing work team effectiveness. *Academy of Management Review*, 22 (3), 730–757.

Kolb, D.A. (1984). *Experiential Learning: Experience as the Source of Learning and Development*. Englewood Cliffs, NJ: Prentice Hall.

Meadows, D. (2008). *Thinking in Systems: A Primer*. White River Junction, VT: Chelsea Green Publishing.

Meyer, E. (2014). *The Culture Map: Breaking through the Invisible Boundaries of Global Business*. New York: Public Affairs.

Milbrandt, J. and Zwieg-Daly, N. (2016). Cultural intelligence: A 21st century organizational advantage. Presentation at the OD Network Annual Conference, October, Atlanta, GA.

Olson, E.E. and Eoyang, G. (2001). *Facilitating Organization Change: Lessons from Complexity Science*. San Francisco, CA: Jossey-Bass.

Schein, E.H. (1983). The role of the founder in creating organizational culture. *Organizational Dynamics*, (Summer), 13–28.

Schein, E.H. (1990). Organizational culture. *American Psychologist*, 45 (2), 109–119.

Stacey, R. (2001). *Complex Responsive Processes in Organizations*. New York: Routledge.

APPENDIX

BOX 13A.1 PART I ACTIVITY CARD (GROUP "A")

Welcome to the Culture and Change Challenge! You have been selected to complete an important group task. You are to follow group norms and assumptions below. In addition to your culture guidelines, you will be assigned a culture expert to support your process. This person will observe your group while you work on your task and norms and be available to clarify questions you have about your organizational culture. Good luck!

- Roles, expectations, and leadership are communicated through formal titles and rank defining power-status within the group. (Drawing cards from the deck to determine this status may be one option to get started).
- When making decisions, the group norm is to share relevant insights through the appropriate channels and defer to the leader to make the final decisions.
- In your culture there is not a word for "NO" instead members make a clicking sound to express "NO."
- Individuals who do not follow the rules are ostracized.
- The group prefers information to be organized in a logical sequence, from beginning to end.
- Completing tasks and having a proven track record to get things done on time is of the utmost importance. The group norm is to minimize risk and maximize efficiency.
- Emotions are private; expressing emotions (even laughter) is discouraged.

Your task is to organize the deck of standard playing cards you have been given using the culture rules stated above. At the end of the allotted time you will be asked to STOP.

If you complete early, you may begin your individual reflections responding to the questions on the reflection worksheet.

BOX 13A.2 PART I ACTIVITY CARD (GROUP "B")

Welcome to the Culture and Change Challenge! You have been selected to complete an important group task. You are to follow group norms and assumptions below. In addition to your culture guidelines, you will be assigned a culture expert to support your process. This person will observe your group while you work on your task and norms and be available to clarify questions you have about your organizational culture. Good luck!

- Roles, expectations, and leadership emerge out of the interactions within the group.
- When making decisions the group norm is to build consensus. This means every member has a voice and when differences emerge efforts are made to reach agreement.
- In your culture there is no word for "YES" – instead a non-verbal signal is used (raising both eyebrows at the same time).
- Individuals who try to enforce rules are ostracized.
- The group prefers information to be organized categorically, grouping things by similarity and connection to one another.
- Relationships and social connections are highly valued – letting each member of the group make a contribution is of utmost importance.
- Expression of feelings is encouraged; those who are unexpressive are deemed untrustworthy.

Your task is to organize the deck of standard playing cards you have been given using the culture rules stated above. At the end of the allotted time you will be asked to STOP.

If you complete early, you may begin your individual reflections responding to the questions on the reflection worksheet.

BOX 13A.3   PART I REFLECTION WORKSHEET
             (ALL GROUPS)

The Change and Culture Challenge Reflection Worksheet

Personal reflection: Part I
Take 2–3 minutes to reflect on your experience of the task and culture.

1. How well did the assigned group behaviors fit with your personal work preferences?
2. How did you feel as an individual?
3. What was confirming or distancing?
4. What surprised or confused you?
5. What seemed to help or hinder the process?
6. What, if anything, might you do differently?

Group reflection: Part I
As a group take a few minutes to discuss your personal experiences. Then as a group discuss the following questions. Afterward capture key points on flipchart paper used to report out to the larger group.

1. What common or unique themes emerged related to the experience of your group culture in this activity (for example surprises, confusion)?
2. What seemed to help or hinder the group process?
3. What strategy did the group use to complete the task?
4. What was the process for completing the task?
5. What was the end result? (What did you do?)
6. What if any questions did this experience raise for you?

BOX 13A.4   PART II ACTIVITY INSTRUCTIONS
             (ALL GROUPS)

Congratulations! You have all been promoted for the great work you did on Task I and have been placed in cross-functional teams. The organization expects you to apply what you have learned from your experience and therefore you will be given less time to complete. This task is more complex – but you are now experts! Your team has been given two decks of standard playing cards to sort.

Use what you learned during Part I of the activity to inform your strategy.

You will be given an allotted time to finish and at that time will be asked to STOP. If your group completes ahead of schedule you may begin your personal reflections on your experience of Part II. Good luck!

BOX 13A.5   PART II REFLECTION QUESTIONS (ALL GROUPS)

Personal Reflection: Part II

Take 2–3 minutes to reflect on your experience of the task and culture.

1. How did you feel as an individual?
2. How did you fit your "new" groups' behaviors?
3. What aspects of what you learned in part one helped or hindered your group two process?
4. What surprised or confused you?
5. What did you learn? Based on the outcomes and your reflections what, if anything would you do the same? Differently?

Group Reflection: Part II

1. What did you find in common or different about individual experiences during part two of this activity?
2. What parts were challenging or surprising about repeating this task?
3. What strategy did the group use to complete the task?
4. What was the process for completing the task?
5. What was the end result? (What did you do?)
6. What if any new questions did this experience raise for you?

14. Building exchange relations and brokerage positions within groups

Keith Hunter

A typical text on organization development, organizational change, or change leadership will feature topics such as the foundations of organizational behavior and theory, data collection and analysis, and interventions at multiple levels, as well as values and ethics. Research and practice around the area of organizational networks has made solid contributions to all of these areas; see network research from Landis (2016) on personality, Brass (2018) on organizational citizenship behavior, Borgatti and Cross (2003) on information-seeking and learning, Maak (2007) on leadership and social capital, Cross et al. (2002) on strategic collaboration, and Flynn and Wiltermuth (2010) on ethical decision-making. The naturally occurring web of human interactions within organizations has been shown to have significant, even a critical, impact on both the success of organizational change and the impact of such change. Work associating networks with change has addressed many important topics, including use of network insight for successful change management (McGrath and Krackhardt, 2003), response to crisis (Krackhardt and Stern, 1988), sense-making, and innovation (D'Andreta et al., 2016; Perry-Smith and Mannucci, 2017; Tortoriello et al., 2014).

The learning exercise described in this chapter provides an experiential basis regarding important factors that drive the emergence of social networks and the extraction of value from those networks. The exercise focuses on improving participant understanding of social capital, exchange, and power in social networks. The core activity of the exercise entails participants engaging in multiple dyadic interactions with the aim of maximizing the value of the resources (cards) they hold, negotiating with counterparts to obtain resources (cards) that improve their respective situations. Using a rich, targeted debrief emphasizing critical themes in organizational change and development, facilitators of this exercise can deliver important lessons that help learners to understand why informal networks have tremendous impact on the success of change initiatives, and how the power to drive change can be developed through a basic understanding of how exchange relationships form, key network structures, and the importance of network centrality.

This exercise primarily focuses on the network as a dynamic collection of channels for the exchange of information and material resources among a group of people. In undertaking the exercise with the objective of enhancing their resource base (obtaining the highest scoring combination of cards that they can), each participant is faced with multiple challenges that are relevant to building and exploiting networks, including establishing new connections, establishing and sustaining trust, and increasing awareness of the network's structure beyond their knowledge of the network ties that they have formed directly with others. Finally, participants gain a stronger perspective of how network structure emerges, and that value within networks takes on multiple forms.

This exercise has been effective with a range of audiences including undergraduate college students, executive MBA students, and educators in management and organizational behavior. The executive MBA and educator populations in particular have typically included members who engage in significant organizational management or development practice.

Specifically, this learning activity is designed to promote participant learning on a number of different levels and for different outcomes:

- identifying tendencies and biases in choosing people to interact with;
- examining communication patterns or tactics that enhance or impede cooperative outcomes with other people;
- developing understanding of how network ties facilitate discovery and accessing of resources within a network;
- critiquing different approaches to seeking and obtaining resources within a network;
- explaining how power accrues not only to those who are central in social networks but also to those who are aware of social networks.

THE EXERCISE

This exercise is built around a simple game using standard playing cards used for many popular card games such as Poker or Blackjack. All players begin with a set of cards for use in either: (1) creating scoring combinations according to a set of scoring rules provided; or (2) negotiating the exchange of cards with other participants in order to create better scoring opportunities. Whoever possesses the collection of cards that is worth the highest number of points by the end is declared the winner of the game.

In spite of its simplicity, this game provides the opportunity for a group of participants to examine rather complex and influential processes that are associated with the accumulation, adoption, and sustaining of organizational change. Much like a real organization, the group of participants is composed of individuals who operate under a need to maximize their local interests; with their capacity to do so highly dependent on exchange relationships with at least some others, who have their own local priorities. In some cases, local needs make it difficult to support the needs of others, while in other cases desired resources are easier to provide on request. Also similar to real organizations, players in this game may be not only direct participants in exchange but also act as brokers for relationships and interactions between other people. This bridging and facilitation behavior is an important component of system-wide innovation and change, and it also grows the power and influence of individuals within networks. Even the more fundamental consideration of how individuals choose who to approach or accept for interaction under uncertainty can be explored using this simple game.

Preparation

Basic requirements include an appropriate number of participants (20–30), sufficient space, and minimal materials. In terms of physical space, at a minimum, the exercise should be run within an area that allows all participants to move comfortably and fluidly to engage in dyadic encounters, with at least 5 feet of space around each dyad, and a comfortable speaking distance between members of each dyad. Obstructions such as tables and chairs should at least be spread out sufficiently to support flexible movement on the part of the participants. If participants are allowed to be seated during the exercise, care should be taken to ensure that spacing requirements are still satisfied.

The following materials are necessary:

- three decks of regular playing cards;
- one adhesive or lanyard type ID tag for each participant, large enough for a one- or two-digit number to be easily read from a distance of at least 10 feet;
- one information sheet for each participant (see Appendix 14.1 and 14.2);
- a means of visually presenting information (for example, whiteboard, pad and easel, projector).

Overall the exercise can be successfully completed in under two hours. As an example:

- Phase I – distribution of materials and explanation of rules: 20 minutes.
- Phase II – networking and exchange: 30–40 minutes.
- Phase III – debrief 1: 20–25 minutes.
- Phase IV – debrief 2: 20–25 minutes.

Facilitator Pre-work

The preparation for facilitators is minimal:

1. Prepare one envelope for each exercise participant and mark each with a distinctive identification (ID) number.
2. Place within each of these envelopes a name tag marked with the same ID number that appears on the envelope.
3. Remove any Joker cards, then combine and shuffle all three sets of playing cards together to form one well-shuffled stack.
4. Place within each numbered envelope exactly five randomly chosen playing cards taken from the stack.
5. Place within each numbered envelope one blank information sheet (see Appendix 14.1 and 14.2).
6. (Optional.) Include within each envelope a piece of scratch paper for participants to use as they see fit as they proceed through the exercise. Some may decide to carefully track details about their interactions or make note of who seems to have which resources (cards).

The exercise has been used successfully without any pre-work on the part of participants. In such cases, Phases III and IV (debriefing, identified above) tend to focus more on delivering fundamental understanding of organizational networks and associated analysis. Deeper progress with respect to learning outcomes involving situational contexts and network-oriented behaviors is clearly enabled by participant study of the general topic of social networks or organizational networks before experiencing this exercise. Hence, we recommend a lesson and/or readings covering some or all of the following basic concepts prior to running this exercise, depending on which themes you intend to pursue most richly during your debrief:

- Definition of a social network and its basic components.
- Definition of social capital.
- Identification of some basic drivers of network formation (for example, homophily, structural balance).
- Basic definitions and examples of network centrality. These should definitely include popularity centrality and betweenness centrality, structural holes and structural equivalence.

Although the learning outcomes of this exercise do not require coverage of the methodology behind centrality or other structural measures associated with social network analysis, participants are typically curious about these later on. Some articles I have found useful for building initial familiarity with network analysis include classic pieces from Krackhardt and Hanson (1993) and Cross and Prusak (2002). More in-depth readings that include considerable treatment of applications in the field include Cross and Parker (2004), McCulloh et al. (2013), and Scott (2017).

Running the Exercise

Having secured the exercise requirements and accomplished the pre-work noted above, you are in position to run this activity for 20–30 participants. This number of participants has seemed to me to be the "sweet spot" between having enough participants for the network to display some interesting complexity, and having few enough participants for a highly interactive debrief that allows everyone a good chance to get their reactions and ideas out into the open.

The following is an illustrative introduction script for the exercise. Please note that it may be helpful to prepare handouts, slides, or visual aids in order to help participants keep on track with your instructions:

- Today you are about to play a game that is designed to improve your understanding of social networks, how they grow, how they are used, and what they make possible. Each of you will have an objective that can only be met through productive interactions with other participants. You should expect to move around the classroom in order to accomplish this, and only interaction in pairs is allowed.
- First, you will receive important instructions regarding the rules you are to follow and how points are scored. Once these instructions and rules are understood, you will each pick up an envelope containing the following contents:
  - an ID tag that you should attach to a highly visible place on your upper body;
  - five playing cards you should not show to anyone, leaving them inside your envelope;
  - an information sheet that you should remove and prepare to write on when instructed to do so. [At this point, students should only fill out the part of the form that asks for their assigned ID number.]

With the materials handed out and the exercise introduced, students are then given the core instructions they need in order to play and win the game. These instructions are as follows:

1. Interactions:
   a. This game is driven by one-on-one interactions. Once the game begins, students may only speak to one other person at a time.
   b. Anything at all may be discussed during an interaction, but a key function of the interaction within this game is the negotiated exchange of playing cards that individual players use to accumulate points.
   c. Both parties must agree to begin an interaction for an interaction to occur, and third parties are not allowed to join the discussion or listen in.
   d. At the very beginning of each interaction, students must check a new box next to the ID number of their partner on their own information sheet (see Appendix 14.3). Each partner who a given student interacts with should have at least one check mark next to their ID number on that student's information sheet. If multiple interactions occurred with the same partner, multiple check marks should appear next to that partner's ID number.
   e. Each interaction may persist for as long as both parties wish. An interaction may be ended at any time by any single party currently engaged in the interaction.
   f. Each player has full discretion to share or withhold any information or make any claims that they wish to during any interaction.
2. Accumulation of points:
   a. The objective of each player in this game is to accumulate the highest number of points possible by putting together high-scoring combinations of playing cards. Score values for card combinations are defined in Appendix 14.1 and 14.2.
   b. Every player begins the game with a randomly selected combination of cards that represent a certain starting point total that should be calculated by each player at the beginning of the game and noted in the appropriate place on the player's information sheet.
   c. Through interactions with other players (one player at a time), each player may attempt to improve their score by obtaining different cards. As shown in the table of scoring combinations, there are many different ways to put together valuable combinations of cards. Hence, exchanges can be beneficial to both parties engaged in an interaction.

3. Ending the game:
    a. After the prescribed amount of time has passed, the game is halted by the facilitator. [It is a good idea to provide time checks at various points during the exercise so that the final countdown does not come as a total surprise.]
    b. Once time has expired, all interactions must cease and participants should return to their seats with no further discussion or exchange of cards.
    c. Participants should then examine the cards they have in hand and calculate their final scores.

Once the time period for the exercise is concluded, the facilitator then brings the room to order and instructs students to take their seats and abstain from any discussions as they silently reflect on the experience they have just had. You might prompt them to consider specifically their own behaviors, the behaviors of others, what made the game harder, what might have made the game easier, and so forth.

The Debrief

The first part of debriefing the exercise should focus on the impact that behavior has on task accomplishment. Initially, participants face the question of who to approach and how to do it. For a group of participants who have already spent some time together, initial interactions tend to be driven by already established friendships or affiliations. Ongoing interaction during the exercise continues to be dominated by this factor, consistent with the findings of Casciaro and Lobo (2005). But as these contacts become exhausted, or less free when needed (or when students get the feeling that the correlation between who is their friend and who has the cards they need may not be high), outreach begins to involve other factors. One of the simplest factors involved tends to be the "law of propinquity," participants turning to whoever is physically near them in the room. Non-verbal communication also plays a part both in the establishment agreement or interest in an interaction, and in the perception that someone is even willing to interact. Considerations of who the student believes they can negotiate with most successfully may also come into play, contributing to opportunities to examine the basis of such perceptions in past experience and specific histories with specific individuals.

A second focus is on the behavior and tactics during a given encounter that come into play. Participants negotiating for a favorable exchange of cards during this exercise receive the opportunity to develop their ideas regarding trade-offs between competitive and collaborative thinking.

They also receive the chance to learn about the effects of positive and negative emotion and how they are communicated and reacted to while an interaction is under way, including the importance of how the interaction is initiated and the way it is concluded.

The check-sheet (Appendix 14.3) that students fill out as they do the exercise sometimes reveals individual patterns of access and exchange that reflect biases, preferences, or rational responses to prior experience during the session. Reputation can come into play, in the event that participants share information about their encounters with others. Also, sharing of information about other participants can lead to students realizing that the value of a new connection lies not only in which cards that connection has control over, and how pliable that party is when certain cards are sought, but also in the knowledge that connection may hold regarding other players, what cards they have or need, or what they are like to negotiate with.

Brokerage is a very important behavior within networks, illustrating the value that knowledge of the network can itself be useful currency, even when one does not possess desired resources. Brokerage is possible when a person's position within or awareness of the social network, and where resources are located among a group of people, makes it possible for that person to act as a bridge between people who have resources and those who need those resources. For example, let us say that Player A needs a King of Hearts card and Player B knows that Player C has that card. If Player B becomes aware of Player A's need, Player B has the opportunity to act as a broker, connecting Player A to a potential opportunity to gain a needed card from Player C by sharing information or even making the effort to facilitate an introduction. Burt et al. (2013), among others, have been informing the field of the importance of network brokerage and other positional effects for quite some time. In brokerage roles, individuals can become key facilitators of organizational change and innovation through better awareness of existing social networks, and by occupying and using positions of high "betweenness" that connect otherwise unconnected individuals. Brokers may also derive considerable benefit from their exposure to novel ideas, or from their uncommon awareness of where distinctive resources reside within a group of people or collection of subgroups.

The following are some illustrative questions that I have found useful in debriefing this aspect of the exercise:

1. What did you find to be challenging during this exercise?
2. Reflect on the moments you experienced during this game in which you had to decide who to talk to. What were some of the reasons why you approached the people you did?
3. What tactics or behaviors did you find yourself engaged in?

4. What are some examples of competitive behavior that you observed or perceive to be possible in this game? Collaborative?
5. What sources of power do you think you had during the exercise?
6. Did anyone obtain a card without giving a card? If so, describe what happened. Sometimes a card is exchanged for information about where another card may be found, requiring both capital and trust. Sometimes liking alone influences surrender of a desired card, or (more rarely) apathy or resignation to a low-scoring outcome (low self-efficacy, which can also be discussed).
7. Describe how you felt during some of your interactions. What do you think caused those feelings? Did trust play a part in any of your interactions?
8. When organizations undergo change, local interests sometimes find themselves in competition for scarce, diminishing, or shifting resources. During such times, leaders often encourage units to work together in support of both shared and individual interests. Given what you have just experienced in playing this game, what more specific advice or action do you think a change leader might consider in order to increase the likelihood that stakeholders will interact in a manner that maximizes value during the course of organizational change?

To end the initial debrief, participants are asked to calculate the value of their current collections of cards. Facilitators can provide a fun reward for those having the top score(s) in the class, encouraging applause and celebration of these successful deal-makers. Discussion of relative scores may or may not have come up by this time in the discussion. It should be noted that this game provides a window on a very complex system, even though it is highly simplified relative to that within a real organization during change. In essence, there are many determinants of individual outcomes, and each provides an important perspective on how value is discovered, created, and mobilized within an organization. Individual factors that may encourage more numerous or more lucrative interactions include:

- Verbal and non-verbal communication of openness. ("It is safe to approach me.")
- Signaling empathy or win–win perspectives. ("I want both of us to benefit from this interaction.")
- Positive energy around interactions. ("I want for us to enjoy this activity.")
- Extraversion or comfort with opening up socially within less familiar contexts.

- Ability to establish a friendly or trustworthy tone early in a relationship. ("I will not exploit or take advantage of you.")
- Ability and inclination to apply proper focus to learning the needs and resources of others.
- Luck. This activity simulates a complex system in which little is predetermined besides the rules of the game (and those rules may be bent or even violated in some way during the activity). While there are available explanations for why any particular beneficial exchange occurs, the processes that lead to each interaction are far from predictable. Notably, though, the argument should be made that, in repeated situations, knowledgeable and intentional actions are likely to yield desirable outcomes at a rate substantially better than pure chance.

The second part of debriefing the exercise focuses on the impact of social networks. The ID numbers recorded on each information sheet reveal each individual's network structure within the game, as well as the overall network structure of the entire class during the evolution of the exercise. Ideally, Debrief II occurs during the day following the exercise, when sufficient time has been spent capturing the network data from all participants, and some visualizations are made from that data (as an example, see Figure 14.1).

Whether or not strong correlations exist between those who are central in the network and those who score best in the exercise, participants will still gain much from seeing the actual structure their activities essentially

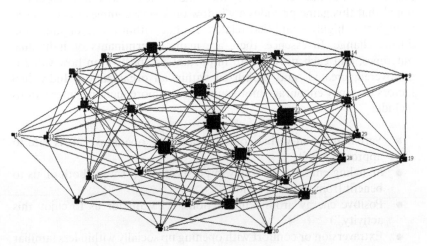

Figure 14.1   Illustrative network visualization

produced as they each sought to obtain favorable exchanges with each other. Highly central participants may have different perceptions of the group's overall behavior, or of the exercise itself. It may also be useful to have the group try to identify how certain people wound up being more central than others. Note that either degree or betweenness centrality (or both) are quite sufficient for driving this examination.

Research has shown that power accrues both to those who are central in social networks and to those who are aware of social networks (Krackhardt, 1990). Debrief II aims to help participants understand the impact that centrality may have on both collective and individual outcomes as a group of people interacts under shared constraints, even to address their own respective narrow interests. Visualizations sometimes reveal how some participants were at the periphery of all of the action, while a few people engaged in more interactions, or interacting with more people who did not interact with each other. This can support some very informative follow-up questions and probes into what strategies, reactions, or circumstances were located where within the network. It can be enlightening to many to realize and discuss how multiple tendencies, behaviors, and circumstances may lend themselves to similar structural positions within the network. But it can also be illuminating to look at the overall network density and whether or not interaction was among small clusters of individuals. Pre-existing affinity groups may even be identifiable simply by looking at the network structure (for example, participants who work together, attended the same college, or who have been sitting near each other prior to the exercise). Illustrative discussion questions for the social network portion of the debrief include:

1. How much awareness do you think you developed of what cards other people had?
    - Use at least a rough scale here (for example: essentially none, a small amount, a significant amount, a great deal). An excellent way to accomplish this would be through use of a tool that provides for instant feedback such as PollEverywhere. A show of hands for different levels of response can also provide an immediate and visible response.
    - This feedback can be used to drive discussion about how such insight was gained, or of what was perceived to stand in the way of developing this insight. This can be the beginning of a fruitful discussion of how one may come to understand the needs or resources of individuals or units within organizations.
    - Of particular interest may be indirect methods outside of roles and responsibilities within a formal structure or direct

communication regarding needs and resources. Included among these more subtle sources of insight may be observed responses to available options, discussions about strategy, or expressions of interest in specific types of card combinations. Ultimately, the point that can always be made here is that a narrow focus on just what one seeks in an exchange relationship (or any other context that lends itself to negotiation) may not be as helpful as one might think.

2. Did you use your awareness of what cards other people had in any particular way during the game?

    - The purpose of considering this question is to, first, acknowledge the most obvious use of information about the needs of other players, for targeting of efforts to obtain a beneficial exchange of cards with those players.
    - The second and more nuanced aspect of this question is to identify and discuss the use of knowledge regarding what other players need and who else may have the capacity to address that need. The value of having interacted with different people than some others can wind up being discussed here. Even if few or no participants endeavored to use brokerage as part of their game strategy, a very useful discussion about this can arise from the question.
    - Show the overall network drawing. Looking at the overall network for the entire class, are you surprised at your centrality within the game? Why, or why not?
    - This question may be the one that begins the discussion of how network structure and one's position within it leads to (or reflects) real differences in capacity to influence others or gain access to resources. Bridging otherwise unconnected individuals may emerge as valuable within this game.
    - Whether or not forming a bridge between individuals is present as a strategy during your facilitation of this exercise, participants may now be in a better position to discuss how to gain awareness of organizational networks, and the value of occupying brokerage positions within them. Examples that come up may be engagement in positive "water cooler talk," seeking assignments to diverse teams formed from personnel throughout the organization, observing which individuals or subunits are dependent on which others and how, and making note of informal affinity groups (for example, who goes to lunch, on hikes, discusses books, or plays video games together).

Variations

Small groups
Another way to conduct the exercise is to assign participants to small groups and have each group pursue the goal of obtaining the highest total sum of all group member results.

Costly interactions
Especially in the early minutes of the exercise, the best strategy might well be to circulate broadly and quickly, gaining knowledge of who has which cards and of who seeks which cards. A player bent on seeking value (either points, credibility, or simply fun) through brokerage might use a less deliberative approach rather successfully early in the exercise. However, some facilitators may wish to experiment with fostering some learning regarding how environmental structure and process may affect the development of networks. This can be done simply by assessing a one-point cost or benefit for every interaction engaged in. Experience of a communication cost makes the notion of economy of interaction more salient, potentially motivating participants to be more thoughtful and strategic in their interactions, or spawning slightly less open behaviors among those being approached. Experience of an incentive for interaction may create opportunities to discuss efficiency and effectiveness, not only when it comes to how much yield individual participants feel they gained during each interaction, but also in consideration of how well the group did as a whole given a highly active pattern of engagements. Diversity of partners may also be worth observing here, as some participants may simply revisit the same small number of people rather than make sure they talk to many different people.

Incentives for brokerage
Without any modifications to the exercise format as presented so far, brokerage behavior sometimes emerges as some people learn about the strategies other players have and what those players need in order to pursue those strategies. When this has occurred during my runs of this exercise, the exchange is usually information for a card or simply information for a little gratitude. In order to encourage more attempts at brokerage, facilitators may wish to assign bonus points for successful referral events. If Player A subsequently approaches Player C and obtains that King of Hearts, all three players can add three points to their total. This may also support ongoing participation on the part of those who have obtained a fairly high scoring hand early in the activity. Such people may decide to apply themselves to trying out some brokerage, creating value for the

collective while also enriching themselves thanks to a structure and process that rewards this engagement.

CONCLUDING THOUGHTS

Facilitating this exercise has consistently provided me and my students with a buzzy, interactive experience that reinforces learning about the behaviors and structures associated with social networks. Insights developed through the debriefs and ensuing discussions have never failed to expand beyond questions such as "How do I get what I want from the network?" to address more encompassing issues such as what affects openness and willingness to support others within networks, how power and influence materialize within networks, and how the consequences of even an exchange interaction extend beyond the simple result of who winds up with which resources. The dynamic network perspective featured in this exercise is an important companion to the key lessons of organization development and change. Network effects have always been essential to successful change and influence at the group and organizational levels, whether the challenge is that of building a shared sense of urgency, managing resistance, or fostering a culture of support and interaction around the meaning of change itself. Ultimately, my fundamental objective when I run this exercise is to have learners understand that "networking" is not simply working a room or getting what you want from a collection of people through your political prowess. Change leaders and those who would be effective drivers of positive change need to realize that engagement with and understanding of social networks is also a key avenue for building insight about the people affected by change, what people may have to contribute to change, and to both assess and establish trust.

REFERENCES

Borgatti, S.P., and Cross, R. (2003). A relational view of information seeking and learning in social networks. *Management Science*, 49(4), 432–445.

Brass, D.J. (2018). A social network perspective on organizational citizenship behavior. In Podsakoff, P.M., MacKenzie, S.B., and Podsakoff, N.P. (eds), *The Oxford Handbook of Organizational Citizenship Behavior* (pp. 317–330). New York: Oxford University Press.

Burt, R.S., Kilduff, M., and Tasselli, S. (2013). Social network analysis: Foundations and frontiers on advantage. *Annual Review of Psychology*, 64, 527–547.

Casciaro, T., and Lobo, M.S. (2005). Competent jerks, lovable fools, and the formation of social networks. *Harvard Business Review*, 83(6), 92–99.

Cross, R., Borgatti, S.P., and Parker, A. (2002). Making invisible work visible: Using social network analysis to support strategic collaboration. *California Management Review*, 44(2), 25–46.

Cross, R.L., and Parker, A. (2004). *The Hidden Power of Social Networks: Understanding how Work Really Gets Done in Organizations*. Boston, MA: Harvard Business School Press.

Cross, R., and Prusak, L. (2002). The people who make organizations go – or stop. In Cross, R., Parker, A., and Sasson, L. (eds), *Networks in the Knowledge Economy* (pp. 248–260). New York: Oxford University Press.

D'Andreta, D., Marabelli, M., Newell, S., Scarbrough, H., and Swan, J. (2016). Dominant cognitive frames and the innovative power of social networks. *Organization Studies*, 37(3), 293–321.

Flynn, F.J., and Wiltermuth, S.S. (2010). Who's with me? False consensus, brokerage, and ethical decision making in organizations. *Academy of Management Journal*, 53(5), 1074–1089.

Krackhardt, D. (1990). Assessing the political landscape: Structure, cognition, and power in organizations. *Administrative Science Quarterly*, 35(2), 342–369.

Krackhardt, D., and Hanson, J.R. (1993). Informal networks. *Harvard Business Review*, 71(4), 104–111.

Krackhardt, D., and Stern, R.N. (1988). Informal networks and organizational crises: An experimental simulation. *Social Psychology Quarterly*, 51(2), 123–140.

Landis, B. (2016). Personality and social networks in organizations: A review and future directions. *Journal of Organizational Behavior*, 37, S107–S121.

Maak, T. (2007). Responsible leadership, stakeholder engagement, and the emergence of social capital. *Journal of Business Ethics*, 74(4), 329–343.

McCulloh, I., Armstrong, H., and Johnson, A. (2013). *Social Network Analysis with Applications*. Hoboken, NJ: John Wiley & Sons.

McGrath, C., and Krackhardt, D. (2003). Network conditions for organizational change. *Journal of Applied Behavioral Science*, 39(3), 324–336.

Perry-Smith, J.E., and Mannucci, P.V. (2017). From creativity to innovation: The social network drivers of the four phases of the idea journey. *Academy of Management Review*, 42(1), 53–79.

Scott, J. (2017). *Social Network Analysis*. Thousand Oaks, CA: SAGE.

Tortoriello, M., McEvily, B., and Krackhardt, D. (2014). Being a catalyst of innovation: The role of knowledge diversity and network closure. *Organization Science*, 26(2), 423–438.

APPENDIX 14.1:   SCORING INFORMATION AND RULE SUMMARY

Basic Rules

- Connect with only one person at a time. No broadcasting information. No third person hanging around. Give all connecting pairs at least 3–5 feet of space.
- Check the next open box beside the ID number of each person you connect with, each time you connect with them.
- Discuss anything you like for as long as you like. Interaction ends whenever you desire.

Your Objective

- Work out exchanges of playing cards with other players in order to obtain the highest score you possibly can before time expires.

How to Score in this Game

- Use the information below to determine the score you have obtained from any set of cards in your possession.

Combo	Description	Points
Twin Aces	Two IDENTICAL aces (same suit)	100 points
Royal Triplets	Three IDENTICAL "face" cards (same suit) All Jack, all Queen or all King	100 points
Royal Run	Jack, Queen, and King all of same suit	80 points
Royal Twins	Two IDENTICAL Jack, Queen or King (same suit)	65 points
Runner	Consecutive sequence of at least two non-face cards of same suit (Ace is low) Does not include Jack, Queen or King	2 cards → 40 points 3 cards → 90 points 4 cards → 150 points 5 cards → 200 points
Bonus	Use all 5 of your cards as part of one or more scoring combinations	25 points

- No card may be used in more than one scoring combination.
- All players must have exactly 5 cards at all times.

APPENDIX 14.2:   CARD SCORING EXAMPLES

A♥ A♥ 7♠ J♦ 4♠	Twin Aces (Aces–Hearts) 100 Points!
Q♣ Q♣ Q♣ 4♦ 5♠	Royal Triplet (Q – Clubs) 100 Points!
J♦ Q♦ K♦ 7♠ J♣	Royal Run (J, Q, K – Diamonds) 80 Points!
J♦ J♦ K♠ 2♣ A♥	Royal Twins (J – Diamonds) 65 Points!
6♥ 7♥ 8♥ J♦ Q♠	Runner (consecutive Hearts) 90 Points!
3♠ 4♠ 5♠ A♦ 2♦	Two Runners using Spades and Diamonds and Bonus Spades → 90 points Diamonds → 40 points Use 5 cards to score → 25 points Total of 155 Points!

APPENDIX 14.3: EXERCISE WORKSHEET

Section I: Getting Started

Please indicate your ID number: _____

Please list your initial cards (e.g., "4-Clubs," "J-Hearts," "7-Diamonds," "A-Spades")

_____, _____, _____, _____,

_____

Initial Score (see Appendix 14.1 and 14.2): _____

Section II: Interactions

Place a check mark for each time you connect with each of these people:

1		11		21	
2		12		22	
3		13		23	
4		14		24	
5		15		25	
6		16		26	
7		17		27	
8		18		28	
9		19		29	
10		20		30	

Section III: Final Result

Final Cards (e.g., "4-Clubs," "J-Hearts," "7-Diamonds," "A-Spades")

_____, _____, _____, _____,

_____

Final Score: _____

15. UGH! Generational conflict amidst a change effort

Therese F. Yaeger

The chapter presents a case for understanding different age groups working in United States organizations today. The aging of the workforce and the advent of younger generations entering the workforce present a major demographic phenomenon that may create tensions (conflict) in organizations. With people in their twenties working with colleagues in their seventies, companies will be faced with the need to accommodate a mature set of workers with the needs and expectations of a younger generation, which can readily lead to unanticipated challenges in organizational practices. The traditional three-stage life pattern of education, work, and retirement – which historically has been geared to set age ranges – is transitioning to a more flexible, multi-stage life with more generational diversity than we have ever experienced. Thus, in an effort to create increased awareness of potential conflicts and to prevent the "UGH! and grumbling" from generational conflicts, this case exercise provides opportunities and insights to explore different generational perspectives.

OUR GENERATIONALLY DIVERSE WORKFORCE

For the first time in history, four generations are working side by side in organizations. These four generations, as defined by Strauss and Howe (1991) are: the Greatest Generation (those born between 1922 and 1945); the Baby Boomers (those born between 1946 and 1964); Generation X (those born between 1965 and 1978); and Generation Y (those born after 1978). Because each generation has its own unique values, set of skills, and characteristics, having employees from different generations has created opportunities for differences and conflict among co-workers. According to the Society for Human Resource Management (2004), dissimilar work values are the source of many significant challenges among generations, and a major source of conflict in the workplace. An explanation of the four generations follows.

The Greatest Generation

The Greatest Generation, sometimes referred to as the Silent Generation or Traditionals, were born between 1922 and 1945. This generation witnessed the Stock Market Crash of 1929, where 9 million Americans lost their life savings, and one in four American workers lost their jobs. They experienced the Dust Bowl, the New Deal, and a World War. As adults in the workforce, this group was exposed to early stages of participative management but never really felt compelled to change their style (Zemke et al., 2000). In their early life, their use of technology involved listening to a radio in the home with family members. In organizations today, this generation believes in the values of working hard, adhering to rules, and that authority is based on seniority.

Baby Boomers

This generation is called Boomers because of the boom in children born between 1946 and 1964. This generation experienced the Kennedy and King assassinations and Watergate. Boomers are reported to have generally positive attitudes; they have the most consistent attendance in the workforce today as well as greater practical knowledge of their work. This generation witnessed the new era of color televisions, early computers, and cordless phones. In organizations today, the Baby Boomers are ambitious and they want to make a difference. They value teams and group involvement, have a strong work ethic, and they "live to work."

Generation X

This is the generation born between 1965 and 1978 that was brought up playing *Atari* and *Asteroid* games. This cohort is 93 million people strong; they learn by doing, and if they are stuck, they will go online to figure out a solution. Gen X-ers have high job expectations, and they are known to lack organizational commitment and loyalty. This generation values work–life balance, craves independence, and wants their input evaluated on merit (not seniority).

Generation Y

Generation Y workers (born after 1978) typically do not know a world without computers, an Internet connection, or cell phones. Also called Millennials, these employees emphasize immediacy (24/7 information availability), curiosity, and intellectual openness. This generation values digital media, is tech-savvy, self-confident, and has high expectations of their bosses. They value meaningful work, want constant feedback and affirmation, and need to be treated respectfully.

THE EXERCISE

The purpose of the exercise is to gain appreciation of the challenges of four different generations in the workforce today. Through an experiential role play, participants will gain an appreciation of the values and needs of different age groups and how it can impact decisions. More importantly, participants may even realize their own shortcomings when working with other age groups. In this exercise, participants will experience how workers present themselves as the best person for a new leadership role at "Universal Gadget House" (UGH).

This exercise has been used:

- in a hospital setting with newly hired nurses assigned to work alongside very senior nurses, which caused conflict;
- with a Human Resources (HR) team stuck in creating different incentives for new hires;
- to address an unexpected corporate turnover due to a younger generation's feelings of not fitting in.

The discussion should illuminate that different work values can be the source of significant challenges among generations, but if addressed properly they can also be a source of potential team strength.

Setting Up the Exercise

Group size
Unlimited, but with a balanced distribution of the four different generations (age groups). An observer can be an option, if available.

Time required
Minimum one hour, depending on the size of the group, and the debrief time needed.

Materials
An UGH employee script for each participant to role play.

Process

(All timings are suggested.)

1. Facilitator welcomes the participants and explains that they will be engaging in a role play in the UGH case (five minutes).
2. Facilitator reads out loud the characterizations of the four different generations in the workforce (ten minutes).
3. Facilitator distributes a role to each participant to play. Remind the audience of the importance of role playing as seriously as possible. Intentionally distribute each role to a person not of the age of the role they must play (without having participants disclose their real age or generation). Depending on the size of the group, there may be multiple participants role playing for a generation (ten minutes).
4. Facilitator presents the UGH case. Then in role-playing fashion, participants engage in a discussion of how they would like to participate in the upcoming information technology (IT) implementation at UGH. As UGH employees, participants should express their generational values to the group and why they should be selected for the assignment (20 minutes).
5. Role play ends. The facilitator asks each participant to share their learning from the exercise, allowing for discussion and understanding of conflict when different values impede the situation (15 minutes). As the facilitator leads the debrief, some questions might include:
   - What did you learn as you presented the perspective of a different generation?
   - What was different for you in your role?
   - What are the benefits/challenges of having different generations (age groups) on the implementation team?
   - What are the challenges for the role you played? For other generations?

THE UGH CASE

(To be read out loud by the facilitator.)

The Universal Gadget House (UGH) has a 50-year history of success in manufacturing, beginning decades ago, gradually shifting from the use of carbon copy colored order forms to a more electronic form of product ordering for its gadgets. Recently the chief executive officer (CEO) realized the need for an enterprise-wide solution to its technology and IT needs.

The firm prides itself on the longevity of its staff – some employees have been with the firm for three decades. Some very respected employees were around for the last IT upgrade, which includes employees now in their sixties and seventies. There are some new and promising employees who provide creative tech-savvy skills. More recently, new college graduates with degrees in IT and supply chain management have been hired to strengthen UGH's talent pool as well.

The new implementation will encompass HR records, supply chain, manufacturing, and finance; in short, this will be the largest technology upgrade the firm has ever experienced. The CEO realizes that the new IT team selection will be critical to the success of the implementation's success. Time management for this project is also critical, as powerful external customers have commented that there can be no delays on this upgrade; and UGH's CEO agrees.

Selection for the best-suited team members will begin soon, which will also include the selection of the IT Team Lead. The role of Team Lead is particularly important as this person will interface with team members, external vendors, clients, and UGH's CEO. The CEO has sensed recently that there has been an atmosphere of competitiveness and conflict with potential candidates for the new IT team leader. He struggles with the ability of the employees to address all of the challenges, including people issues in the IT Department.

Four potential team members who bring different strengths to the upcoming IT implementation are Pat, Dale, Alex, and Jordan. A discussion with the four different UGH employees is about to begin. Let us hear from each member regarding why they would be the best Team Lead for UGH's upcoming IT project.

UGH Employees

One role should be handed out to each participant.

Pat

I am PAT. I am the IT Director here at Universal Gadget. I've been here for more than 30 years, and I'm proud to be 71 years young. It is my civic responsibility to make sure everything at UGH runs smoothly, but lately that has not been the case. I know all the old-timers here – heck, I was one of the first hires by the CEO. But with new folks and new projects here, I don't know what others think of me specific to the upcoming change efforts. Worse, I can't even understand what the younger staff wants, or what they mean. Often these younger workers are coming from other parts of the world (at least to me, they look foreign). The change effort to improve UGH's technology operations is being rolled out in a few months and this is creating a conflict among the staff. I'm hunching that the boss might include me on the new IT team.

I feel responsible for the success of this change implementation but it's doomed to fail with all the conflicting age groups and mindsets here – it's a boon-doggle! I may be a senior, but my long-term understanding of UGH is reason enough to lead the upcoming IT effort.

Dale

I am DALE. I am 55, and I work at UGH on the Project Management side of the IT Department. I've been told I'm a Baby Boomer, which supposedly means I'm used to being in large groups, and that I enjoy rock and roll music on my CD player. A change effort to improve UGH's operations is being rolled out soon and this is creating a conflict among the staff. I sense tensions between the old folks and the young kids because of turf and different knowledge bases. I show up on time and do my work. I care a lot about the people here at UGH. But younger staff wants it all: more time off, more money, and the ability to run the upcoming IT implementation. I pity the old folks that have to tell the younger staff that they don't rule the world at UGH.

I was with UGH for the last IT upgrade, which was successful although not as comprehensive. If selected to lead this IT effort, I would work on the people side of this implementation, and address the noticeable conflict around here. There is work to be done and people have to get along!

Alex

I am ALEX. I'm a 35-year old Gen-Xer, which means I know technology and the Internet and the bigger global world. I've been at UGH for ten years now. I used to love it, but not any more. I was hired even before I finished college, and I was promoted quickly at first because of my creative technical skills. But I feel stuck here after ten years with no experience outside of UGH. In the middle of the age pack, I'm too young to get promoted again, but too old to be the up-and-comer. The change effort to improve UGH's operations is creating a conflict among the staff. This upcoming implementation is sure to get the best of me. Amidst my technological expertise, I'm frustrated by the seniors, the newbies, and the upcoming IT effort, which I know needs my expert creativity.

If it wasn't for all the divisiveness between old and young employees, I wouldn't be so disconnected from my job. If I was selected for the new IT team, I would demonstrate my tech-savvy skills and rise above the clashes.

Jordan

I am JORDAN. I'm a 23-year old "up-and-coming" IT Coordinator at UGH. I recently finished my college degree in technology and big data, and I'm ready to jump into the big change implementation. I'm a millennial multi-tasker! But the minute I get a compliment from my boss for my timely deliverables, the older folks just sneer at me. They, like, don't get me. I have plans to be an executive here very soon because of my degree and tech knowledge. Older workers don't catch on to technology as fast as I do, and they get so much vacation time from their longevity that it's a wonder they get anything done. I have a crazy busy social life outside of work, so when I am at my work station I just plug in my ear buds and crank out the work so I can become the leader for any upcoming technology effort.

A change effort to improve UGH's operations is being rolled out soon and I think this is creating conflict around me. Whatever – they don't even think green around here! My boss knows I am capable of leading the new IT team; in fact I can't imagine anyone but me to roll-out the upcoming IT effort!

CONCLUDING REFLECTIONS

In the post-discussion phase, the challenge is to: (1) realize that one's generation can be a contributor to organizational tensions; and (2) gain appreciation of different mindsets of various generations and the positive contribution each generation can contribute to an organizational group. The dialogue among different age groups at UGH is not merely to decide who might be best for the lead role in IT; instead it illustrates the different mindsets that often are not recognized by different co-workers. Remember that dialogue is key to understanding the positive impact of different age groups.

Variations

This case provides non-gender names to avoid gender issues. To address gender conflicts, this case can also be presented as an all-female team with Stella, Sarah, Susie, and Skylar; or an all-male group with Theodore, Thomas, Terrence, and Tapper. For additional work involving generational conflict, this case has been resituated in a highly competitive real estate organization as the organizational members must make a final agreed-upon decision requiring input from all four generations.

Also, a new Generation Z, born after 1992, is entering the workforce, which will create even more values differences in the work environment. Will these younger workers have different needs and expectations from their employer and their co-workers? What might be the conflicts that emerge? As this exercise draws out, it is vital for managers to understand the underlying values and needs of each generation, and differences among those generations, if they want to create and maintain a supportive work environment that fosters collaboration and generational synergy (Smola and Sutton, 2002). Remember that generational differences can also be used as a source of strengths and opportunities.

REFERENCES

Smola, K., and Sutton, C. (2002). Generational differences: Revisiting generational work values for the new millennium. *Journal of Organizational Behavior: The International Journal of Industrial, Occupational and Organizational Psychology and Behavior*, 23(4), 363–382.
Society for Human Resource Management (SHRM) (2004). *Generational Differences Survey*. Alexandria, VA: Society for Human Resources Management.
Strauss, W., and Howe, N. (1991). *Generations: The History of America's Future, 1584–2089*. New York: Quill William Morrow.
Zemke, R., Raines, C., and Filipczak, B. (2000). *Generations at Work: Managing the Clash of Veterans, Baby Boomers, Xers, and Nexters in Your Workplace*. New York: American Management Association.

PART V

The experiential exercise end game: end-point engagement

16. Debriefing change exercises: end-point engagement

Gary Wagenheim

Have you ever had the frustrating experience of answering endless student questions about "What happened?" in an experiential learning activity, instead of progressively asking them to assess their own learning and insights? Or, your questions seemingly get answered, but result in an endless ebb and flow of unrelated remarks leading nowhere. Many of us have experienced such disappointing outcomes with experiential exercises. Instructors can spend an enormous amount of time developing lesson plans for an experiential student-centered class on organizational change, only to unwittingly sabotage their own effort by trying to facilitate learning without a proven debriefing method. Although facilitating debriefing is one of the essential instructor skills necessary in the experiential learning classroom, ironically such debriefing is all too often underdeveloped or completely lacking. Thus, a focused debriefing method can provide more structure and help to effectively improve the entire learning process.

THE SIGNIFICANCE OF A DEBRIEFING METHOD

In the absence of reflection, students fail to critically analyze their individual experience, missing an opportunity to gain further insights into their learning. Instructors who use experiential learning activities to connect theory to practice should recognize that students need focused debriefing questions to prompt reflection in constructing their learning. Helping students to understand the connection between theory and practice increases both their knowledge and their effectiveness. Theories are useful because they provide explanations for our actions, frame issues, and serve as catalysts for reflection. Reflection on experiences is important, because if someone becomes aware of what they are doing in a situation they have the ability to reframe the experience in ways that may generate different outcomes and produce new learning. The social interaction of collectively reflecting in the classroom helps students to make better sense of their learning.

Student responses to questions posed during debriefs are often superficial, merely recounting what they did, instead of critically understanding how or why they did it. The problem may be the instructor's questions, rather than the lack of student capacity for reflection. The question instructors should ask themselves is, "How can I effectively facilitate debriefing an experiential learning activity so that students understand the organizational change lesson and develop the capacity for future learning from experience?"

Debriefing a meaningful class learning activity is more than just standing in front of the class and asking, "What did you think of the simulation?" Good facilitation creates an empowering learning environment by allowing students to take ownership of their learning. The process is intended to help students uncover: (1) their immediate learning of the lessons embedded in the experiential activity; and (2) their own developmental learning of how to debrief their own experiences. Debriefing facilitation is important for instructors to master, and a role model for students to gain new insights.

It is important to keep in mind that facilitating experiential student-centered learning is more than technique and protocol, as it represents a fundamental change in the teaching paradigm and a resultant change in the class culture. The instructor shifts from teaching "about the discipline of organizational change" to facilitating "how to do organizational change." The instructor, of course, still needs subject matter expertise, but will now be better equipped with the ability to facilitate student learning through their experiences.

The Facilitative Instructor

Students in a didactic class may expect the instructor to provide both the framework and the information to solve organizational change problems. A first step in a facilitative experiential class, therefore, is to encourage students to change their view that instructors represent the main source of knowledge. In essence, students need to understand their responsibility for developing skills to create their own knowledge. Ideally students will develop their own points of view, not just repeat the instructor's teaching.

The facilitative instructing approach shifts the emphasis from teaching content to managing the learning process. Through facilitation, the instructor becomes more of a coach who empowers students to own their learning. This chapter highlights facilitative instructing to enhance focused debriefing, and those new to this approach would be wise to consult Richard Schwarz (1994), who provides many guidelines as to the roles the facilitator plays.

Roles and Goals of the Facilitative Instructor

As a facilitator, the instructor becomes responsible for helping to improve the learning process – how students take in and process information to create knowledge – not just presenting the topic material. The facilitative instructor needs to construct an open, supportive classroom that encourages student engagement. The facilitative instructor is trying to achieve a "we are all in this learning together" classroom culture where students are empowered to take ownership and responsibility for the course and their own learning needs. Using experiential learning the instructor facilitates co-generated knowledge with each student and the entire class. Students provide the input through questions, answers, comments, and suggestions about the topic, the course, and their own learning in a collaborative way. Thus, the facilitative instructor's role is more about setting the classroom culture, providing resources, and facilitating discussion than transmitting facts about the topic. In this way, the goals of facilitative instructing and specifically debriefing experiential learning are to:

- help students reflect on and learn from the immediate experience;
- connect change theory to change practice; and
- create life-long learners who are knowledgeable about how to gain insights from future experiences.

This method requires more than just content knowledge from instructors. Instructors need to be more mindful of class time, have a sensitivity about where students are in their development and topic knowledge, and be equipped with the energy, interest, and skill to successfully facilitate an experiential learning debrief. This approach requires instructors to develop facilitative skills and the knowledge of how and when to use them (see Appendix 16.1: Facilitative Instructor Tips).

While it is important to master facilitating a focused debrief, one should remember that this approach is ideally a subset of questions that should be used regularly in a student-centered classroom within the context of good facilitative instruction skills. However, it does not minimize the value and importance of instructors' expertise in organizational change content that is necessary to ensure successful student learning.

A note of caution: instructors stepping out of a more didactic philosophy to a facilitative student-centered philosophy need to be aware of their responsibility to create a safe environment for students to experiment with their learning, as the outcomes associated with facilitation are not without limitations. Facilitation skills take time to learn and time to use in class.

This requires the instructor to think critically about issues that may be in question. Facilitation requires a different approach to preparing for class than the more traditional approach of teaching. Instructors need to be willing to role-model openness, genuineness, and trust while respecting differences between individual students. Instructors teaching an organizational change course may find it particularly challenging as they may need to be open to making personal change themselves in how they are in the classroom. Instructors would be wise to consider how to model their own reflection by thinking aloud at occasional points in the class regarding direction, and making those issues discussable.

I often share assumptions, feelings, and thoughts I have during the activity or debrief. For example, I will say, "Let me take you behind the curtain, this is what I was trying to do," or "This is why I did it this way," or "I was surprised it turned out that way." Similarly, I may answer some of the same facilitative reflection questions, after students have responded, to show what I was thinking and feeling at the time. My sharing is intended to build a trusting, safe, and open environment that encourages all to participate. While I keep my comments brief, I want to model reflection. In pursuit of deeper learning, I want students to answer questions previously unconsidered or that they initially found too forward or too personal.

Adopting a set of ground rules for debriefing as well as for the class in general may help to ensure an acceptable code of student conduct and create an appropriate classroom culture for learning. This is best done at the beginning of the course, with student input and agreement, although the instructor might suggest some possible ground rules to jump-start the list (see Appendix 16.2: Sample Ground Rules). It is important that these ground rules are developed, accepted, and owned by the students.

Debriefing that Prompts Reflection and Learning

The experiential learning cycle (Kolb, 1984) emphasizes using real concrete experience (feeling), reflective observation of oneself in the experience (watching), abstract conceptualization of considering theory (thinking), and active experimentation using the feedback of the observation in the experience to change behavior in the next experience (doing). Experiential learning is essentially a learning loop that is developmental and focuses on change as a way of knowing. Debriefing experiential activities is one of the key points in that learning loop, and is therefore a critical skill for facilitative instructors to master and use regularly. While one can certainly debrief an activity without embracing all the tenets of facilitative instruction, the process works best when it is closely coupled.

Instructors utilizing experiential learning are helping students to construct their knowing throughout the activity and, most importantly, to make meaning of that experience and learning through the debrief. Debriefing is essentially a meaning-making system, where the collective classroom conversation becomes data for informing individual meaning-making. The process of debriefing encourages learners to analyze assumptions that influence outcomes, and surface cognitive and behavioral alternatives for future experiences. Students are trained as life-long learners who can eventually do their own debrief of not just experiential classroom activities, but also of real-life situations in the future that will allow them to continuously learn, grow, and develop. In the absence of a true debrief, individuals fail to develop the ability for meaning-making, and class experiential activities get remembered, if at all, as little more than fun play times.

As instructors, we want to help students learn reflection skills so that they can recognize and modify their actions to effect better outcomes. Instructors cannot reflect on experiential learning for their students, but they can use a debriefing method that prompts reflection and makes the practice more explicit and deliberate in the classroom. Acknowledging the paradox that students can only learn debriefing by debriefing – which is to say, practicing a skill they do not know or completely understand – leads instructors to consider facilitating the debriefing process in a more structured and focused manner. In other words, students may require scaffolding to first learn how to debrief before they can put it into action for themselves. Facilitating debriefing goes beyond experiential activities to create a classroom that encourages social interaction and uses dialogue for constructing collaborative and individual meaning-making through co-discovery.

Focused Debriefing

Focused debriefing is a proven easy to learn and useful method that I adapted from the group facilitation discussion method called Technology of Participation (ToP) developed by the Institute of Cultural Affairs (Spencer, 1989; Stanfield, 1997). This discussion method has been used to help solve social and economic problems in community development projects around the world. As a certified ToP facilitator, I edited and adapted the method for use in the classroom. I have personally used this adapted methodology for constructing dialogues and debriefing experiential learning activities for over 20 years.

Figure 16.1 captures the essence of focused debriefing. Essentially the method uses a series of open-ended questions presented in a sequential

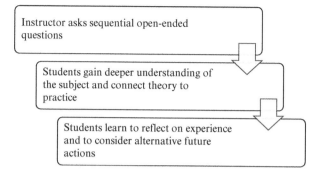

Figure 16.1   Process of focused debriefing

manner paralleling the way the human mind absorbs and processes new information: observation, reflection, interpretation, and decisional. The main goal of this focused discussion method is to help a group come to a deeper understanding of the subject they are studying and to direct their thinking toward making a decision.

A focused debriefing method is valuable scaffolding for supporting experiential learning, promoting reflection, connecting theory to practice, questioning students' assumptions, transferring the onus for learning onto students, and supporting students' learning reflection skills. I adapted and use this focused debriefing method for four reasons:

1. Congruent with Kolb's experiential learning cycle, the method moves from sensory stimuli to action.
2. The sequence of questions is easy to remember and effective to use.
3. While the model was designed for helping direct a group toward making a decision, only slight modification was necessary for debriefing experiential learning activities.
4. This approach has proven to be highly effective in debriefing experiential activities and facilitating student learning.

It is also important for instructors to use variations of the debriefing method for more than processing experiential learning activities. As an example, this approach can be used as an everyday technique for guiding class check-ins and check-outs as well as processing lectures, as it is consistent with a student-centered facilitative approach. It serves as an important reminder for students developing reflection routines. In this way, the richness of debriefing emerges and grows through the semester, as students and teacher develop trust and become more comfortable with the reflection process.

The focused debriefing questions

The twin goals of this methodology are: to provide a protocol for debriefing to increase reflection and learning in a specific activity; and to guide, practice, and support students in developing their own reflection skills. The focused debriefing questions guide students though four levels of the reflective process: objective, reflective, interpretive, and decisional (ORID):

- Open-ended objective questions inquire about data and facts, and focus the discussion. I typically start with questions that ask students to recount observable information – such as: What did you notice in the activity? What did you hear? Who was doing what? What was your role? – that focuses the conversation, invites low risk input, and prompts student voices.
- Reflective questions serve to elicit emotions and feelings immediately associated with the experience, and may provide clues for students about hidden emotions or assumptions triggered in the experience or conversation. Reflective questions serve to connect personal reaction with learning, and questions may include: What surprised you? What was challenging? What was most frustrating? How did you feel during the activity? What event in your life would you associate with this one? What specifically impacted you in this experience? Where have you experienced similar feelings?
- Interpretative questions draw out underlying assumptions, biases, values, and learning significance, by asking: What was your intent? What assumptions did you make? How does this affirm or disconfirm your assumptions? How does this connect to the theory? What did you learn? Why is this of value? What is the meaning of this experience for you? How are you different after this event? How does this change your perspective? What new insights have you gained?
- Decisional questions challenge students to connect action with reflection by bringing the class and individual students to potential alternative solutions for future implementation. Questions include: What will you do with these new insights? What will you do differently next time? Where will you apply your learning? How will you follow up? What else do you need to know?

Appendix 16.3 includes a sample of focused debriefing questions.

The ORID method also aligns well with Kolb's (1984) experiential learning cycle: (1) concrete experience (feeling) is similar to reflective questions: How did you feel?; (2) reflective observation (watching) similar to objective questions: What did you observe in the exercise?; (3) abstract conceptualization (thinking) is similar to interpretative questions: What theory from our readings might relate?; and (4) active experimentation (doing) is similar to decisional questions: What would you change in your behavior to achieve a better outcome next time?

Practical considerations in debriefing

In practice, debriefing is not as linear as the questions might suggest, for students tend to drift between questions, get stuck on issues, run out of energy, and think in ways that run counter to the sequence. In fact, dialogue is circular, sometimes messy and sticky, and occasionally dull; it never seems efficient or purposeful in covering all points of the lesson. You will find that certain questions readily provoke answers, while others are met with silence; it is thus important to dig deeper with the questions that gain responses, probing for more information and simply moving on to other questions if there are no responses. It is not necessary to ask all questions in a category, as usually one or two or sometimes three are enough to prompt appropriate student responses within these categories: observable data, feelings, learning, and future change action. Keep in mind that the debrief dialogue will go back and forth between categories, and you will need to manage the process within class time constraints toward conclusion. It is important, however, to get through all categories to complete the learning.

Using a focused debrief does change the classroom communication dynamics from telling to asking, and the focus from instructor to students. However, this debriefing method has many advantages over just asking "What do you think?" or telling students, "This is what you should have learned" in an experience.

Advantages of using focused debriefing

The debriefing gets richer and deeper with practice and when the instructor uses experiential organizational change activities that engage students. In addition, the debriefing method has several advantages, as it:

● focuses the discussion;
● appreciates multiple perspectives;
● uncovers assumptions;
● surfaces feelings;
● encourages student voices;
● appreciates multiple interpretations;
● promotes divergent and convergent thinking;
● connects theory and practice;
● emphasizes student-centered learning.

Of course, not all experiential organizational change activities go according to plan or readily produce obvious learning. If the activity fails, do not give up, and continue to move forward with the debrief. Thoroughly debriefing disastrous experiential learning activities, including an admission by the instructor of "What went wrong?" ironically often promotes the best learning. This is especially true in the field of organizational change and the change classroom, where unintended consequences are to be expected, providing a wealth of "lessons learned."

Enhancing the Use of Focused Debriefing

To get the most out of the focused debrief process, instructors need to go beyond the questions in the protocol and utilize an array of prompts to encourage additional information. By utilizing good active listening skills – probing for details or examples, asking for clarification, expressing empathy for students' emotion, and recruiting all students to participate – the dialogue is enriched and the learning enhanced. Thus, follow up student responses to the focused debrief questions with such prompts as: Go on. Tell me more. Why? What's an example of that? I understand. So, what? Now what? Thank you. At the same time as the instructor is focusing on these debriefing task questions, and behaviors and student responses, they need to pay attention to the facilitation process in terms of their own enthusiasm, positive regard for students, body language, and eye contact. Facilitating a focused debrief is not easy; it is more than a line of questioning: it requires keen concentration and abundant energy.

Progression of Focused Debriefing

Typically, the instructor's expert voice is not so necessary as students glean the important points and genuinely access and analyze their experience, apply change theory to change practice, and generate potential new ways of solving future organizational change problems on their own. If this is not the case, instructors can always supply the missing information at any time during the debrief. Instructors can use mini versions of the ORID debrief questions, one or two questions per level, for discussing readings, lectures, check-ins, and all sorts of classroom activities. Making the debriefing protocol transparent and discussable is developmental. Often, later in the semester the need for the instructor to be the sole facilitator providing reflection structure begins to disappear, as students manage the debrief, for the most part, by themselves. This is the development aspect of routinized reflection debriefing, which is equipping students with the skill to debrief their own situations in the future. Also, as students learn the process and gain trust they are more forthcoming in their participation and more revealing of their emotional and behavioral issues. Therefore, the instructor needs to be mindful and supportive of student disclosure around these issues.

This dynamic can be an interesting phenomenon to witness: the increasing quality of reflective communication that students share, and their capacity to self-manage the dialogic process with thoughtful interventions and questions. Not only is the dialogue substantively improved relative to reflection, but also student action in subsequent experiential activities is more engaged with greater transferability of theory to practice. Observable new student actions and post hoc personal debriefing reflection accounts provide further evidence of the deeper learning.

Exemplars and takeaways

An example from a recent Executive MBA course where I used the focused debriefing method may illustrate this point. My leadership course was designed to illuminate the complex intersection of theory and practice. A cognitive model for comprehending organizational theory that could simultaneously be used for leadership practice was introduced in the course. The course also provided students with an opportunity to develop an understanding of leadership issues as well as organizational change through an experiential pedagogy.

I regularly used the focused debriefing methodology throughout the course to encourage reflection about the activities, and more generally about their individual leadership styles, analyzing personal and organizational change, raising assumptions, and exploring connections between theory and practice in their leadership in their organizations. The most significant reflective learning I observed was a hastily convened student meeting during a coffee break. Students were huddled together, changing the format for a major corporate presentation scheduled for later in the week at their international headquarters. They were changing the content, framing, and presentation style based on their learning in an experiential organizational change activity that morning. They demonstrated the ability to question their assumptions and generate alternative courses of action: the hallmark of learning from a successful reflective debrief.

While my initial reaction was "Let's get back to class," I gave in to their plea for more time by granting an extra ten minutes to wrap up. It was during this time that I realized this was a teachable moment – where students seemed to understand that reflection on their experience informed new actions – and I wanted to reinforce their knowing by debriefing the meeting. However, I did not assume that they understood what they were doing as they were doing it, so I announced, once the class reconvened,

"I want us all to understand what just happened during the break. Let's go through the debriefing process just like we do with our classroom exercises."

I would encourage experimentation and practice with the focused debrief. Using the same method of focused debrief for oneself, for example, is helpful in acquiring the necessary facilitation skills. As with any skill acquisition, understanding the concept, practicing the skill, debriefing and reflecting, and then implementing the new actions, are keys to learning. As a general guide, you can use self, student, or peer scoring on a feedback form (see Appendix 16.4: Focused Debriefing Skills Feedback Form) combined with focused debriefing to gain the necessary feedback for improvement.

Focused debriefing can and should be used in conjunction with other reflective techniques and methods. For example, consider setting aside a small amount of time at the end of class for student journal writing after the debrief. A reflection paper at the end of the semester that affords students the opportunity for meaning-making from the myriad of learning experiences is a powerful assignment. If the debriefings were effective and documented in their journals, students should be able to do more than simply recount various experiential exercises: they should be able to make sense of their organizational change learning by finding common themes from their actions, feelings, and behaviors. Combined with the integration of theory, such journaling can help students to learn course content in the present, and gain skills for managing organizational change in the future.

CONCLUSION

This chapter introduced a focused debriefing method to guide student reflection and learning about organizational change. This method enables students to take ownership of their learning, providing an easy to use effective set of questions for debriefing and helping to promote life-long reflective learners. The focused debriefing method is ideally best used in a facilitative manner within the context of an experiential student-centered class.

Readers are encouraged to experiment and customize questions to fit course content and student learning needs. As the debriefing process itself is more art than science, it is important to be more mindful of student energy, interest, and voice than rigidly following any protocol. Once mastered, however, it is also important to understand that this powerful debriefing method can create empowered students who need you less and less, altering your classroom role as the semester moves on and they take more responsibility for their own reflection and learning.

REFERENCES

Kolb, D. (1984). *Experiential Learning: Experience as the Source of Learning and Development*. Englewood Cliffs, NJ: Prentice Hall.

Schwarz, R.M. (1994). *The Skilled Facilitator: Practical Wisdom for Developing Effective Groups*. San Francisco, CA: Jossey-Bass.

Spencer, L.J. (1989). *Winning through Participation: Meeting the Challenge of Corporate Change with the Technology of Participation*. Phoenix, AZ: Institute of Cultural Affairs.

Stanfield, R.B. (ed.). (1997). *The Art of Focused Conversation: 100 Ways to Access Group Wisdom in the Workplace*. Gabriola Island, BC: New Society Publishers.

APPENDIX 16.1:　FACILITATIVE INSTRUCTOR TIPS

- Ask more; tell less.
- Ask open-ended questions; avoid yes/no questions.
- Encourage students to build on others' comments.
- Ask for specific examples if comments are too general. Consider asking students to make "I" statement rather than "we" statements.
- Ask students to check out assumptions they may be making. Are inferences accurate?
- Intervene if ground rules are violated.
- Intervene at the class level, not the individual student level, if you are not receiving the type of responses that will lead to learning.
- Keep the conversation focused on the learning activity and class topic.
- Look for and appreciate a range of perspectives.
- Ask simple understandable questions.
- Listen to the first thing students say as it's often a clue to the real issues and learning.
- Show empathy and a positive attitude for all responses.
- Be respectful and reserve judgment for all.
- Beware of silence; give students time to think.
- Be willing to contribute content if students are missing the point.
- Use eye contact, head nodding, and attentive posture to show listening.
- Clarify unclear points.
- Pay attention to students' body language, level of interest, and energy.
- Be flexible and willing to change the topic, focus, or activity.
- Have fun.

APPENDIX 16.2: SAMPLE GROUND RULES

1. All students participate.
2. Start and end on time.
3. All responsible for learning.
4. One voice at a time.
5. Keep discussion focused.
6. Share all relevant knowledge.
7. Test assumptions.
8. Be specific.
9. Discuss undiscussable issues.
10. Monitor how long and how often individual students speak.
11. Be open, be direct, be honest.
12. Respect all opinions.
13. Avoid "killer" phrases.
14. Minimize the use of electronics (phone/computer).
15. Maintain confidentiality.

APPENDIX 16.3: ORID SAMPLE FOCUSED DEBRIEFING QUESTIONS

(Adapted from the Institute of Cultural Affairs: Spencer, 1989; Stanfield, 1997)

Objective Questions

- What did you see during the activity?
- What are some actions you did?
- What are some actions others did?
- What is something new you noticed?
- What were you doing?
- What were others doing?
- What did you hear?
- What was your role?
- What caught your attention?
- What do you remember most from the activity?

Reflective Questions

- What surprised you?
- What most challenged you?
- What most frustrated you?
- What did you feel during the activity?
- What event in your life would you associate with this one?
- What specifically impacted you in this activity?
- Where have you experienced similar feelings?
- What were the highlights?
- What made you uneasy?
- What most excited you?
- What engaged you?

Interpretive Questions

- What specifically did you learn?
- What assumptions did you make about yourself, others, or the outcomes of the activity?
- How does this affirm or disconfirm your assumptions?
- Why is that important?
- What was your intent in the activity and was it realized?
- What theory applies to explain your (others) behaviors and outcomes?

- What was the value of this experience?
- What was the meaning of this activity?
- What new insights did you gain?
- What is the impact of _____ on your learning?
- How will this change your future actions?
- How are you different after this event?
- How does this change your perspective?

Decisional Questions

- What will you do with this knowledge?
- What specific new actions will you take in the future?
- When and where will you use this learning?
- What obstacles do you need to manage to implement your new learning?
- Where else might you use this knowledge?
- Where do you go from here?
- How do you intend to follow up?
- What else do you need to learn?
- What additional resources do you need?
- What is an unanswered question that remains?
- How can we recognize or celebrate this activity?

APPENDIX 16.4

Focused Debriefing Skills Feedback Form

Please check off the number of times the instructor exhibited the
following behaviors.
Make additional notes with specific examples or quotes for clarification
in the feedback process.

ORID Questions	✓	Comments
Objective: What did you observe? What did you hear? What actions did you take? What did you see?		
Reflective: What was most challenging? Frustrating? Surprising? Interesting? How did you feel?		
Interpretive: What did you learn? What new insights were gained? What assumptions did you make? What theories apply?		
Decisional: What will you do with this new knowledge? What new actions will you take?		

Task Behaviors	✓	Comments
Probing: Seeking additional information, "Would you provide more detail?"		
Elaborating: More information, "Go on."		
Clarifying: Explaining meaning, "Could you give me a specific example?"		
Reflective or paraphrasing – Greater depth exploring feelings by mirroring what was said,		

"Let me say what I think you said to see if everyone understands."		
Empathy statements: acknowledging feelings, "I hear you say you're upset, that's understandable."		
Summarizing: Synopsis of session, "Let me see if I have the whole picture. . .."		
Acknowledging: Recognizing and thanking students, "thanks for your insightful comment."		
Gaining full participation: Including all students, "I am aware we haven't heard from everyone so I would like to hear other voices on this topic."		
Enforcing ground rules: Improving the group process. "We agreed to limit stories so I would like to remind the group to please be concise in their responses."		

Process behaviors ✓ **Comments**

Encouraging, friendly attitude: Creating a welcoming and safe environment.		
Good eye contact: Looking at the students, and making eye contact with all students.		
Congruent body language: Appropriate to the message and topic.		
Voice: Clear, appropriate volume.		

Enthusiasm, genuine interest: Displaying interest in the students and the topic.		
Positive regard for students: Respecting all students and their opinions.		

Ineffective behaviors   ✓   **Comments**

Attacking: "That was a dumb thing to do."		
Blocking: "I don't think that will work."		
Excessive talk: Answering one's own questions; talking too much.		
Dominating or drawing attention to self.		
Not facilitating: Being co-opted; not enforcing ground rules; not performing the debriefing role.		

Additional Comments:

17. Facilitating focused debriefing: connecting experience with theory and reflection – the Three-Part Journal

Anthony F. Buono

In Chapter 16, Gary Wagenheim examined the nature and process of "the debrief," a critical yet often overlooked or downplayed part of experiential learning. His assessment provides useful insights into how instructors can guide their students toward focused debriefing, drawing on how the mind absorbs and processes new information – from observation and reflection, to interpretation and subsequent decisions. As part of his concluding discussion, he also draws attention to the utility of journaling, suggesting a reflection paper at the end of the semester to provide students with the opportunity for their own "meaning-making" from the different aspects of the course. As he notes, if the debriefing process is successful, students should be able to do more than simply recount various experiential exercises. Focused debriefing throughout the semester should enable them to make sense of their organizational change learning by drawing out common themes from their understandings, feelings and attitudes, and behaviors. As Wagenheim concludes, "combined with the integration of theory, such journaling can help students to learn course content in the present, and gain skills for managing organizational change in the future."

The concept of reflective journaling, of course, is not a new idea. Going back to Schön's (1983) classic volume *The Reflective Practitioner*, a vast literature has emerged on the significance of enhancing student ability to engage in reflective learning (see Muncy, 2014). As Schön (1987) has convincingly illustrated, in a broad range of occupational fields professional development is substantially improved when people develop the ability to engage in reflective learning, developing their own insights into the nature of their own attitudes, behaviors, and possibilities. This type of "mindful concentration" has also been suggested to stimulate the parts of the brain that are active when not engaged in directed activity – helping us to process disparate bits of information, finding patterns, and creating meaningful dialog and action over time (McNulty, 2018).

One of the challenges with experiential learning is to simulate direct experience for students – and provide them with the opportunity to think deeply about that experience – so that they can more fully appreciate the possibilities as well as limits of theory in an unpredictable world (see Kenworthy-U'Ren, 2005). We can try to simulate the experience of and discussions about practice day in, day out in the classroom, but unless students experience it on a personal level – in essence face it up close and in person through experience – the necessary insight does not translate. Journaling can facilitate this process.

The underlying challenge is that students – especially those at the undergraduate level – are not that good at such reflective exploration. As a growing body of research suggests, simply giving students a journal-based assignment does not ensure that reflective learning will actually occur. The reality is that student journals are often little more than descriptive accounts of their experience, rather than what they were supposed to do – connecting to theory and reflecting on its meaning (see Muncy, 2014; O'Connell and Dyment, 2004; Wessel and Larin, 2006). As this research strongly indicates, instructors must be very clear about expectations; otherwise journaling assignments will fall well short of desired educational outcomes (Muncy, 2014; O'Connell and Dyment, 2011; Sharma, 2010).

One of our Bentley University colleagues, Edward Zlotkowski, a Professor of English and co-creator of the institution's Service-Learning program, devised a simple yet powerful approach to enhance the reflective journaling process. The Three-Part Journal was initially created to facilitate student ability to turn their civic engagement and service experiences into academic learning, by clearly differentiating three levels of learning in journal entries in different fonts:

1. Normal font: an objective, detailed description of what was done in the field or at the client, organized into half-hour segments.
2. **Bold** font: a discussion of the experience in terms of course-related concepts and themes, with the objective to demonstrate ability to make connections between project experiences and class concepts as well as skill in using those concepts to analyze project experiences.
3. *Italics* font: a personal response to the experience, including feelings, thoughts, judgments, and what was learned (about oneself, one's assumptions, reactions, and so forth). This section of the journal is particularly concerned with discoveries about ourselves and our attitudes toward other people we encounter.

This type of structured journaling can be very useful in an experiential organizational change course. Going beyond the individual exercises and simulations per se, what we are attempting to do is to enhance student ability to think deeply about the material – pushing them toward greater attentiveness, insight, empathy and compassion, and understanding (see Stein, 1994), enabling them to draw connections between experience, theory, and their own feelings and development – the essence of reflective learning:

1. Journal sections with normal font describe the experience, drawing out observations of actions and responses to the stimuli in the exercise or simulation.
2. Journal sections in **bold** font relate that experience to relevant course concepts – theories, frameworks, and so forth – using those concepts to probe, analyze, and explain the behaviors or experience, pointing out the utility and futility associated with the concepts.
3. Journal sections in *italics* then probe and reflect on the material presented in sections 1 and 2 above, focusing on the personal aspects of the learning process, from testing assumptions and beliefs, to contemplating new attitudes and behaviors as part of their own growth and development.

Through this type of three-level learning, students can also be encouraged to contrast their former beliefs with their new beliefs, examining how this new way of thinking has expanded the thoughts they now have about themselves and others, and their understandings of the nuances and complexities associated with organizational change.

This type of journaling exercise can be done in a number of ways, from periodic journals submitted throughout the semester, to a final, culminating experience. Regardless of the approach taken, it is important to stress all three levels of learning. As a general guide, I typically tell students that they do not necessarily have to think about their Three-Part Journal as having equal thirds across the different levels, but their paper should clearly reflect the three levels. My experience is that students typically struggle at first, being far more comfortable with descriptive content; but over time, they get better and better at the bold face and italics content in their journals.

As many of the chapter authors in this volume have underscored, a critical starting point for reflective journaling – as with experiential exercises in general – is the instructor's role in creating a sense of openness in the classroom. If we truly expect students to engage in this type of deep, potentially transformative learning, we must provide them with a safe learning environment— in essence, creating a climate of trust (Castelli, 2011) – that will encourage them to delve into, explore, and share their learnings.

REFERENCES

Castelli, P.A. (2011). An Integrated Model for Practicing Reflective Learning. *Academy of Educational Leadership Journal*, 15, 15–30.

Kenworthy-U'Ren, A. (2005). Toward a Scholarship of Engagement: A Dialogue between Andy Van de Ven and Edward Zlotkowski. *Academy of Management Learning and Education*, 4 (3), 355–362.

McNulty, E.J. (2018). Journaling Can Boost Your Leadership Skills. *Strategy+Business*, May 15. https://www.strategy-business.com/blog/Journaling-Can-Boost-Your-Leadership-Skills?gko=e748f&utm_source=itw&utm_medium=20180517&utm_campaign=resp (accessed February 5, 2018).

Muncy, J.A. (2014). Blogging for Reflection: The Use of Online Journals to Engage Students in Reflective Learning. *Marketing Education Review*, 24 (2), 101–114.

O'Connell, T.S. and Dyment, J.E. (2004). Journals of Post-Secondary Outdoor Recreation Students: The Result of a Content Analysis. *Journal of Adventure Education and Outdoor Learning*, 4 (December), 159–172.

O'Connell, T.S. and Dyment, J.E. (2011). The Case of Reflective Journals: Is the Jury Still Out? *Reflective Practice*, 12 (February), 47–59.

Schön, D.A. (1983). *The Reflective Practitioner: How Professionals Think in Action*. New York: Basic Books.

Schön, D.A. (1987). *Educating the Reflective Practitioner*. San Francisco, CA: Jossey-Bass.

Sharma, P. (2010). Enhancing Student Reflection Using Weblogs: Lessons Learned from Two Implementation Studies. *Reflective Practice*, 11 (April), 127–141.

Stein, H.F. (1994). *Listening Deeply*. Boulder, CO: Westview Press.

Wessel, J. and Larin, H. (2006). Change in Reflections of Physiotherapy Students Over Time in Clinical Placements. *Learning in Health and Social Care*, 5 (September), 119–132.

18. Afterword: the change game – moving from toolkits to "That was great!"

Susan M. Adams, Gavin M. Schwarz, and Anthony F. Buono

In the tradition of providing pragmatic, useful, and realistic organizational change outcomes, this book focuses on improving our understanding of and experience with organizational change through focused, high impact change-related simulations and experiential exercises for teaching, facilitating, and coping with change. If organizational change and transformation involve a combination of understanding, fixing (or unfixing), and practiced behavior, and as part of improvements to the conceptualization, formulation, and implementation of change, then the process of learning from experience is recognized as a means of deeper learning about change. This effect is especially relevant when we acknowledge the scale and significance of just how many organizational change efforts end in failure or are limited in their outcomes (e.g., Beer et al., 1990; Hughes, 2011), suggesting the role that experience can play. Rather than concentrate on explaining change or focusing on how to manage change in this context, however – as illustrated throughout this book – when it comes to organization development and change, emphasis should be placed on the processes of and strategies for learning from active experimentation to increase individual and organizational effectiveness. It is this focus on engaged techniques for improvement and well-being through practice that the exercises in this book address – a focus incorporating "That was great!" outcomes for both participants and facilitator.

This emphasis on the value of learning from change and about change through personal experience is an important part of helping organizational members to improve the many factors that bring about organizational effectiveness. It is this key feature of the book – the importance of experience in learning about change – that is our focus: learning by doing. The underlying lesson is fairly straightforward – experience counts. So, understanding how to incorporate participatory learning into change is a basic feature of effective change intervention. Continuing an established tradition, making sure that we fully appreciate and engage with simulation and experience is an intrinsic part of educational efforts to facilitate changing. Having read this far in the book, you are already aware of the essential place and value of using experience to facilitate change. Yet, this aspect of learning is often minimized or overlooked in favor of other features of pedagogy or attempts to change behavior. Moreover, despite the voluminous extent of work dedicated to understanding change and its features through "toolkit" approaches or ways toward sustainable change, we appear to repeatedly and regularly fall back or focus on a direct training approach: "how to" change and manuals describing such development. The value of this book is in asserting, as we do in the introductory chapter to this volume, that this common approach is too restrictive in today's fast-paced, limited-attention, and constantly changing world. Training people for organizational change in traditional, "mapped out" ways also fails to recognize that today, organizational members living change and university students learning about change look at their learning environment through a different lens, heavily influenced by their experiences. Change is more meaningful when we reflect and incorporate our experiences.

The exercises in the book should not hold any dramatic surprises. After all, there is a rich tradition of preparing people for change through simulation and application. Rather, we set out to highlight the value of bringing experience and hands-on learning about change to the forefront of producing change; something that has slowly receded from view in discussions on change. Behavioralists, of course, have identified the "curse of knowledge" (Camerer et al., 1989) that limits our ability to teach effectively; and conversely, that learning by teaching leads to benefits for all groups involved (Koh et al., 2018)–these types of effects have long been realized in organizational development. In this context, the book is both an acknowledgment of the history of previous exercise material on facilitation (such as the *Handbook* series by Pfeiffer and Jones, starting in 1972 and published through 1980), and a recognition of the tendency in contemporary learning debate to theorize the power and application of experiential learning or its basis (building from Kolb, 2014). A critical outcome has led to the study of pedagogy and intellectualizing "management education" over the actual experience, as Schwarz and Stensaker (2014) note, the basis of which is increasingly related to a limited outlook on how we view organizations and knowledge.

With a hands-on showcasing of high impact methods for engaging with organizational change in different contexts and different forms, the exercises in the book promote a path toward self-learning and reflective development for change, rather than providing another all-purpose mechanism for change or for making sense of management learning. It is intended to be a resource. Thinking about different ways of transforming organizations and facilitating change, the chapters highlight that there are many different ways to deal with or to understand change, with considerable value for trainers and consultants as well as those teaching in formal, classroom settings.

It is our hope that readers and exercise participants take away key lessons and insights, from recognizing and managing their own reactions to change, the challenges of dealing with incomplete information and tight time frames, and the ways in which communication can facilitate as well as stifle change efforts, to the human experience inherent in any change process. In this sense, through the book we hope to further stimulate an ongoing conversation on how to facilitate better change, with the objective of extending the practice of constructive change management and organization development – the process of learning (about change) by doing. There are many different ways to formalize the next steps in this context, such as: developing frameworks that help to analyze, understand, and cope with change through experience; advancing knowledge and understanding of management consulting on change through experience that aids the development of different views on change; and building a multiple-perspectives approach to experiencing change, which assumes that a variety of learning styles, assumptions, and methodologies can be employed to explore the many areas associated with learning through change. In keeping true to the book's title, we hope that readers will use these exercises as a practical guide, working toward a better understanding of and commitment to experiential learning in preparing organizations and their members for high impact change.

REFERENCES

Beer, M., Eisenstat, R., and Spector, B. (1990). Why change programs don't produce change: Effective corporate renewal starts at the bottom, through informal efforts to solve business problems. *Harvard Business Review*, 68(10), 158–166.

Camerer, C., Loewenstein, G., and Weber, M. (1989). The curse of knowledge in economic settings: An experimental analysis. *Journal of Political Economy*, 97(5), 1232–1254.

Hughes, M. (2011). Do 70 per cent of all organizational change initiatives really fail? *Journal of Change Management*, 11(4), 451–464.

Koh, A.W.L., Lee, S.C., and Lim, S.W.H. (2018). The learning benefits of teaching: A retrieval practice hypothesis. *Applied Cognitive Psychology*, 32(3), 401–410.

Kolb, D.A. (2014). *Experiential Learning: Experience as the Source of Learning and Development*. Hoboken, NJ: Pearson.

Pfeiffer, J.W., and Jones, J.E. (1972). *The 1972 Annual Handbook for Group Facilitators*. Iowa City, IA: University Associates Press.
Schwarz, G.M., and Stensaker, I. (2014). Time to take off the theoretical straight-jacket and (re-)introduce phenomenon-driven research. *Journal of Applied Behavioral Science*, 50(4), 478–501.

Index

Printed and bound by CPI Group (UK) Ltd, Croydon, CR0 4YY

23/04/2025

14660957-0004